LEARNING THE TAROT

LEARNING THE TAROT

Joan Bunning

A Tarot Book for Beginners

SAMUEL WEISER, INC.

York Beach, Maine

First Published in 1998 by
Samuel Weiser, Inc.
P. O. Box 612
York Beach, Maine 03910-0612
www.weiserbooks.com

Library of Congress Cataloging-in-Publication Data
    Bunning, Joan.
        Learning the tarot / Joan Bunning.
            p.   cm.
        Includes bibliographical references and index.
        ISBN 1-57863-048-7 (alk. paper)
        1. Tarot.   I. Title.
    BF 1879.T2B835   1998   98-23461
    133.3*'2424—dc21   CIP

VG

Cover design by Ed Stevens

Illustrations from the Universal Waite Tarot Deck reproduced by permission of U.S.
Games Systems, Inc. Stamford, CT 06902 USA. Copyright © 1990 by U.S. Games Systems, Inc. Further reproduction prohibited.

Typeset in OptiBerling-Agency with PostAntiqua and Bernhard Modern as display faces

Printed in the United States of America

05 04 03 02 01 00
10 9 8 7 6 5 4 3

The paper used in this publication meets all the minimum requirements of the American National Standard for Permanence of Paper for Printed Library Materials Z39.48-1984.

Contents

Section II—Exercises

Section III—Suggestions for Exercises

Section IV—Card Descriptions

Part 1 ▩ Major Arcana

Part 2 ▨ Minor Arcana

Section V—The Celtic Cross Spread

Appendices

Preface

Welcome to *Learning the Tarot*—my course on how to read the tarot cards. The tarot is a deck of 78 picture cards that has been used for centuries to reveal hidden truths. In the past few years, interest in the tarot has grown tremendously. More and more people are seeking ways to blend inner and outer realities so they can live their lives more creatively. They have discovered in the tarot a powerful tool for personal growth and insight.

My main purpose in this course is to show you how to use the cards for yourself. The tarot can help you understand yourself better and teach you how to tap your inner resources more confidently. You do not have to have "psychic powers" to use the tarot successfully. All you need is the willingness to honor and develop your natural intuitive abilities.

I began writing this course in 1989. I had been studying the tarot for some years, and I found that I was developing some ideas about the cards and how they could be used as a tool for inner guidance. In October 1995, I created my *Learning the Tarot* website to share my thoughts with others in the Internet community.

Since that time, thousands of people from all over the world have visited my website. Many have written to share their experiences with me via email. Often they tell me they have always been curious about the cards, but didn't know how to begin with them. It has been very exciting to hear how my course has given them the start they were looking for.

Learning the Tarot is divided into five sections:

Section I contains the 19 lessons that make up the course. They begin with the basics and gradually move into more detailed aspects of the cards. You can do the lessons at any pace you like. They are geared toward beginners, but experienced tarot users will find some useful ideas and techniques as well.

Section II contains exercises and practice activities that reinforce the concepts presented in each lesson. The exercises are completely optional.

Section III contains sample responses for some of the exercises. These are not answers in the usual sense, but simply suggestions to give you an idea of the kind of interpretations that are possible.

Section IV contains information on each of the tarot cards. You'll be referring to this section as you go through the lessons, but it will also prove useful later as you work with the tarot on your own.

Section V contains information on the Celtic Cross Spread—a popular pattern for laying out the cards. I refer to this spread throughout the course. Section V also contains some sample readings based on the Celtic Cross.

The only real requirement for taking this course is a tarot deck. This workbook is illustrated with the Universal Waite Tarot which is based on the popular Rider-Waite. These are both good decks to start with because they have pictures on every card which helps when you are learning. However, if you already have a different 78 card deck, you may use it with the course. The principles of tarot work are much the same no matter what deck you use.

You can buy tarot decks in many places now. Bookstores often carry them, and many Internet websites offer a variety of tarot decks for sale. If you have trouble finding a deck in your area, you can order one from me. Simply visit my website for more information.

Some people worry that working with the tarot will involve them in occult practices or create conflicts with their religious beliefs. My approach to the cards is simple and natural. I try to show that the cards are not dark and mysterious, but wonderful tools for self-discovery. In fact, I feel that using the tarot can expand your spiritual awareness in many positive ways.

Others may believe that the tarot is unscientific—a plaything at best, but certainly not to be taken seriously by those who know better. I ask only that you indulge your curiosity and be willing to explore the cards with an open mind. After all, that is the true spirit of scientific endeavor!

I hope you're intrigued enough to try this course. If you're still not sure, read lesson 1. It explains in more detail why using the tarot cards makes sense. I think you will find *Learning the Tarot* interesting at least, and perhaps the tool you have been looking for to develop your unrealized potential.

Acknowledgments

I want to thank my husband Steve for his love and confidence in me and for his technical prowess. Without it, my website would have self-destructed long ago.

Much love goes to my sons David and Jonathan who have filled my days with incredible experiences.

I wish to express my gratitude to my mother for always being there; to my brother, sister, and dad for what we've shared; and to my friends and extended family, young and old. Each one of you is precious to me.

I extend my gratitude to all those who contributed to my tarot understanding over the years, in particular Eileen Connolly, Mary Greer, Shoshanna Hathaway, Rachel Pollack and all the knowledgeable folks on the "tarot-l discussion list."

A nod of thanks goes to Ragu Pasupulati for his intuitive insight, Paul Caskey for his scanned tarot images, Kent Stork for his inventive tarot program, and David Cook for his ISP generosity.

A big hug to my long-term cyber-friends for their support and tarot insights: Rhys Chatham, Linda Cortellesi, Elizabeth Delisi, Asher Green, Hairani Hardjoe, Joe Holtslag, Roger Mewis, Patty Pidlypchak, Gary Pinsky, Brett Shand, Ray Simon, Phyllis Stevens, Hazel Stitt, Lou Violette, Curtis White, and Judy Lenzin for her warmth and inspiration.

I wish to thank "Jill" and all the others who have allowed me to dip into their lives through the cards. Your tales have enriched my book and my life.

A special thanks goes to Robin Robertson for seeing the potential in my course and acting on it.

Finally, I wish to thank all those who wrote to share their tarot knowledge and experiences. I learned from each of you, and your words of encouragement made all the difference.

For Steve
Technical Wizard and
King of Pentacles

I

LESSONS

Introduction to the Tarot

Years ago, when I told my brother I was studying the tarot, his first comment was, "How can a deck of cards possibly tell you anything about anything?" I laughed because I thought his reply summed up pretty well the common sense view of the cards. I, too, had my doubts about the tarot, but I found out that the cards can make a real difference in the way you perceive and deal with the challenges in your life. In this introduction, I'll try to explain why.

The origin of the tarot is a mystery. We do know for sure that the cards were used in Italy in the fifteenth century as a popular card game. Wealthy patrons commissioned beautiful decks, some of which have survived. The Visconti-Sforza, created in 1450 or shortly thereafter, is one of the earliest and most complete.[1]

Later in the eighteenth and nineteenth centuries, the cards were discovered by a number of influential scholars of the occult. These gentlemen were fascinated by the tarot and recognized that the images on the cards were more powerful than a simple game would suggest. They revealed (or created!) the "true" history of the tarot by connecting the cards to Egyptian mysteries, Hermetic philosophy, the Kabbalah, alchemy, and other mystical systems. These pursuits continued into the early part of the twentieth century when the tarot was incorporated into the practices of several secret societies, including the Order of the Golden Dawn.[2]

Although the roots of the tarot are in the occult tradition, interest in the cards has expanded in the last few decades to include many perspectives. New decks have been created that reflect these interests. There are Native American, herbal, mythological, and Japanese decks, among others.[3]

The tarot is most commonly viewed as a tool for divination. A traditional tarot reading involves a seeker—someone who is looking for answers to personal questions—and a reader—someone who knows how to interpret the cards. After the seeker has shuffled and cut the deck, the reader lays out the chosen cards in a pattern called a spread. Each position in the spread has a meaning, and each card has a meaning as well. The reader combines these two meanings to shed light on the seeker's question.

A simple process, but rarely presented in a simple way. In films, we always see the tarot being used in a seedy parlor or back room. An old woman, seated in shadows, reads the cards for a nervous, young girl. The crone lifts her wrinkled finger and drops it ominously on the Death card. The girl draws back, frightened by this sign of her impending doom.

---

1. Michael Dummett, *The Visconti-Sforza Tarot Cards* (New York: George Braziller, Inc., 1986), p. 13.
2. Cynthia Giles, *The Tarot: History, Mystery and Lore* (New York: Simon & Schuster, 1992), chapters 2 and 3.
3. J. A. and Magda Gonzalez, Native American Tarot Deck; Michael Tierra and Candis Cantin, The Herbal Tarot; Koji Furuta and Stuart R. Kaplan, The Ukiyoe Tarot, all published by U.S. Games (Stamford, CT); and Juliet Sharmon-Burke and Liz Greene, *The Mythic Tarot*, a book and deck set published by Simon & Schuster.

DEATH.

This aura of darkness clings to the tarot cards even now. Some religions shun the cards, and the scientific establishment condemns them as symbols of unreason, a holdover from an unenlightened past. Let us set aside these shadowy images for now and consider the tarot for what it is—a deck of picture cards. The question becomes, what can we do with them?

The answer lies with the unconscious—that deep level of memory and awareness that resides within each of us, but outside our everyday experience. Even though we ignore the action of the unconscious most of the time, it profoundly affects everything we do. In his writings, Sigmund Freud stressed the irrational, primitive aspect of the unconscious. He thought that it was the home of our most unacceptable desires and urges. His contemporary Carl Jung emphasized the positive, creative aspect of the unconscious. He tried to show that it has a collective component that touches universal qualities.

We may never know the full range and power of the unconscious, but there are ways to explore its landscape. Many techniques have been developed for this purpose—psychotherapy, dream interpretation, visualization, and meditation. The tarot is another such tool.

Consider for a moment a typical card in the tarot deck, the Five of Swords. This card shows a man holding three swords and looking at two figures in the distance. Two other swords lie on the ground. As I look at this card, I begin to create a story around the image. I see a man who seems satisfied with some battle he has won. He looks rather smug and pleased that *he* has all the swords. The others look downcast and defeated.

What I have done is take an open-ended image and project a story onto it. To me, my view is the obvious one—the only possible interpretation of this scene. In fact, someone else could have imagined a totally different story. Maybe the man is trying to pick up the swords. He's calling to the others to help him, but they refuse. Or, maybe the other two were fighting, and he convinced them to lay down their arms.

The point is that of all possible stories, I chose a certain one. Why? Because it is human nature to project unconscious material onto objects in the environment. We always see reality through a lens made up of our own inner state. Therapists have long noted this tendency and have created tools to assist in the process. The famous Rorschach inkblot test is based on such projection.[4]

Projection is one reason why the tarot cards are valuable. Their intriguing pictures and patterns are effective in tapping the unconscious. This is the personal aspect of the tarot, but the cards also have a collective component. As humans, we all have certain common needs and experiences. The images on the tarot cards capture these universal moments and draw them out consistently. People tend to react to the cards in similar ways because they represent archetypes.

---

4. Hermann Rorschach, *The Rorschach (R) Test* (Switzerland, Hans Huber, 1927).

Over many centuries, the tarot has evolved into a collection of the most basic patterns of human thought and emotion.

Consider the Empress. She stands for the Mother Principle—life in all its abundance. Notice how her image conjures up feelings of luxuriance. She is seated on soft, lush pillows, and her robe flows in folds around her. In the Empress, we sense the bounty and sensual richness of nature.

The power of the tarot comes from this combination of the personal and the universal. You can see each card in your own way, but, at the same time, you are supported by understandings that others have found meaningful. The tarot is a mirror that reflects back to you the hidden aspects of your own unique awareness.

When we do a tarot reading, we select certain cards by shuffling, cutting, and dealing the deck. Although this process seems random, we still assume the cards we pick are special. This is the point of a tarot reading after all—to choose the cards we are meant to see. Now, common sense tells us that cards chosen by chance can't hold any special meaning—or can they?

To answer this question, let's look at randomness more closely. Usually we say that an event is random when it appears to be the result of the chance interaction of mechanical forces. From a set of possible outcomes—all equally likely—one occurs, but for no particular reason.

This definition includes two key assumptions about random events: they are the result of mechanical forces, and they have no meaning. First, no tarot reading is solely the product of mechanical forces. It is the result of a long series of conscious actions. We decide to study the tarot. We buy a deck and learn how to use it. We shuffle and cut the cards in a certain way at a certain point. Finally, we use our perceptions to interpret the cards.

At every step, we are actively involved. Why then are we tempted to say a reading is "the chance interaction of mechanical forces?" Because we can't explain just how our consciousness is involved. We know our card choices aren't deliberate, so we call them random. In fact, could there be a deeper mechanism at work, one connected to the power of our unconscious? Could our inner states be tied to outer events in a way that we don't yet fully understand? I hold this possibility out to you.

The other feature of a random event is that it has no inherent meaning. I roll a die and get a six, but there is no purpose to this result. I could just as easily roll a one, and the meaning would be the same—or would it? Do we really know these two outcomes are equal? Perhaps there is meaning and purpose in every event, great or small, but we don't always recognize it.

At a party many years ago, I had the sudden urge to pick up a die sitting on the floor. I *knew* with great conviction that I would use this die to roll each number individually. As I began, the laughter and noise of the party faded away. I felt a growing excitement as a different number appeared with each roll. It was only with the last successful roll that my everyday awareness returned, and I sat back, wondering what had happened.

At one level, these six rolls were unrelated, random events, but at another level, they were very meaningful. My inner experience told me this was so, even though an outside observer might not agree. What *was* the meaning? At the time, it was a lesson in the strange interaction between mind and matter. Today, I know it had another purpose—to be available to me now, some twenty-five years later, as an illustration for this very lesson!

Meaning is a mysterious quality that arises at the juncture of inner and outer realities. There is a message in everything—trees, songs, even trash—but only when we are open to perceiving it. The tarot cards convey many messages because of the richness of their images and connections. More importantly, tarot readings communicate meaning because we bring to them our sincere desire to discover deeper truths about our lives. By seeking meaning in this way, we honor its reality and give it a chance to be revealed.

If there is meaning in a reading, where does it come from? I believe it comes from that part of ourselves that is aware of the divine source of meaning. This is an aspect of the unconscious, yet it is much more. It acts as a wise advisor who knows us well. It understands what we need and leads us in the direction we need to go. Some people call this advisor the soul, the superconscious, or the higher self. I call it the Inner Guide because that is the role it plays in connection with the tarot.

Each of us has an Inner Guide that serves as a fountain of meaning for us. Your Inner Guide is always with you because it is part of you. You can't destroy this connection, but you *can* ignore it. When you reach for your tarot deck, you signal to your Inner Guide that you are open to its wisdom. This simple act of faith allows you to become aware of the guidance that was always there for you.

We are meant by nature to rely on the wisdom of our Inner Guide, but somehow we have forgotten how to access it. We trust our conscious minds instead, and forget to look deeper. Our conscious minds are clever, but unfortunately, they just don't have the full awareness we need to make appropriate choices day by day.

When we are operating from our conscious minds, we often feel as if events are forced upon us by chance. Life seems to have little purpose, and we suffer because we do not really understand who we are and what we want. When we know how to access our Inner Guide, we experience life differently. We have the certainty and peace that comes from aligning our conscious will with our inner purpose. Our path becomes more joyous, and we see more clearly how we bring together the scattered elements of our lives to fulfill our destinies.

I use the tarot because it is one of the best tools I have found to make the whispers of my Inner Guide more available consciously. The ideas, images, and feelings that emerge as I work through a reading are a message from my Inner Guide. How do I know there is a message, and it's not just my imagination? I don't, really. I can only trust my experience and see what happens.

You do not really need the tarot to access your Inner Guide. The cards serve the same function as Dumbo's magic feather. In the Disney movie, Dumbo the Elephant really could fly on his own, but he didn't believe it. He placed all his faith on the special feather he held in his trunk. He thought this feather gave him the power to fly, but he found out differently when it blew away, and he was forced to fall back on his own resources.

The tarot cards may help you fly until you can reach your Inner Guide on your own. Don't worry for now about how this might happen. Just play with the cards, work through the lessons and exercises, and see if you don't experience a few surprises.

Part 1

Elements of the Tarot

The Major Arcana

The standard tarot deck consists of 78 cards divided into two sections, the major and minor arcanas. The word *arcana* is the plural of *arcanum*, which means "profound secret." To the alchemists of the Middle Ages, the arcanum was the secret of nature. The tarot cards are therefore a collection of the "secrets" that underlie and explain our universe.

The 22 cards of the major arcana are the heart of the deck. Each of these cards symbolizes some universal aspect of human experience. They represent the archetypes—consistent, directing patterns of influence that are an inherent part of human nature.

Each card in the major arcana has a name and number. Some names convey a card's meaning directly, such as Strength, Justice, and Temperance. Other cards are individuals who personify a particular approach to life, such as the Magician or the Hermit. There are also cards with astronomical names, such as the Star, Sun, and Moon. They represent the elusive forces associated with these heavenly bodies.

The major arcana cards are special because they draw out deep and complex reactions. The images on the Universal-Waite deck[1] are evocative because they combine esoteric symbolism with recognizable figures and situations. The symbolism is subtle, but effective.

A major arcana card is always given extra weight in a reading. When one of these cards appears, you know the issues at stake are not mundane or temporary. They represent your most basic concerns—your *major* feelings and motivations. In later lessons, I show in more detail how you can recognize and interpret the themes of the major arcana in a reading.

The major arcana is often considered as a unit. Different schemes have been developed to show how the cards form patterns that cast light on the human condition. Numerology, astrology, and other esoteric sciences often play a role in these schemes.

Many interpreters view the major arcana as showing the different stages on an individual's journey of inner growth—what some call the Fool's Journey (see exercise 2.2, p. 67). In these systems, each card stands for some quality or experience that we must incorporate before we can realize our wholeness.

We all travel this road to self-actualization, though our trips more often involve detours, backups, and restarts than smooth progression! Our specific paths are unique, but our mile-

---

1. The Rider-Waite deck was authored by A. E. Waite. Pamela Coleman did the illustrations. The deck was originally published in England by Rider and Company, hence the "call tag" of the Rider-Waite deck. The illustrations in this book are from the Universal Waite deck, which is a new version whose colors more closely resemble the original. Both decks are published by U.S. Games Inc. and are available from most metaphysical bookstores.

stones are universal. The 22 major arcana cards are markers on the path of inner development leading from earliest awareness (card 0) to integration and fulfillment (card 21).

The Fool's Journey seems to move smoothly from one order of experience to the next, but our learning adventures are usually not so tidy. We make mistakes, skip lessons, and fail to realize our potential. Sometimes we lack the courage and insight to discover our deepest levels. Some never feel the call of the Hermit to look inward or never experience the crisis of the Tower that might free them from their ego defenses.

THE WORLD.

Many times we try to overcome our difficulties, but fail repeatedly. The lesson of the Hanged Man—to let go and surrender to experience—is one that is particularly hard and may need to be faced over and over before it is fully incorporated.

Often we experience lessons out of order. A person may absorb the qualities of Strength early in life due to a difficult childhood, but only later develop the Chariot's mastery and control. Someone may overcome the attraction of the Devil's materialism through a life of seclusion, but then need to learn about relationships and sexuality—a lesson of the Lovers—at a later time.

The major arcana contains many levels and models of experience. These cards hold all the patterns of growth, whether they occur within one segment of a life or a whole life span. We could even say that an entire lifetime is really just one growth episode within the larger saga of our soul's development.

No matter what our pattern of self-discovery, the major arcana shows us that wholeness and fulfillment are our destiny. If we keep this promise as our polestar, we will eventually realize our true nature and gain the World.

The Minor Arcana

While the major arcana expresses universal themes, the minor arcana brings those themes down into the practical arena to show how they operate in daily events. The minor arcana cards represent the concerns, activities, and emotions that make up the dramas of our everyday lives.

There are 56 cards in the minor arcana divided into four suits: Wands, Cups, Swords, and Pentacles.[1] Each of these suits stands for a particular approach to life.

Wands

The Wands are the suit of creativity, action, and movement. They are associated with such qualities as enthusiasm, adventure, risk-taking, and confidence. This suit corresponds to the yang, or masculine principle, in Chinese philosophy and is associated with the element Fire. A flickering flame is the perfect symbol of the Wands' force. This energy flows outward and generates passionate involvement.

Cups

The Cups are the suit of emotions and spiritual experience. They describe inner states, feelings, and relationship patterns. The energy of this suit flows inward. Cups correspond to the yin, or feminine principle, in Chinese philosophy and are associated with the element Water. The ability of water to flow and fill up spaces, to sustain and to reflect changing moods makes it the ideal symbol of the Cups suit.

Swords

The Swords are the suit of intellect, thought, and reason. They are concerned with justice, truth, and ethical principles. Swords are associated with the element Air. A cloudless sky, open and light-filled, is a symbol of the mental clarity that is the Swords' ideal. This suit is also associated with states that lead to disharmony and unhappiness. Our intellect is a valuable asset, but as an agent of ego, it can lead us astray if it is not infused with the wisdom of our Inner Guide.

Pentacles

The Pentacles are the suit of practicality, security, and material concerns. They are associated with the element Earth and the concrete requirements of working with matter. In Pentacles, we celebrate the beauty of nature, our interactions with plants and animals, and our physical experiences in the body. Pentacles also represent prosperity and wealth of all kinds. Some-

---

1. Many decks use names other than these for the four suits. The names chosen often reflect the themes of the deck.

times this suit is called the Coins, an obvious symbol of the exchange of goods and services in the physical world.

• • •

Each minor arcana suit has a distinct quality all its own. Our everyday experiences are a blend of these four approaches. Your tarot readings will show you how the different suit energies are impacting your life at any given moment. (See Appendix B for lists of the suit qualities.)

The suits are structured much as our everyday playing cards with ten numbered cards (Ace–Ten) and four court cards (King, Queen, Knight, and Page). Each card has a role to play in showing how its energy is expressed in the world.

Aces

An Ace announces the themes of a suit. The Ace of Cups stands for love, emotions, intuition, and intimacy—ideas that are explored in the other cards of the Cups suit. An Ace always represents positive forces. It is the standard-bearer for the best its suit has to offer.

Middle Cards

Each of the middle, numbered cards presents a different aspect of a suit. The Wands explore such themes as personal power (card 2), leadership (card 3), excitement (card 4), and competition (card 5). A card may approach an idea from several angles. The Five of Pentacles shows the many faces of want—hard times (material want), ill health (physical want), and rejection (emotional want).

Tens

A Ten takes the themes introduced by an Ace to their logical conclusion. If you take the love, intimacy, and emotions of the Ace of Cups to their ultimate, you have the joy, peace, and family love of the Ten of Cups.

Court Cards

The court cards are people with personalities that reflect the qualities of their suit and rank. The court cards show us certain ways of being in the world so that we can use (or avoid!) those styles when appropriate.

A King is mature and masculine. He is a doer whose focus is outward on the events of life. He demonstrates authority, control, and mastery in some area associated with his suit. A King's style is strong, assertive and direct. He is concerned with results and practical, how-to matters.

A Queen is mature and feminine. She embodies the qualities of her suit, rather than acting them out. Her focus is inward, and her style, relaxed and natural. A Queen is less concerned with results than with the enjoyment of just being in the world. She is associated with feelings, relationships, and self-expression.

A Knight is an immature teenager. He cannot express himself with balance. He swings wildly from one extreme to another as he tries to relate successfully to his world. A Knight is prone to excess, but he is also eager and sincere, and these qualities redeem him in our eyes. We can admire his spirit and energy.

A Page is a playful child. He acts out the qualities of his suit with pleasure and abandon. His approach may not be deep, but it is easy, loose, and spontaneous. He is a symbol of adventure and possibility.

• • •

You now have a basic idea of the role of each card in the tarot deck. You have a feel for how they all fit together and what each one contributes to the whole. In the following lessons, you will learn more about these cards and how to interpret them in your readings.

The Spread

A spread is a preset pattern for laying out the tarot cards. It defines how many cards to use, where each one goes, and what each one means. A spread is a template guiding the placement of the cards so they can shed light on a given topic. It is within this template that the meanings of the cards come together so beautifully.

The most important feature of a spread is the fact that each position has a unique meaning that colors the interpretation of whatever card falls in that spot. For example, the Four of Pentacles stands for possessiveness, control, and blocked change. If this card were to fall in Position 4 of the Celtic Cross Spread (the "Past" position), you would look at how these qualities are *moving out* of your life. In Position 6 (the "Future"), you would instead view them as *coming into* your life—a quite different interpretation.

Tarot spreads can be any size or pattern. Rahdue's Wheel includes all 78 cards and creates a vast tableau of one person's life.[1] A spread can also contain just one card. In lesson 5 I show how a one-card spread is useful for daily readings.

Most spreads contain between six and fifteen cards. This range is small enough to be manageable, but large enough to cover a topic in some depth. The pattern of a spread often forms a design that reflects its theme. For example, the Horoscope Spread is in the shape of the traditional circle that forms a person's birth chart.[2] The twelve cards of this spread correspond to the twelve houses of astrology.

When cards are related to each other in a spread, an entirely new level of meaning is created. Combinations appear, and a story line develops with characters, plots, and themes. The weaving of a story from the cards in a spread is the most exciting and creative aspect of a tarot reading. It is an art, but there are many guidelines you can follow. I discuss these in later lessons and give examples of the story-making process.

In these lessons, I refer to just the Celtic Cross Spread. I think you will be able to concentrate more on developing your intuition if you stick to just one spread at first. Once you know the cards well and feel comfortable reading them, you can expand your tarot practice by exploring other layouts. Before continuing with the lessons, become familiar with the Celtic Cross Spread (see exercise 4.1, p. 70). We'll be using this spread throughout the course.

---

1. Eileen Connolly, *Tarot: A Handbook for the Journeyman* (North Hollywood, CA: Newcastle, 1987), pp. 128–157.
2. Sandor Konraad, *Classic Tarot Spreads* (Atglen, PA: Whitford Press, 1985), pp. 96–97.

The Daily Reading

You are now ready to begin putting your tarot knowledge to work. Lesson 5 describes the Daily Reading. In this reading, you select a single card that becomes your theme for the day. The purpose is to heighten your awareness of one approach to life for a single twenty-four-hour period. It also helps you learn the tarot without strain or tedium.

Let's say you have drawn the Two of Cups for a daily reading. As you go through the day, you will watch for signs of this card's special energy. The keywords for the Two of Cups are connection, truce, and attraction. In the morning, you notice that a colleague, who has been rather hostile, comes to your office to talk. You sense a TRUCE, and you take advantage of it. In the afternoon, while working on a problem, you look for the CONNECTION between two approaches and find your solution. Later, at a party, you talk to someone who ATTRACTS you. On each occasion, you access the energy of the Two of Cups and allow it to guide your decisions.

At first, you may want to choose your daily card deliberately so you can avoid repeat selections and learn the deck more quickly (see exercise 5.1, p. 72). If you prefer, you can choose your card without conscious intervention (see exercise 5.2, p. 72). Here is the procedure:

1. Shuffle the deck once or twice.
2. Hold the deck face down in one hand and cover it with your other hand.
3. Pause a moment to become calm and centered.
4. Ask your Inner Guide to give you the guidance you need for the day.
5. Place the deck face down in front of you.
6. Cut the deck to the left and restack it.
7. Turn over the top card as your card of the day.
8. Return this card to the deck, and shuffle once or twice.

This procedure is easy to do on a daily basis, and it gives you an opportunity to connect with your Inner Guide regularly. Choose a time that works for you. Mornings are good because you can pick a card during your wake-up routine. You can also select one at night. You will be ready to put your card to use as soon as you wake up. It isn't necessary to pick one time since your schedule may change. The main goal is to make the Daily Reading a part of your day so that your tarot work progresses.

Keep a journal of your selections. Later, you will find it interesting to trace the pattern of your choices. I started studying the tarot in earnest when I was spending my days caring for my two boys, then under five. One day I calculated the distribution of my daily cards to that point and found the following:

- Wands—24
- Cups—44
- Swords 41
- Pentacles—57
- Major Arcana—56

How clearly this describes my life at that time—heavy on the real world (Pentacles) and basic forces (major arcana) and not so heavy on individual creativity (Wands).

In your journal, jot down a few highlights of the day next to your entry. This will help you correlate the cards with your moods and activities; but keep it simple, or you will soon tire of the effort.

I wrote my journal entries using five pens of different colors, one for each category:

- Wands = Red (Fire, passion)
- Cups = Blue (Water, moods, emotion)
- Swords = Yellow (Air, mentality)
- Pentacles = Green (Earth, growth, plants, nature, money)
- Major Arcana = Purple (spirituality, higher purpose)

Color coding helps you see at a glance the shifting tarot patterns of your weeks and months.

You will probably be surprised to find that you draw certain cards over and over. Of the fifty-seven Pentacles I recorded early on, I drew the Ace and Queen eleven times each! At home with my children, so many of my days reflected the themes of these two cards. The Queen of Pentacles is the ultimate nurturing mother. The Ace of Pentacles offers opportunities to enjoy the material side of life, and it doesn't get more material than cleaning dirty diapers!

I picked these two cards so often that I became suspicious about them. I examined them closely one day to see if I had damaged them in such a way that I would be more likely to select them. They appeared no different from the others. I was simply drawn to them because they expressed my situation at that time. The cards you select frequently will also tell you about your concerns.

The most important step in learning the tarot is to take the cards out of the box regularly. The Daily Reading is the ideal solution. If you do one each day, you will absorb the character of each card quickly and easily.

The Environment

The environment of a tarot reading includes the physical setting and your internal state. There are five inner qualities that are beneficial. These are:

Being Open. Being open means being receptive. It is an attitude of allowing—being willing to take in what is offered without denial or rejection. By being open, you give yourself the chance to receive what you need to know.

Being Calm. It is hard to hear the whispers of your Inner Guide when you are in turmoil. Tarot messages often arrive as gentle hints and realizations that can be easily overwhelmed by a restless mind. When you are calm, you are like a peaceful sea in which every ripple of insight can be perceived.

Being Focused. Focus is very important for a tarot reading. I have found that when I feel a question strongly, I receive a direct and powerful message. When I'm scattered and confused, the cards tend to be the same. Your most insightful readings will be those you do when the desire is very strong.

Being Alert. When you are alert, all your faculties are alive and awake. A cat is alert when it is watching a mouse or bug. Of course, you won't be stalking your cards, but you *will* find them difficult to read if you are tired or bored.

Being Respectful. Being respectful means treating the cards as you would any valued tool. You acknowledge their role in helping you understand yourself better. You honor the choice you have made in deciding to learn the tarot, and handle the cards accordingly.

Even though these five qualities are important, they are not necessary. You can have a meaningful reading without them, but it may be more difficult. The best way to decide if the time is right for a reading is to look inside. If something feels wrong, postpone the effort, but if your inner sense says go ahead, then all is well.

Besides the inner environment, there is the setting of a reading to consider. The ideal place is one that elicits feelings of quiet, peace, even reverence. You could do a reading in a crowded airport, but the noise and distractions would make inner attunement difficult. Since you will probably be doing most of your readings at home, let's look at how you might create an agreeable environment there.

Set aside a place in your home where you will do your readings. By using the same spot over and over, you build up an energy that reinforces your practice. If you meditate or pray, you can do these activities here as well, as they harmonize with the tarot in spirit and intent.

Try to create a sense of separateness about your spot. When you use the cards, you want to turn away from the everyday world and go into a space that is outside time and the normal flow of events. A separate room is ideal, but a corner set off by a screen, curtain, pillows, or other divider can work too.

Try also to create an atmosphere of beauty and meaning. Place some items nearby that are special to you. Objects from nature, such as shells, stones, crystals, and plants are always appropriate. A talisman, figure, or religious icon may help you shift your focus from the mundane to the inspirational. Consider pictures and artwork, especially your own, and appeal to your senses with such items as flowers, incense, candles, textured materials, and quiet, meditative music.

These touches are nice, but all you really need is a space large enough to lay out the cards. You can use a table or the floor. There is a grounded feeling to the floor, but, if that position is uncomfortable, a table is better. Choose a table of natural materials such as wood or stone.

If you like, you can cover the table or floor with a cloth to create a uniform area. The material should be natural, such as silk, cotton, wool, or linen. Choose the color with care as colors have their own energies. Black, dark blue, and purple are good choices. There should be little or no pattern, so the images on the cards stand out from the background.

Store your cards in a container to protect them and contain their energies. Any natural substance is fine, such as wood, stone, shell, or a natural cloth. I know of one woman who sewed herself a silk, drawstring bag and embroidered it with stars, moons, and other designs. Consider keeping your cards wrapped in silk cloth when inside their container. Silk has a luxurious feel that will remind you of the value you place on your cards.

Tarot cards pick up the energy and character of those who use them. For this reason, set aside a tarot deck that is just for you, if you can. These cards are going to be your personal tool of communication with your Inner Guide. You want to bond to them closely.

When you do your tarot work in a place of your own, the experience can be quite powerful, but extra preparations are never necessary. All you have to do is use the cards. That's the important part.

Writing a Question

Most of the time you will consult the tarot because you are facing a problem or challenge. Something about your life is troubling you, and you want to understand why it is happening and what you can do about it. The best kind of tarot reading for this situation is the Question Reading. You write a question about your problem, and you receive your answer by interpreting the cards. The question helps you relate the guidance you receive to your situation in a way that makes sense. In this lesson, I describe how to create a question for a reading you do for yourself.

The first step is to review your situation thoroughly. Think about all the people involved, directly or indirectly. Go over your options for the future. Let your mind wander freely. You want to look at your problem without judging or censoring any part. Jot down the ideas that occur to you, but try not to be too systematic. You want to use your intuition, not logical analysis.

Once you have finished your review, you can write your question. Here are some suggestions.

Accept Responsibility

Write your tarot question to show that you accept responsibility for your situation. Consider these two questions:

1. Should I put my father in a nursing home, or take care of him in my house?
2. What do I need to know to decide on the best living arrangements for my father?

In the first question, the writer gives up her responsibility for making a decision. She wants the cards to *tell* her what to do. In the second question, she is simply asking the cards for more information. She knows the decision lies with her.

It's tempting to write the first kind of question. We all seek the certainty that we're making good choices, but, the tarot can't make our decisions for us. Avoid questions that deflect responsibility, such as:

1. Questions to be answered "Yes" or "No"
   Will I get the job at the ad agency?
   Can I stick to my diet this month?
   Am I ready to retire?
2. Questions beginning with "Should . . . "
   Should I let my daughter live at home?
   Should I go out with José?
   Should I apply to more than one university?
3. Questions asking only about time
   When will George ask me to marry him?

How long will it take to find a new car?

When will I get my promotion?

Instead, begin your questions with phrases such as:

Can you give me insight into . . .

What do I need to understand about . . .

What is the meaning of . . .

What is the lesson or purpose of . . .

What are the circumstances underlying . . .

How can I improve my chances of . . .

How might I . . .

Keep Your Options Open

Write your question to show that you are keeping your options open. Consider these:

1. How might I encourage my mother-in-law to move out?
2. What do I need to know to get along better with my mother-in-law?

In the first question, the writer is not keeping his options open. He has decided on one solution—having his mother-in-law move out. The second question is more open-ended. It's OK to narrow the scope of a question as long as you don't decide on the answer ahead of time. Both of the following are open questions, but the second is more specific:

1. How would a switch to sales impact my career?
2. How would a switch to a sales position at Purdue Insurance impact my career?

Find the Best Level of Detail

Seek the fine line between wording that is too vague and too detailed. Here are three questions on the same topic:

1. How can I improve my work situation?
2. How can I reorganize my desk so that Tom can find my files?
3. How can I improve the flow of work between Tom and me?

The first question is unfocused. It doesn't specify which work area is of interest. The second question is too detailed. It looks at one minor aspect of the problem. The third question is best because it finds the balance between the two. Include only the details necessary to make clear what you want to know.

Focus On Yourself

When you do a reading for yourself, you are always the central character. Your question should focus on you. There are times when questions about others are fine (see Lesson 9), but not when you are concentrating on your own concerns.

Sometimes you may not realize you are orienting your question around someone else. Consider these:

1. What is behind Arthur's drinking problem?
2. How can I assist Arthur with his drinking problem?
3. What role do I play in Arthur's drinking problem?

The first question focuses totally on Arthur and his problem. In the second question, the writer is included, but his *attention is still on Arthur*. The third question is best because it is grounded solidly in the writer's own experience.

Stay Neutral

Stay as neutral as possible when writing your questions. It is easy to begin a reading convinced that your position is the right one, but if you truly want to receive guidance, you need to be open to other points of view. Consider these sets of questions:

1. Why am I the only one doing chores?
2. How can I foster a spirit of cooperation concerning the chores?

1. How can I make people listen when I'm talking?
2. What is going on when I try to communicate, but feel others aren't listening?

1. How can I make my boss stop asking me to do overtime?
2. Why have I had to do so much overtime recently?

In the first questions, the writer feels his position is the correct one—others are not getting with the program! The second questions are more neutral and open-ended.

Be Positive

Be positive when writing your questions. Consider these:

1. How come I can never get my research published?
2. How can I find the ideal forum in which to publish my research?

1. Why can't I overcome my fear of public speaking?
2. How can I improve my ability to speak to groups effectively?

1. Can you help me understand why I always blow a tournament in the last round?
2. Can you help me find a way to push on to victory in a tournament?

The first questions have an air of defeat. The second questions are more confident. The writer knows she will be successful given useful advice.

• • •

You may be wondering why I have gone into so much detail about writing a question. This process is a focusing exercise that prepares you for the reading that follows. Writing a question usually takes no more than three or four minutes, but, for that small investment in time, you reap big rewards. You understand your situation better and can interpret your reading with more insight.

The Question Reading

In this lesson, you will finally learn how to do a full tarot reading for yourself. I describe a simple procedure you can use to explore a personal question. Having a procedure to follow is important in tarot work. When you follow the same steps over and over in a certain way, they help you center yourself in the moment. The details of the steps are not that important; in fact, you can change any of them if you wish. The goal is to maintain a spirit of mindfulness. Doing a reading with loving concentration will make your tarot practice very powerful.

Here is the procedure for a Question Tarot Reading. (See Appendix F for a step-by-step outline.)

Setting the Mood

Your first step is to create a conducive mood. Lesson 6 offers some suggestions on how to set up a pleasing environment. You can try these ideas, if you like. Focus on what will make you feel comfortable and secure.

When you are ready, sit down on the floor or at a table leaving some empty space in front of you. You should have your tarot cards and your question written on a piece of paper. (See lesson 7 for how to write a question.) At first, a full reading will probably take at least thirty to forty minutes. Try to arrange your affairs so you won't be interrupted. With experience, you will be able to shorten this time, if you wish, but it is always better to feel unhurried.

Begin to relax and still your mind. Put aside your worries and concerns for now. (You can always get them back later!) Settle fully into the present moment. Take a few deep breaths, relax all your muscles, and feel the quiet as you turn away from the outside world. Take as much time as you need for this calming process.

Asking Your Question

When you feel centered, take your cards out of their container. Hold them cupped in one hand while you place the other hand on top. Close your eyes and bring the cards into the circle of your energy.

Now, make an opening statement, if you wish. Some possibilities are:

> a prayer;
> an affirmation;
> a description of how you are feeling;
> a simple hello to your Inner Guide.

You can write a phrase to say every time, or you can speak spontaneously. It is more important to speak from your heart than to mouth an empty formula. Say your statement out loud, as sound adds energy and conviction.

Next, ask your question, either from memory or by reading it. Be sure to say your question exactly as you wrote it. One of the mysteries of the unconscious is that it is very literal; the cards you choose will often reflect the precise wording of your question.

Shuffling the Cards

Open your eyes and begin shuffling. It is important to shuffle the cards because this is how you sort through all the forms your reading could take and arrange at a subtle level the one you will receive.

There are a number of ways to shuffle the cards. Each method has its pros and cons. Choose one that is most comfortable for you. (See appendix E for some shuffling choices.) Certain methods mix the cards so some are right side up (upright) and some, upside-down (reversed). If this is your first reading, do not worry about reversed cards. I will explain these in lesson 17.

Concentrate on your question while you shuffle. Focus on the overall intent rather than the details. Don't strain to stay fixed, but do keep the question in mind as much as you can.

Cutting the Cards

When you feel you have shuffled long enough, stop and place the cards face down in front of you with the short edge closest to you. Cut the deck as follows:

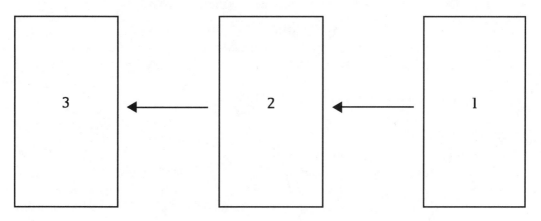

1. Grab some number of cards from the complete pile.
2. Drop this smaller pile to the left.
3. Grab some part of this second pile and drop it further to the left.
4. Regroup the cards into one pile in any fashion.

It's best to regroup the cards in one quick motion. Don't try to figure out which pile should go where. Just let your hand move where it will. The cut is an important finishing step that marks the end of the card-arranging stage. Once you have regrouped the cards, the pattern of the reading is fixed, and all that remains is to lay out the cards and see what they reveal.

Laying Out the Cards

Follow the steps for the spread you have chosen. If this is your first reading, use the Celtic Cross. (Before actually laying out the cards, read the next step, "Responding to the Cards.")

1. Pick up the deck and hold it in one hand with the short edge closest to you.
2. With your other hand, turn over the first card as you would the page of a book.
3. Place this card in Position 1. (The position number corresponds to the placement order.)
4. Turn over the second card, and place it in Position 2.
5. Continue in this way until you have placed all the cards.
6. Turn any reversed cards around if you are not using them.

Responding to the Cards

Pay attention to your reactions to each card as you lay it out. At first, you will not know or remember the usual meaning of a card. Your thoughts and feelings will be based mainly on the images. As you practice, your reactions will become more informed, but also more predictable. Try to keep some of your original openness as much as possible. Pay attention to any responses that seem unusual or out of place.

When all the cards are laid out, take a moment to respond to them as a whole. Do you get an overall impression? Do you have any new reactions? Jot down some of your thoughts, if you wish. Don't worry if you can't remember all of them. Just as with dreams, you will recall the most important. Try not to get too involved in your notes as that can break the flow of the reading. You simply want to capture a few ideas quickly.

Analyzing the Cards

In the beginning, use the section about individual cards for help. Later, you can examine the cards on your own, but you may still find this section useful. (I use it myself from time to time!)

Begin your review with Position 1 and proceed in position order. Here are the suggested steps:

1. Look up the card in section 4.
2. Read through all the keywords and actions.
3. Look for actions that make you say "Yes, that one really fits!" I experience a kind of jolt of recognition when I see one. Don't shy away from actions that seem less pleasant. Trust your reactions, and reserve judgment until you've seen all the cards. Note any stray thoughts or "irrelevant" feelings that come to mind.

When you've considered each card, look for relationships between them. Apply the principles of interpretation. (These are covered in lessons 11–18.)

You could ponder a reading for hours without running out of insights, but, of course, this isn't practical or desirable. Do try to spend some time, however. Your reward will be equal to your effort.

Creating the Story

At some point, you need to pull everything together. I call this creating the story (see lesson 18). Your story will help you understand your situation and give you guidance for the future—what you have been seeking all along.

I recommend that you create your story spontaneously. Once you have finished your card review, let that analytical approach go. It's no longer appropriate. Your story will be more authentic if it arises freely from within. When you feel ready, simply begin speaking your story, saying whatever comes to mind. Use any notes you have to help, but don't focus on them too much.

I encourage you to tell your story out loud. Writing is too slow, and just thinking your ideas is too vague. Your story will gather strength and power as it is spoken. If you begin to ramble or lose your train of thought, don't be concerned. Simply pause, regroup, and start again. As you practice, you will get better at speaking on the fly. You may want to tape your story. When you play back the tape, you will be amazed at what you hear. You will truly feel you are your own best tarot reader.

Writing the Summary Statement

Your story is done when your words slow down and stop naturally. Your next step is to distill the main theme of your story. What is the essence of your guidance? Ask yourself these kinds of questions:

What is the problem or conflict?
What is my role?
What does my Inner Guide want me to understand?
What is the projected outcome?
How do you feel about that?
Do I sense any recommendations for action?

What you are doing is forming the answer to your question. Before the reading, you posed a question that had meaning for you. Your Inner Guide has responded, and now you want to capture that wisdom in a form you can remember. Try to summarize your story in one or two sentences. Concentrate on the message in the cards and not the mechanics of your interpretation.

Finishing Up

The main event is over, but as with any ceremony, there are a few final steps to take to end your reading and leave your cards ready for next time.

If you have not already done so, write down the cards you selected and their positions. It is easy to forget them. Then, *clear the deck* to remove all traces of the energy patterns of this reading. I clear a deck by scrambling the cards together gently. It reminds me of erasing letters in the sand with a sweep of my hand. You may enjoy this technique as well, but any shuffling method will do (see Appendix E). Take a few moments now to clear your deck. Make sure the cards are face down or turned away from you. Stop when you feel you've shuffled long enough, and gather the cards together. Your deck is ready for your next reading.

Before putting the cards away, hold them again for just a moment. Place your deck in one hand with the other hand on top, and close your eyes. Say what you feel you have learned from this reading. Express your gratitude to your Inner Guide for helping you via the tarot cards. Gratitude is a wonderful sentiment. It provides the ideal frame of mind in which to end your reading.

When you began, you initiated a cycle. You created meaning in the form of a reading, and now you have completed that cycle by returning the cards to their resting state.

Using What You Have Learned

The reading proper is over, but the inner work is just beginning. Your goal is to integrate what you have learned into your life in some way. If you don't, your tarot practice will remain a beautiful pastime with no power to help you.

Decide on one or more actions you can take to put your guidance to work. You can reinforce what you're doing now or make some changes, either radical or minor. Specific actions are usually more helpful than vague plans.

If you are keeping a journal, write down what you intend to do. Commit only to what you know you will actually carry out. I know how easy it is to lay out some cards, look at them briefly and then never think about that reading again, especially when your reaction is less than positive!

As the days go by, think about your reading and how it meshes with your life. Ask yourself these questions:

How meaningful was my story?
How well did the guidance fit?
Did I miss any clues?
Did I carry out an action, and, if so, what happened?
Did something unexpected occur?
Can my Daily Readings add anything?

You may be tempted to do another reading, but it's probably best to wait until there are important changes in your situation. Assume that your first reading covers all you need to know. If you are puzzled about certain elements, mine your first reading for more insights. By going deeper, you will get closer to the heart of the matter.

Using what you have learned in a reading is probably the most important step—and the most difficult. It involves moving beyond playing with the cards. When you actually commit to integrating your tarot insights into your life, you have realized the true and lasting benefit to be gained from the cards.

This is my ideal tarot session, but, to be truthful, I don't always follow it. Sometimes I linger over these steps, sometimes I neglect quite a few of them. I encourage you to adopt whatever procedure suits your interests and needs. If you don't enjoy the cards, they'll just gather dust on the shelf. The details aren't that important; it's the intention that counts!

The Other Reading

You can do a tarot reading that is centered on another person or subject. I call this the Other Reading. An Other Reading is appropriate whenever you are simply curious about someone or something that doesn't involve you directly. Other Readings are *about* someone, not *for* him or her. When a reading is for someone, that person writes the question and you simply help interpret the cards.

Other Readings are fun and informative. They are also a good way to learn the tarot. When you use the cards for yourself, you only get to look at a limited set of problems—your own! Other Readings let you explore much more.

Except for choosing the subject, the procedure for an Other Reading is basically the same as the one in lesson 8. The few differences are noted below. (See Appendix G for a step-by-step outline.)

1. Your first step is to decide on the subject of your reading. You can focus on just about anything—a person, animal, place, problem, or news event—as long as you identify the subject ahead of time. Usually it will be the central figure in a situation, but it doesn't have to be.

   Your subject can be a group entity, such as a marriage, family, team, or neighborhood. You can focus on a country or the Earth, but for such large entities, the information will be very general.

   You may be tempted to do an Other Reading about someone who is close to you—a relative, friend, or colleague. In lesson 7 I talk about the importance of focusing on yourself in readings that concern you. Here is a simple test you can take to decide whether an Other Reading is advisable. Ask yourself three questions:

   Do I feel *strong emotions* when I think about this person in this situation?
   Do I have a vested interest in this situation?
   Do I desire a particular outcome in this situation?

   If your answer is yes to any of these questions, you should probably do a reading centered on yourself rather than an Other Reading.

   You now need to write a question. Follow the suggestions in lesson 7, but write the question about your subject. Focus on the aspect of your subject that interests you. If you are wondering about a politician who is running for president, your question might be: "What are the factors impacting Mr. or Ms. Candidate's chances to become the next president?"

2. When setting the mood, place a picture of your subject nearby to help you focus during your reading. An object that reminds you of your subject works well too.

3. When asking your question, say something about the other person or why you are

doing an Other Reading. Request guidance that is in the best interest of all concerned, and mention that you hold only good intentions toward your subject. (If you can't say this truthfully, consider a reading for yourself instead!)

4. As you respond to the cards, remember they refer to the other person, not to you. However, don't be surprised if you see in the cards some interesting correspondences with your own life!

5. When analyzing the cards, in an Other Reading, you are seeing the situation from your own point of view. What you see in the cards may or may not be related to what the subject actually experiences.

6. Even though an Other Reading focuses on someone else, there is still a lesson for you in the cards. Try to identify this lesson so you can apply it in your own life.

The Open Reading

An Open Reading is a request for guidance that is not tied to a particular problem. You don't write a question. You simply give your Inner Guide an opportunity to communicate what you most need to know at a given moment.

For most occasions the Question Reading is the best type because it zeroes in on the issue that is most important to you. Just as with the telephoto lens of a camera, a question lets you move in to focus more narrowly on a subject, but it also keeps you from seeing the bigger picture. An Open Reading has more scope. It covers your long-term growth and development. It offers a higher level of guidance that embraces the larger patterns that are shaping your everyday experiences.

Open Readings can be quite powerful. I try to use them sparingly to preserve their out-of-the-ordinary quality. Consider them for special occasions, such as: birthdays, anniversaries, ceremonial days, equinoxes, and first days (new job, date, trip).

Open Readings are useful when you are standing on the threshold of a new phase, such as after the birth of a child or move to a new house. Open Readings can help you adjust to new or unpredictable situations ahead of time. Whenever an expanse of unknown is opening out before you, that is a perfect time for an Open Reading.

The procedure is basically the same as the one in lesson 8. The few differences are noted below. (See Appendix H for a step-by-step outline.)

1. To prepare for an Open Reading, you want to avoid the analysis that goes into writing a question. Simply let your mind empty of all cares and concerns. There is nothing you have to do or arrange except a gentle quieting of the mind.

2. Instead of reading a question, say a more general message of intent such as: *I welcome a message of wisdom and open myself to receive the guidance that I most need at this time.* You can narrow the focus a little as long as you avoid specific people and events. If you're interested in your health, you can add a phrase to that effect: *I welcome a message of wisdom about my health and open myself to receive the guidance that I most need at this time.*

3. Keep your mind free and open while you shuffle. If a thought drifts by, let it gently pass without fixing on it. Ideally, you should feel like an empty house with all the windows open to every soft breeze.

4. As a rule, when analyzing the cards, you want to step back from the details of your life and let the cards show you the larger themes. Concentrate on the patterns as revealed in the reading. View everything in a wider context. Open Readings are not about the everyday.

5. It is not necessary to commit to specific actions. Simply absorb the spirit of the message and allow it to guide you in a general way.

Part 2

Principles of Interpretation

Introduction

You're seated in front of your first tarot reading. You've shuffled, cut, and laid out ten cards for the Celtic Cross. Your first thought is probably, "Now, what do I do?"

When I first began learning the tarot, I sought the answer to this question everywhere—in classes, conversations, books, and practice. I was looking for the one, *true way* to interpret the cards. Of course, I never found such a system because it doesn't exist. Reading the tarot is an art, not a science. There can be no set rules that apply all the time because every person is unique. How could a set of formulas ever provide guidance that honors that uniqueness?

On the other hand, there are some ways to approach the cards that have proven valuable time and again. They work because they bring form and focus to intuitive responses. They provide a framework around which you can build the special message of each reading.

In the next nine lessons, I share some of the principles of interpretation that I have discovered. I offer these as guidelines to help you develop a feel for readings and what they can tell you. Take from them what works for you and use them to create a tarot approach that is uniquely your own.

Interpreting a Single Card

When I interpret a reading, I go back and forth between sensing the cards as a whole and examining each one individually. The two approaches reinforce each other. In this lesson, we will look at how to interpret one card in a reading on its own. There are four sources of meaning:

1. The first is your unique response to a card based on your background, personality, and state of mind. This element keeps the meaning of the card personal and fresh.
2. The second is the set of meanings that have built up around a card over the years. These vary with different tarot writers and teachers. My suggestions for each card are given in section 4.
3. The third is the set of meanings associated with the *position* of a card. These are also based on convention and common experience. My suggestions for the Celtic Cross are given in section 5.
4. The fourth is your question or life circumstances. This element provides a framework for your responses. It sets boundaries and helps you relate a card to one area of your life.

To interpret a card, you need to combine these four sources of meaning into some composite that makes sense to you. This is a fluid process. These areas seem separate, but in practice, they blend together, and your response just happens.

At first, you will probably rely on the card and position meanings to guide you. Later, your personal reactions will be more important. Your reaction may be triggered by a card's image. The scenes on the cards can seem to relate to your situation very directly. For example, if you are building a house, the document on the Three of Pentacles may strike you as a set of blueprints.

Assume that you have drawn the upright Seven of Cups in Position 5. Your question is: "How can I improve my chances of receiving a bonus this year?"

To begin reviewing this card, you would first note your reactions. Perhaps your glance falls on the cup filled with jewels. The figure in the foreground seems to be looking directly at this cup. You identify with him as he reaches out for treasure. This fits your question—you're *reaching out* for a bonus.

Next, you look at the keywords for the Seven of Cups. They are:

wishful thinking
options
dissipation

When you read through the actions, you are struck by the following:

> kidding yourself about the facts
> waiting for your ship to come in
> lacking focus and commitment

These phrases suggest someone who is passive and unrealistic, who lacks the energy and desire for success. They reinforce the idea of wishful thinking.

On reading over the meanings for Position 5, you feel a pull toward:

> your delusions and illusions
> what you're obsessed about
> what you've set your heart on

The sense of this card is beginning to take shape for you. The card seems to be suggesting that you are too busy daydreaming to act constructively. The figure now strikes you as awed by the cup dangled in front of him. You decide that this card represents for you at this time an attitude of unreasonable hopes and unproductive dreaming. This is your *first* feeling about what the card is saying. You may modify that assessment later when you examine the other cards.

Clearly there are other possibilities. You might have been struck by the array of delights floating in front of the shadowy figure. He seems to have many *options*, another meaning of the Seven of Cups.

There is never just one right answer in tarot work! Both of these interpretations make sense. You may wonder how you can decide on the best meaning when there are so many possibilities. You must trust your intuition. Your Inner Guide will give you hints that will lead you toward the ideas that are most important for you. An insistent thought may keep popping into your mind. You may circle around a meaning—thinking about it, moving off, then finally coming back. When one meaning hits you with particular force, you know you're on the right track. This is the "Aha" reaction. An "Aha" reaction may not happen for every card, but when it does, you know it is important. These are the ways that inner knowing manifests.

Major and Minor Arcana Cards

Certain cards in the tarot naturally form into groups. These cards have unique meanings, but they also have a common identity with the other cards in their group. The two largest subgroups are the major and minor arcanas. The terms *major* and *minor* reflect the relative weights of these two groups.

A major arcana card represents an energy that is deep, strong, decisive, or long-term. When a major arcana card appears in a reading, you have tapped into a powerful energy in some area of your life. The minor arcana cards do not carry the same weight, but they are still important. They chart the ups and downs of daily life and register changes in feelings and thoughts. These dramas are gripping while they occur, but they pass with time as new concerns take their place.

Compare the interpretation of two cards with similar meanings, but different weights—the Hermit (major) and the Eight of Cups (minor). The Hermit is the archetypal symbol of one who seeks truth and deeper meaning. He stands for the impulse to renounce superficial pleasures to seek understanding within. In a reading, the Hermit could hint that you are feeling a strong urge to find answers even if it means giving up aspects of your current way of life. This is not a passing fancy, but a major desire that could last for some time.

With the Eight of Cups, your interpretation *might be* much the same, but, as a minor arcana card, this card implies your search does not have the same force. Maybe you've been a little bored at work. Some days you feel like chucking everything to go make hats on the beach, but you don't really mean it. You *are* seeking, but the urge is not yet a heartfelt desire.

Let's say you have been happily married for many years, but suddenly find yourself attracted to an acquaintance. You consult the tarot and draw the Two of Cups in Position 1.

One of the meanings of this card is attraction—being drawn toward a person, place, or idea

that is pleasing. As a minor arcana card, the Two of Cups tells you your attraction is probably based on surface elements such as common interests or sexual desire. The feelings are strong, but they're mainly coming from the give-and-take of everyday adventure—*for now.*

If you had drawn the Lovers instead, you would have to give this attraction greater weight. As a major arcana card, the Lovers implies this relationship is not simple. The attraction is coming from a deeper place. There are elements that go beyond the casual and require more understanding.

You could draw a minor arcana card in one reading and then draw a major arcana card about the same subject in a later reading. What started as *minor* has become more important over time. Similarly, a *major* matter can fade and lose its urgency as your life changes. You can assume that a major arcana card brings greater energy to whatever area it represents. Give that aspect extra consideration and take advantage of the power building there.

Aces

Each Ace represents the qualities of its suit in their purest form. An Ace always adds something special to a reading. It stands out from the other cards as if in a circle of its own light. The images on the Aces are all similar. A strong hand, glowing with energy, comes out of a cloud grasping the token of its suit. An Ace "hands" you a gift that comes from some unknown source hidden in the clouds. The nature of the gift is symbolized by the suit token.

Ace of Wands

A wand is a strong, masculine object, alive with potent force. Leaves are growing as new life bursts forth. The wand reminds us of a magic wand used to perform miracles and create wonders. The gift of the Ace of Wands is creativity, enthusiasm, courage, and confidence.

Ace of Cups

A cup is an open, feminine object—a receptacle designed to hold nourishing liquids. Water pours from the cup showing there is a never-ending supply of refreshment flowing into the world. The gift of the Ace of Cups is emotion, intuition, intimacy, and love.

Ace of Swords

A sword is a weapon—a finely crafted tool to cut through any obstacle or confusion. A sword extends the power of its user to fight and prevail. It can wield a cruel force, but also a clean, sharp one. The gift of the Ace of Swords is mental clarity, truth, justice, and fortitude.

Ace of Pentacles

The pentacle is a magical sign for the mystery of nature and the everyday world. It is stamped on a coin, the token of material exchange. With money and raw materials, we have the wherewithal to make our dreams real. The gift of the Ace of Pentacles is prosperity, practicality, security, and the ability to manifest.

Aces are portals between the realms of the major and minor arcanas. They allow powerful, but impersonal forces to come into your life. An Ace in a reading shows that its qualities are becoming available to you. If you take advantage of them, you will achieve greater happiness and success. An Ace is always interpreted as beneficial, positive, and life-enhancing.

An Ace can indicate a new adventure is beginning. I once saw the Ace of Cups in Position 1 for a friend's reading about her new love affair. What better card to signal the beginning of love and intimacy? (Well . . . possibly the Fool, but that's another story!)

An Ace can also represent a window of opportunity that is opening. The Ace tells you to pay attention so you don't miss it. Think of an Ace as a seed of possibility that will grow given your attention and care.

A relative once drew the Ace of Pentacles in Position 1 and the Ace of Wands in Position 2—a dynamic combination that says "Look for a real, *creative* outlet for your energies that will bring greater *prosperity*." Several months later, she told me that—encouraged by this sign—she pursued a challenging opening at her workplace and was now making more money with greater personal satisfaction.

When you are working with an Ace, look for the potential in every situation. See how you might take advantage of whatever comes your way because you will have the chance to make real and important changes in your life.

Court Cards

You have probably noticed that people tend to fall into types. Their traits cluster together in familiar ways. We sometimes give these clusters names, such as "loner," "dreamer," or "life of the party." Psychologists have devised elaborate systems that categorize types of people. The popular Myers-Briggs is one such system.[1]

The tarot has its own system of personalities represented by the 16 court cards—the King, Queen, Knight, and Page of each suit. In lesson 3, you learned about the four suits and court card ranks. These are the keys to understanding the court cards because the personality of each one is a combination of its suit and rank.

Kings
The King of Wands is creative, inspiring, forceful, charismatic, and bold. These are typical positive traits of the Wands suit. They are prime examples of its dynamic fire energy, but they also reflect the character of a King. Kings are active and outgoing. They want to make an impact on the world through the force of their personality.

Queens
The Queen of Wands is attractive, wholehearted, energetic, cheerful, and self-assured. These are also Wands qualities. This Queen is upbeat and lively, but she does not wield her personality as a force directed outward. Queens express their suits from the inside, setting a tone without imposing it.

Knights
Knights are extremists; they express their suit qualities to the maximum. Such excessive feelings and behavior can be either positive or negative depending on the circumstances.

For example, the Knight of Pentacles has an excess of caution—a trait typical of the steady, conservative Pentacles nature. This Knight prefers to check and double-check everything. He always proceeds slowly before committing himself—the kind of person you would ask to fold your parachute or guide you through a mine field.

---

1. I. B. Myers, *The Myers-Briggs Type Indicator* (Palo Alto, CA: Consulting Psychologists Press, 1962).

On the other hand, you could also say the Knight of Pentacles is unadventurous. He will never double his money in two months through a risky investment or propose a surprise trip to Paris on a whim. Such daring moves are not in his nature. You would have to check with the Knight of Wands for that!

The keywords for the Knights are positive and negative word pairs (cautious/unadventurous). In readings, you must consider both views when interpreting a Knight. Does he represent a beneficial or harmful approach? The other factors (and your own honesty!) will help you decide.

Pages

Each Page shows a happy child holding the token of his suit. He is fascinated by his plaything. The Pages inspire us to enjoy their interests with them. The Page of Swords can represent the thrill of intellectual discovery or other mental challenges.

Pages also encourage you to "Go for it!" Children do not hesitate when they want something. They reach out and grab. If you want what the Page is offering, don't be afraid. Seize the day!

If the Page of Cups is your card of the day, and a fellow student smiles at you, take this opportunity for friendship. Strike up a conversation or suggest getting a cup of coffee after class. This Page encourages you to bring love and sharing into your life.

In many tarot systems, the court cards represent people of a certain age and type. For example, the Queen of Swords is often a divorced woman. To me, this way of looking at court cards is too limiting. Traits are not limited to certain groups. The King's approach may be more typically masculine, but his style is also available to women. Children are more often playful, but that doesn't mean that a Page must always represent a child.

A court card in a reading is showing you how a certain approach to life is (or could be) impacting your situation. There are several possibilities.

First, a court card can show a side of you that is being expressed or seeking expression. It may be a side you value, or one you neglect. It may be an approach you recognize, or one you deny. How you view it depends on your question, the other cards, and the situation.

Let's say you are trying to decide whether or not to enter into a business partnership. If you draw the King of Swords, you could interpret him as a way for you to act in this situation—to be fair and ethical, to review everything carefully, and to articulate your needs. If you are already taking this approach, the King of Swords affirms your position, but, if you are lying or hiding something, this card asks you to reconsider.

A court card can also represent another person. If you look at a court card and say to yourself, "I know who that is!" then it probably is that person. It may also represent someone of whom you are not yet aware.

KNIGHT of CUPS.

Let's say you have met someone who is very romantic. You spend long hours together and connect on a deep level. In a reading, the Knight of Cups could represent this new lover, but, since he is a Knight, you should look at this relationship closely.

What are you hoping to experience with your lover? You may be enjoying the romance, but are you also looking for dependability and commitment? The Knight of Cups is a signal to you that this relationship may be lopsided: abundant in intimate sharing, but deficient in other ways.

QUEEN of PENTACLES

Finally, a court card can reflect the general atmosphere. Sometimes, an environment seems to take on a personality of its own—one that matches a court card type.

Let's say you consulted the tarot to find out about the group house you just joined and drew the Queen of Pentacles. You wonder if you will get along with your future housemates. This card could be telling you that the atmosphere will be nurturing. Your housemates will be warm and generous with a sensible approach to problems.

On the other hand, you may meet someone in the house who is similar to the Queen of Pentacles, or you may be like her yourself in this situation. Such is the subtle play of the tarot!

The court cards have a human dimension that the other cards do not, so they can give you clear messages about who you are and what you want. The trick is to understand yourself and the situation so you can accept the messages when they come.

Card Pairs

There is a game called *Labyrinth* that consists of a square box with a platform inside. On the platform is a maze punctuated by little holes. The object is to move a ball from one end of the maze to the other without letting it fall into one of the holes. Knobs on the outside let you guide the ball by rotating the platform in any direction.

A simple game, but difficult in practice! The slightest miscalculation, and the ball goes down. If you lean the platform too far in one direction, you lose control. If you try to compensate, you lose control in the other direction. The only strategy that works is a patient shepherding of the ball along the path as you maintain a balance of movement and force in all directions.

I see in *Labyrinth* a metaphor for our navigation along the pathway of life. We travel from birth to death negotiating around the "holes" by continually balancing our approaches. We maintain steady progress forward by making countless life adjustments—first here, then there. Our actions offset each other in a dance that is sometimes delightful, often challenging.

The key is always balance. To achieve balance, we must know how to express all the energies available to us. Personal balance is never static. It comes from the ability to choose dynamically the option that will work in any given moment.

A tarot reading is a map of all the counterbalancing tendencies that are or could be operating in your life at one time. To read this map, you must understand the Law of Opposition—that any quality, once identified, implies its opposite. This is a basic principle of the material universe. The Fool discovers this principle at the very beginning of his journey when he meets the Magician and the High Priestess. These two show him that nothing can be defined in isolation, only as one pole of a balancing pair.

At the deepest level, opposition does not exist. There is just Oneness, but, in physical life, we perceive Oneness as broken up into countless different energies. These are the forces we navigate in our search for balance.

One way to discover balance issues is by looking for two cards in a reading that oppose each other. One meaning of the Eight of Swords is restriction—being trapped in an oppressive or limiting situation. If you ponder this meaning for awhile, you realize that simply by acknowledging the idea of restriction, you imply the opposing idea of freedom—the breaking out of bonds and limitations. This quality is represented by the Four of Wands.

In a reading, these two cards could be showing you the importance of the restriction/freedom issue in your life. They define the extreme ends of a continuum of experience from which you choose the best balance point for yourself. There are three types of card pairs.

Permanent pairs. Certain cards form clear and obvious permanent opposites. The Eight of Swords and Four of Wands are this type of pair. The Magician and the High Priestess are another. The Magician represents action and conscious awareness; the High Priestess, nonaction and unconscious awareness.

Court card and Ace pairs. You can create a pair between any two court cards or two Aces. These pairs reflect the balance patterns that emerge when you contrast two suits or ranks.

Consider the King of Pentacles and the Queen of Cups. Here are the keywords for these cards:

King of Pentacles	Queen of Cups
enterprising	emotional
adept	tenderhearted
reliable	intuitive
supporting	psychic
steady	spiritual

The King of Pentacles acts outwardly (King) in an enterprising, adept way based on his interest in the material world (Pentacles). The Queen of Cups has an inner focus (Queen) that is emotional and intuitive based on her concern with feelings (Cups).

In a reading, this pair could represent a conflict between two people—a can-do type who wants to get the job done, and a dreamer who first wants to see how everyone feels. This pair could also represent a dual approach within you—perhaps a need to focus on worldly concerns versus a desire to concentrate on the spiritual. There are many possibilities, all based on the dynamic between these two styles. Appendices C and D describe how the suits and ranks interact.

Occasional pairs. You can interpret any two cards as a pair, even if their meanings are not clearly opposites. There is so much meaning in every card that useful comparisons can almost always be made. Occasional pairs arise by chance, and their relationship lasts for only that one instance.

The Four of Cups shows a solitary man sitting under a tree. The Ten of Cups shows a happy family celebrating together. If the idea were meaningful to you, you might see these cards as defining the opposites of "being alone" versus "being with others." This understanding would occur to you out of the blue as a possibility.

Reinforcing Pairs. Two cards do not have to oppose each other to form a pair. They can reinforce each other. Both the Empress and the Nine of Cups suggest pleasure, sensuality, and physical enjoyment. Reinforcing pairs show that a certain energy is or could be having an extra impact. Sometimes we have to face circumstances in an unbalanced way for the moment in order to achieve our goals.

Balance issues are everywhere. Your tarot readings will help you identify them through the action of card pairs. In the next lesson, we will see how these pairs operate in the Celtic Cross.

Position Pairs in the Celtic Cross Spread

The Celtic Cross is a powerful spread because it contains many natural pairings. Certain positions complement each other, so the cards that fall there relate in meaningful ways.

Position 1 and Position 2—The Core Situation

The 1–2 pair is at the very center of the Celtic Cross. These cards form an obvious pair because Card 2 sits right on top of Card 1, turned 90 degrees! The 1–2 pair symbolizes the heart of a situation. It shows two factors coming together either on a collision course (example 1) or for mutual support (example 2). Sometimes Card 1 shows the central issue and Card 2 what you must do about it (example 3).

Examples—Position 1 and Position 2

1. Two Forces Colliding

Sharon[1] asked for a reading shortly after she reunited with her boyfriend. They had broken up a few weeks before because she wanted marriage and children, and he was reluctant. Now they were engaged. She drew the Ten of Cups as Card 1 and the Six of Pentacles as Card 2. The Ten of Cups shows the joy of romance and family that is the promise of this couple's future. Card 2 suggests that there are still issues of give-and-take to work out. The Six of Pentacles symbolizes the subtle (or not so subtle!) dance of dominance/submission that is a factor here.

2. Two Forces in Mutual Support

Julia did an Open Reading after quitting her job. She felt she was standing at the threshold of a new chapter in her life. She drew the King of Wands as Card 1 and the Empress as

---

1. Names used in all the examples in this lesson are not those of the actual participants.

Card 2. This striking pair combines two different, but powerful forces. Julia thought these cards meant that her future would include both the creative, inspiring energy of this King and the abundant, nurturing energy of the Empress.

3. What Is True and What That Implies

Nancy drew the Page of Swords as Card 1 and the Nine of Pentacles as Card 2. It turned out that her 8-year-old granddaughter Rose was much on her mind. Rose was quite a handful. During visits, she was often unruly and impossible to control—a real challenge (Page of Swords). The Nine of Pentacles told Nancy she would need to enforce a lot of discipline if she wanted to help Rose improve her behavior.

Position 3 and Position 5—Levels of Consciousness

Cards 3 and 5 represent two levels of awareness. You can learn much about a situation by comparing your innermost knowledge with your conscious attitudes. You can find out:

	Card 3	Card 5
(example 1)	real feelings	expected feelings
(example 2)	deeper truth	surface appearances
(example 3)	wisdom of higher self	beliefs of ego-self

Examples—Position 3 and Position 5

1. Real Feelings—Expected Feelings

Nicole did a reading to find out what to do about her friend Ann. Ann had asked Nicole to lie to her (Ann's) ex-husband about where she and their children were. Nicole drew the Ten of Wands as Card 3 and the Ten of Cups as Card 5. Nicole *thought* she should provide love and support to Ann and try to help keep peace in their family (Ten of Cups). At a deeper level, she was having trouble saying no. She felt burdened by the responsibility of the request and resented being dragged into this messy situation (Ten of Wands).

2. Deeper Truth—Surface Appearances

You have just gone through a bitter, unwanted divorce. You do a reading to try to come to terms with this blow, and you draw the Fool as Card 3 and the Five of Cups as Card 5. On the surface, you are feeling sad and defeated about your loss, but in fact, this change may represent an opportunity for you. The Fool suggests you may be on the threshold of a new, exciting time in your life. Deep inside, your faith in yourself is strong. Your future looks bright despite this apparent setback.

3. Higher Self—Ego-Self

I once did a reading to find out how I could open more to my higher self. I drew the Wheel of Fortune as Card 3 and the Two of Swords as Card 5. At a spiritual level, the Wheel of Fortune suggests the mystery behind everyday life. It indicates a mind ready to expand its personal vision. This card showed that a greater awareness was circling around inside, but I was blocking it. The Two of Swords told me I was choosing not to accept my inner knowing, probably because of my ego's fear.

Position 4 and Position 6—Time

Cards 4 and 6 are mirror images. Time is the theme of these two cards. Card 4 is the past, Card 6, the near future. Together they form the two halves of the circle of time that surrounds the present (Card 1). These cards can show something that is:

	Card 4	Card 6
(example 1)	moving away	approaching
(example 2)	to be released	to be embraced
(example 3)	already experienced	to be experienced

Examples—Position 4 and Position 6

1. Moving Away—Approaching

Sophia was wondering whether or not to have a third child. She drew the Knight of Cups as Card 4 and the Page of Cups as Card 6. These two court cards show exactly what would occur in time if she were to get pregnant. Her emotional (Cups) focus on the older children (Knight) would recede somewhat as her attention turned toward the baby (Page). The Knight and Page take on a special meaning here due to the ages they suggest.

2. To Be Released—To be Embraced

In a reading about a possible career change, I drew the Seven of Pentacles as Card 4 and the Eight of Wands as Card 6. The Seven of Pentacles is a card of assessment—the need to take stock before a decision. Here it suggests that such questioning needs to end. The time for quick action and conclusion is at hand as shown by the Eight of Wands. This pair seems to be saying, "OK, you've thought long enough. Just go ahead and make your move, whatever it is."

3. Already Experienced—To Be Experienced

Jeff had quit his job and was now working part-time while looking for a new position. He drew the Five of Wands as Card 4 and immediately saw this card as a symbol of the petty fighting that was rampant at his old company. The antagonistic atmosphere there was one of the reasons he had left, but Jeff still had another hurdle to face. The Four of Cups as Card 6 suggests he may need to go through a period of withdrawal and introspection before finding the job he is looking for.

Position 7 and Position 8—Self and Other

We may experience ourselves as separate from an outside world, but we are linked to our environment by countless threads of cause and effect, emotion and thought. The 7–8 pair can show us these connections. Card 7 represents you, Card 8, the other. Card 8 can stand for another person (example 1), group (example 2), or the environment in general (example 3).

Examples—Position 7 and Position 8

1. You and Another Person

Cynthia didn't share what was on her mind until she saw Justice as Card 7. When I told her this card can mean having to accept the results of a past action, she volunteered that she was worried about being pregnant. The timing was just not right for her and her boyfriend; however, she was comforted to see the Lovers as Card 8. This card suggests that another person—probably her boyfriend—will be loving and supportive. The Lovers card also reinforces the sexual context.

2. You and a Group

I was concerned about a drug I was being urged to take as part of a treatment program. I drew the Five of Pentacles as Card 7 and the Hierophant as Card 8. I interpreted the Hierophant as the orthodox medical establishment with its strong belief in the value of drug therapy. The Five of Pentacles shows how isolated I felt refusing to go along with the program, even though I was running the risk of illness.

3. You and the Environment

You are an enthusiastic saver. You enjoy the security of having a ready supply of cash in the bank, but now a business venture has come your way. You wonder if you should take it. You draw the Four of Pentacles as Card 7 and the Ace of Pentacles as Card 8. The Four shows your tendency to save, but the Ace suggests that this venture may be offering you the chance for greater financial rewards.

Position 5 and Position 10—Possible Futures

Three cards refer to the future: Card 6 (near future), Card 10 (longer-range future), and Card 5 (possible alternate future). The 5—10 pair lets you compare what you *think* will happen (Five) with what is actually projected to happen (Ten), if all energies continue as they are. There are several possibilities:

	Card 5		Card 10
(example 1)	positive vision	does not match	negative outcome
(example 2)	negative vision	does not match	positive outcome
(example 3)	vision	matches/reinforces	projected outcome

When Card 5 reinforces Card 10, your beliefs are flowing with the thrust of events. If you react positively to both cards, you can stay the course. If you react negatively, you can change your beliefs to change the outcome.

Examples—Position 5 and Position 10

1. Vision (Positive)—Projected Outcome (Negative)

You're working on your Ph.D. and have set the date for your oral presentation. You do a reading to see how well you are progressing and draw the Six of Wands as Card 5 and the

Nine of Swords as Card 10. This pair is giving you a loud wake-up call. You are picturing a triumphant victory parade for yourself, but the projected outcome is the opposite—an anxious experience. You need to take steps to make sure your projected future is more in keeping with your goal.

2. Vision (Negative)—Projected Outcome (Positive)

You've always wanted to quit your job and pursue music, but the reality of the move scares you. You wonder if you will ever have the nerve to try. You draw the Devil as Card 5 and the Three of Wands as Card 10. The Devil shows that even though you feel stuck, you're afraid to change. You think success is out of reach, and you're worried that you could lose everything. The Three of Wands suggests that if you take the leap and leave the secure behind, you may discover a whole new world for yourself.

3. Vision Matches Projected Outcome

You've noticed that Allison, your teenage daughter, has been aloof and secretive lately. You're wondering what's going on. You draw the Seven of Swords as Card 5 and the Tower as Card 10. The Seven shows how worried you are that your daughter is hiding something. The Tower suggests that if you don't talk to Allison soon, the result could be a crisis or angry scene that will be upsetting for everyone.

Position 9—Wild Card

Traditionally, Card 9 represents your "hopes and fears," but it can also be a guidance card. When you read the cards for yourself, you need a card to help you put everything together. Card 9 can explain and integrate the other cards by showing:

(example 1)   approach to take or way to proceed
(example 2)   key person, problem, or obstacle
(example 3)   element of surprise

Examples—Position 9

1. Your Guidance—the Way to Proceed

Two Knights once appeared in a reading for Ralph: Cups as Card 1 and Pentacles as Card 10. I sensed that this man was torn by the need to express two different sides of himself—the artistic and the practical. The key to this interpretation was the Two of Cups as Card 9. It told me that Ralph needed to unite his two impulses—combine the inner aspects that were at odds.

2. Problem or Obstacle

I've learned over the years that the Five of Swords is a special symbol for me. This card almost always implies that I'm putting my own interests before those of others when it is not wise to do so. This card appeared as Card 9 in a reading about the contract for this book. I knew right away I would have to watch my attitude if I wanted the arrangements to go smoothly. Over time you may find that certain tarot cards become personal symbols for you as well.

3. Surprises

One day I received a letter from my son's teacher. She wanted to talk to me about an incident in class. I drew the Five of Wands as Card 9.

I assumed this card meant my son was working at cross-purposes with his environment. Later, I learned the facts: my son had poked another child repeatedly with a pencil. This came as a surprise as he had never done such a thing before. In fact, the image on the Five of Pentacles was showing me the problem—a young person holding a long piece of wood (like a pencil!) and using it repeatedly as a weapon (five figures).

The cards in a reading do not always form pairs. Looking for them is just one technique among many. The pairings in this lesson are only suggestions. Let your intuition guide you to combinations that are meaningful to you.

Reversed Cards

When you shuffle the tarot cards, they often end up facing in different directions. So far, I've suggested that you ignore this effect and simply turn the upside-down cards around. Now you are ready to learn more about reversed cards and what they have to offer.

All life is energy—currents of force that mix and blend to form the patterns of our lives. Each tarot card symbolizes a particular energy, and a tarot reading shows the collective energies that make up a situation. When you do a reading, your actions and intentions align the energies of the moment with the cards to form a picture. The cards capture the energy currents in and around you as you shuffle and cut.

At any given moment, these energies will be at different levels. Some will be strong and powerful, others less so. Some will be entering your life, others, moving away. How you use these energies depends on all the factors that bear on your situation.

When a card is upright, its energy is free to manifest. Its qualities are available and active. When a card is reversed, its energy is not fully developed. It may be in its early stages, or losing power. It may be incomplete or unavailable. The qualities of the card *are* present, at least in potential, but they can't express completely.

The Sun's energy is just what you would imagine—expansive and enlightening. An upright Sun shows the energy of *vitality* is openly available. You feel confident and successful. Now is your chance to shine. A reversed Sun shows this same energy is present, but at a lower level. The vitality is reduced or limited in some way. You may feel lowered pep or enthusiasm. You may have a desire for greatness that is being frustrated. You want success, but something is holding you back.

The Empress reversed once appeared in a reading for a man who

wanted to know if he and his wife might have a child. I guessed they had been trying to have a baby for some time. This card showed that the energy of mothering and birth was present, but held down in some way. This pregnancy was blocked. I told this man that once the block was removed, the chances for a child were good. Something must have happened to free up that energy because now they have a beautiful baby girl!

It is tempting to view a reversed card as undesirable. This man wanted a baby, so he was disheartened by the reversed Empress. Someone else might have viewed the same card differently. Reversed cards are not negative in and of themselves. Everything depends on what you hope to achieve.

The Three of Swords represents the energy of heartbreak and betrayal. If this card is upright, hurtful feelings are a feature of the situation. Reversed, they are also present, but reduced. Perhaps the intensity of a painful episode is fading, or you are feeling lonely, but just a little. A reversed Three of Swords is more agreeable than an upright one, but it is still a cautionary sign. The fact that an unpleasant card appears at all means that its energy is present in some way.

Sometimes a card is reversed even though you are experiencing a high level of its energy. In this case, the reversal hints that you can improve your situation by making a conscious effort to lower the energy.

You have drawn the Seven of Wands reversed in a reading about being pressured to do something you don't want to do. This card represents defiance. Since you are being pushed against your will, you are probably feeling defiant in this situation. The Seven of Wands reversed suggests that you might try to subdue your strong emotions. Lessen your feelings of defiance and find a different way to deal with the problem. (Of course, it's possible that the energy is low because your defiance is being squelched! Only you can tell which interpretation is best.)

The meaning of a reversed card sometimes comes from a twist in the usual interpretation. In this sense, the Emperor reversed could show a powerful authority figure *toppled from his throne*. The Ten of Wands reversed might remind you to *get out from under* burdensome responsibilities. It's surprising how often such meanings apply, but you can't force them. They tend to occur as needed.

You can form pairs that contain reversed cards. Here is an example:

The Sun and Moon are opposites in the area of clarity—the Sun is enlightenment, the Moon, confusion. In a reading, a reversed Sun/upright Moon could show that certainty is low (Sun), and uncertainty is high (Moon), or you are bewildered now (Moon), but greater clarity is possible (Sun).

It's helpful to look at the proportion of reversed and upright cards in a reading. When many cards are upright, your energies are expressing freely and powerfully. The overall situation is well developed, and your purpose is clear. When many cards are reversed, your energies are low, and the situation is not clearly defined. You may lack direction or feel blocked, discouraged, and restricted. You could be in a topsy-turvy state where change is likely. Since energies are not well developed, they are free to go in new directions.

I encourage you to try using reversed cards. When you feel ready, state out loud your intention to use them. You might say, "I have decided to interpret reversed cards in my tarot readings." In this way, you acknowledge your decision with conviction. After a time, if you decide you like using reversed cards, add them to your practice permanently. If not, just let them go. It's better to decide one way or the other, as switching back and forth can be confusing.

Life is a constant energy flow—a marvelous dance guided by Spirit. When we understand that flow and move with it creatively, all things are possible. We can direct energy consciously or just let it take us where it will. In either case, reversed cards add an extra dimension to a reading that will help you appreciate the play of energy in your own life.

Creating the Story

In this lesson, you will learn how to pull together the elements of a reading—to create a tarot story. This is not an easy process to describe because storytelling is an art. Even though you can be shown a few techniques, in the end, you must develop your own style as a tarot artist. This is the challenge (and fun!) of card interpretation.

First, I want you to set aside everything you've learned so far! That's right, just disregard all those fancy principles. In the last seventeen lessons, you've been exposed to pages of information about the cards, and I've only touched on the possibilities! Other tarot books contain system after system for relating the cards to each other. This is fascinating stuff, but what is its real purpose? It is to find a way to release your inner knowing *through* the cards.

The techniques you've learned so far have been based on the idea that you must *figure out* what the cards are saying, but this is not really the case. If you think of a tarot reading as an object to be dissected, you will have trouble grasping its full meaning. A tarot story doesn't come from without; it arises from within. Your stories come from a part of you that is seeking expression and conscious realization.

Of course, I don't really want you to discard your tarot principles. They are valuable, but not because they hold the key to readings in themselves. They simply help you recognize what you already know. They draw you in so you can set up the circumstances to release your story.

The secret of creating a tarot story is getting from intellectual understanding to knowing, from a piecemeal grasp to a unified vision. To do this, you need to recognize and honor your feelings. Feelings in this sense are not moods or emotions. They are the language of your Inner Guide. They are the outward expression of a knowing that is deeper than thought. The main feature of knowing is a sense of rightness. You *know* your insights are correct when you *feel* complete and satisfied with them.

The best way I've found to release inner knowing is through stream-of-consciousness talking—saying your thoughts out loud *as they occur*, uncensored and uncontrolled. You make no attempt to organize or clean up your speech. You simply let the words come out.

This technique is effective because it bypasses the critical ego. It allows the wisdom of your Inner Guide to come forth spontaneously. You feel as if something within has been set free. Your first attempts will probably be awkward, but your stories will improve with practice. You will develop an ability to guide the flow of words without imposing your will on them. Sometimes insights will surface that completely surprise you!

It's not necessary to rush or talk continually. You can pause whenever you want, but avoid thinking when this happens. Simply wait patiently until you feel the impulse to continue. Sometimes repeating the name of a card a few times can help. Queen of Cups . . . Queen of

Cups . . . Queen of Cups. After each repetition, wait to see if anything comes to mind in the form of a thought or image.

Sometimes your story will just flow. You will have no trouble fitting everything together. Other times there will be gaps and empty places. Certain cards will stay stubbornly obscure. The moment may not be right for you to fully grasp these cards, or all the pieces of the story may not yet be in place.

Don't be concerned if you can't always create a beautiful narrative. Sometimes knowing comes in fragments. Stay with a reading only as long as the effort seems worthwhile. A partial understanding may be all you need.

I once drew the Ace of Pentacles reversed in Position 9. I knew right away that this card was telling me not to focus on money or material concerns. This realization hit me as soon as I saw the card. Everything I needed to know was in that one Ace, so interpreting the other cards was not all that necessary.

A good tarot spread makes weaving the pattern of the cards easy. By following the spread's built-in structure, your story unfolds naturally. Each spread has its own character based on its history, form, and purpose. I discuss some features of the Celtic Cross spread in that section.

Your tarot story ends when your talking begins to wind down and come to a stop. A few stray thoughts may still occur to you, but the main theme will have been established. You will know the essential message of the reading.

Stream-of-consciousness talking is an effective style for me, but you may not like it. You may prefer to sit quietly and absorb the meaning of the cards. Some people like to write out their reactions or create charts that cross-correlate the cards in a systematic way. Each of us is different, and our approaches to the tarot will be different too.

I'd like to leave you with one final thought about tarot stories. *Trust yourself and your intuition completely.* Banish right now any concerns you have about reading the cards correctly. You really can't make mistakes. Your tarot realizations are always the right ones for you at a given time and place. They are meaningful *because* they are yours. Know you are truly connected to all that is. You can access an understanding that is far greater than your everyday awareness. Trust that this is so.

Some Final Thoughts

My family loves horse racing. They pour over the statistics on the horses to see if they can pick the winner for each race. Sometimes I go with them and bring a friend who has never been to the races before. Invariably, I wind up sitting between my family, picking winners from experience, and my friend, picking winners from beginner's luck. I'm in the middle with no winners and just enough knowledge to be ineffective!

If you feel the same way right now about the tarot, don't be discouraged. At this point, you have a firm foundation of knowledge about the cards that will sustain you in the days ahead. If you continue to practice, you'll find the techniques become more and more invisible as your intuition takes over. Eventually you will reach a point where you can rely on your tarot abilities consistently. You won't have to continue working with the cards as intensely, unless you want to. These days I go to the cards only when I have a puzzling problem or situation that I know they can help me with. The tarot is a tool I can count on.

I'm sure you've found already that you do not feel neutral about your readings. No matter what the situation, as you lay out the cards, you hope for ones that will be positive and encouraging. This is only natural. In my experience, people want to know right away if their situation looks good. They respond cheerfully to the pleasant cards, but recoil in disappointment if a nasty one appears. Indeed, it *is* difficult to look at the Tower and accept it calmly. We don't want something scary to happen; we want the good!

THE TOWER.

In fact, the good and the bad are so mixed in life that these terms finally become meaningless. If you were to lose a leg in an accident, but then develop great inner strength during recovery, could you really say the accident was completely bad? If you were to be fired from your job, but then find a better one on the rebound, where is the positive and negative in this situation?

The cards in the tarot are not good or bad in themselves. They only describe certain energies or influences. It is up to you to use this information to make conscious choices about your life. Although the Tower can show a shattering breakup or downfall of some kind, you do not have to view this negatively. Sometimes an explosion of feeling or dramatic shakeup provides welcome relief, clearing the air and freeing up new energy.

It is your concentrated clarity about a situation that gives you the power to mold events along the lines of your choosing. This clarity comes from the wisdom of your Inner Guide paired with the fearless confidence you have in yourself. A reading does not deliver news to you as a passive victim, but as a powerful agent who can use that information creatively. It gives you a picture of the energy patterns in and around you so that you can work with them as you see fit.

Always remember that the outcome pictured in a reading is the one projected *for now* from all the influences of the present moment. If you can identify those forces, you can alter or encourage them as you wish. The future is never fixed. The outcome of your story is not a certainty, but a possibility. You can always embrace or change a direction provided you have the desire and courage to take the necessary steps. At the deepest level, you know what your situation is all about. Your tarot story simply lets you recognize what you know so you can act consciously.

Perhaps you are concerned that you aren't objective enough when reading the cards. You suspect that you only see in a reading what you want to see, and not the truth. In fact, that is exactly the point! The tarot helps you find out what it is you *do* believe, so you can acknowledge it. Your unconscious becomes conscious. You can't interpret falsely, but you *can* fail to perceive all that is there. The tarot is a mirror that reflects your own consciousness back to you. As you learn, that mirror becomes clearer, and you perceive at ever deeper levels.

A tarot practice is based on the understanding that wisdom from some Source will come to you through the cards. At first, you may have to accept this on faith, but after awhile you will receive the "proof" you need in the results you experience in your life. If you can approach the cards with trust, your tarot practice will take off. Good luck!

II

EXERCISES

Introduction to the Exercises

These exercises give you a chance to practice the concepts presented in the lessons. Do the ones that appeal to you, and take them at your own pace. You don't have to do any exercises before continuing with the lessons. They are completely optional. The later exercises do build on earlier lessons, so it's best not to skip ahead.

For some exercises, I give examples of possible responses. These are found in the "suggestions" section. My suggestions are *not* answers. They are simply examples of the kinds of insights you can get from the cards. In the tarot, whatever your intuition tells you is valid. Everyone sees the world through a different lens. Your goal is to learn how your own particular lens works.

Introduction to the Tarot

Exercise 1.1—What Do I Believe?

Think over the ideas presented in lesson 1. Write down briefly what you do and do not believe at this time about the tarot. Assign a percentage to your beliefs where:

0% = "I am totally skeptical about using the tarot for anything but fun."

100% = "I am absolutely convinced that the tarot can give me specific, personal guidance."

Exercise 1.2—Getting to Know a Card

Shuffle your tarot deck and choose a card. Look at the image for a while. Ask yourself these questions:

1. What story do I see in the picture?
2. What emotions do I feel?
3. How do the details in the picture reinforce those ideas?
4. What is the overall mood?
5. What do I think this card might mean?

When you are through, go to the information page for the card and read through the actions. Compare these to your impressions. Do not be concerned if your ideas do not match mine. Your intuition is working and already giving you some unique insights! You can repeat this exercise with as many cards as you like.

Exercise 1.3—How Do I Contribute to "Random" Events?

Choose an event from your past in which you felt victimized by forces over which you had little control. List ways you actually did contribute to this event. My camera and typewriter were once stolen from my apartment. I didn't give the robber a map, but I

1. did rent an accessible 1st floor apartment;
2. did leave my items lying around;
3. did invest my money in expensive items;
4. did not invest in a burglar alarm system;
5. did not investigate when I thought I heard someone

This list includes choices I made and those I failed to make. Some relate to the robbery and some to bigger issues. None of these choices is wrong, but they all have effects that contribute to "random" events.

Exercise 1.4—Answers from Nowhere

Try this exercise when you're in a library or bookstore. Think about a problem that concerns you. Close your eyes, and suggest silently to your Inner Guide that you are seeking advice. Ask it to help you learn what you need to know.

Now, wander freely through the aisles. Avoid noticing where you are; just trust your inner promptings to guide you. When you feel ready, pick up a book and open to a page. Read the entire page, and try to relate what is there to your problem. You may be surprised to find just what you needed. If the information doesn't seem related, pretend the message is in a code that you must decipher. Look for a subtle meaning. Meaning is everywhere—literally at your fingertips—but you must seek it out.

Exercise 1.5—You Can Get What You Need

Before going to bed, take a five dollar bill in your hand, close your eyes and ask that you be shown during the day how to use this five dollars to benefit yourself or the world. (A five dollar bill is a practical symbol of the means by which we carry out our purposes in life.)

Place the money under your pillow. In the morning, repeat your request, and then take the bill with you. During the day, keep alert for a sign of how to use it. Stay focused so you don't miss the slightest clue. You will recognize the moment when you feel a little jolt. If nothing strikes you the first day, continue for one week. Give the world a good chance to respond. Try not to forget your morning and evening requests. The strength of your intent and commitment is important.

Later, think about the implications of this approach to the world. Life will bring you what you seek if you ask and trust, but the answer may not be in the form you expect!

EXERCISES FOR LESSON 2

The Major Arcana

Exercise 2.1—Studying the Major Arcana cards

Spend a few minutes looking at section 4 so you understand how to use it. Become familiar with keywords and actions as I use these terms in the lessons. Don't worry about memorizing anything. The goal is simply to get comfortable with the information.

Now, choose any major arcana card from the deck and go to its information page. Notice how the keywords reinforce each other to create a certain kind of energy or focus. Note also how the actions flesh out the keywords. Read the description, but just glance at the "opposing" and "reinforcing" sections for now. You will learn more about these in lesson 15. You can repeat this exercise for as many major arcana cards as you like.

Exercise 2.2—Fool's Journey

The Fool's Journey is an interpretation of how the major arcana symbolizes the stages of inner growth. Read this description now in appendix A. It may deepen your understanding of the major arcana cards and help you appreciate their power as archetypes of the human condition. As you continue the lessons, keep in mind how these 22 cards work together as a unit. Be open to the possibility that you may develop your own ideas about these cards and what they mean.

The Minor Arcana

Exercise 3.1—What are the Suit Qualities?

Review the lists of suit qualities in appendix B. They describe some positive and negative expressions of each suit. Don't try to memorize these lists. They are simply designed to give you a first feel for the energy of each suit. When you're ready, go through the word pairs below. For each pair, give the suit and expression (+ or −) that seems most appropriate *to you.* For "dependable and careful" you might say "Pentacles—positive." See page 93 for my suggestions. When your choices are different from mine, try to figure out why. In this way, you begin refining your own understanding of each suit. You can also have a friend quiz you using new two-word combinations from the lists.

1. sullen and lazy
2. prim and humorless
3. witty and well-informed
4. judgmental and controlling
5. cheerful and bold
6. thorough and practical
7. calm and sympathetic
8. logical and outspoken
9. irresponsible and cocky
10. loyal and down-to-earth
11. critical and arrogant
12. wholehearted and passionate
13. temperamental and sulky
14. sensitive and loving
15. foolhardy and rash
16. moody and frail
17. stubborn and gloomy
18. honest and objective
19. persistent and firm
20. aloof and domineering
21. spiritual and intuitive
22. hasty and unprepared
23. creative and adventurous
24. overcautious and rigid

Exercise 3.2—Suit Qualities: Clear-cut Examples

Many aspects of daily life reflect the energy of one suit in particular. For each activity below, state the suit and expression you believe fits that activity best, and name a few qualities that support your choice. Going skydiving might be a "Wands—positive" activity because you must be "daring, energetic, and confident" (or a Wands—negative activity because it is "foolhardy and reckless"!). See page 93 for my suggestions.

1. always needing to have everything just so
2. getting drunk the night before an important exam
3. being where you say you will, every time
4. solving a math problem
5. using the tarot cards
6. cheering your team on to victory
7. listening to a friend talk about her troubles
8. making a cruel, sarcastic remark
9. refusing to apologize when you're wrong
10. treating those "beneath" you with disdain

11. seeing a project through to the end
12. brooding over a perceived slight
13. volunteering for a dangerous but vital mission
14. quitting your job in a moment of anger
15. arbitrating a dispute
16. finding dirty work distasteful

Exercise 3.3—Suit Qualities: Blended Examples

In most events, the four suit qualities blend together. For each activity below, name two positive suit qualities that would contribute to success and two negative ones that would take away from it. Do this for each suit. For example:

1. To keep love alive:

    Wands—be passionate and enthusiastic, but not impatient and hot-tempered
    Cups—be romantic and loving, but not broody and touchy
    Swords—be honest and honorable, but not cold and judgmental
    Pentacles—be loyal and dependable, but not unexciting and inflexible

2. To manage a project . . .
3. To create a work of art . . .
4. To raise a child . . .
5. To close a sale . . .

Exercise 3.4—Suit Qualities in Yourself

The different suit qualities combine in each person to create his or her personality. Examine yourself in light of the four suits. Ask yourself these questions:

1. Is one suit quality dominant?
2. Is one quality less familiar?
3. In what situations do I take on each quality?
4. Do I reflect the positive or negative side?
5. Do I attract people of the same type, or different?

You can repeat this exercise with another person as the subject.

The Spread

Exercise 4.1—Celtic Cross Spread

Spend a few minutes looking at the section about the Celtic Cross so you understand how it is set up. Don't worry about memorizing anything. The goal is simply to get comfortable with the information.

Now, lay out ten cards of your choice using this spread. Read the page for each position one by one. Think about the meaning each card takes on because it falls in a certain position. You will learn more about this later, but just speculate for now.

Exercise 4.2—Designing a Spread

You can design spreads yourself to suit your needs. Create for yourself now a three-card tarot spread. Follow these steps:

1. Draw a picture of the physical layout—where the cards should go.
2. Number the positions to show order of placement.
3. Write a short phrase or two describing the meaning of each position.

Here's a basic three-card spread that covers events in time:

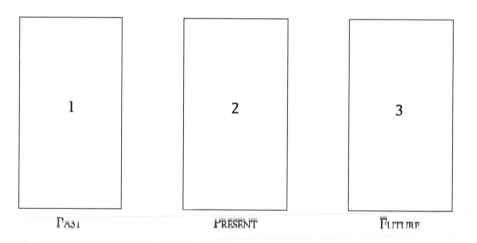

PAST   PRESENT   FUTURE

Here's a spread to use when you belong to a three-person team and want to know the expectations of the members (including yourself):

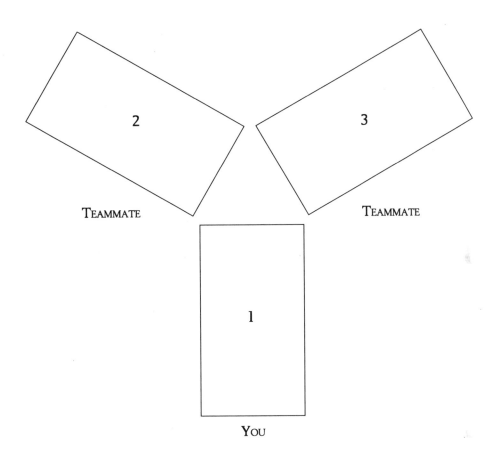

The cards form a "Y" with the tops facing inward. This pattern suggests a meeting of the minds. Design your layout so it reflects the meanings of the positions. To expand on this exercise, work with four, five, or more cards.

The Daily Reading

Exercise 5.1—Learning the Cards One By One

You can become more familiar with each tarot card by concentrating on a different one each day. This exercise takes a minimum of seventy-eight days, so it is quite a commitment, but if you stick with it, you will know the tarot deck very well when you are done.

Decide now how you will choose your daily card during this learning phase. You can be systematic (first the Wands, then the Cups, etc.) or spontaneous. You can pick a card that catches your eye, or one that seems fitting for the day's events. A single day on each card is enough, but you can take longer, if you wish.

When you have selected a card, read its information page at least once. Write down the keywords and try to memorize them. They will help you remember the meanings of a card quickly. Study the details of the card's picture as well. You may want to make a copy of the card's information page to refer to during the day. I don't recommend carrying your card around as it could get lost or damaged. Start a journal, if you wish.

Exercise 5.2—Establishing a Daily Reading Practice

When you have studied all the tarot cards at least once, begin drawing your cards without conscious deliberation. Follow the steps listed in lesson 5. Continue to make entries in your journal, if you have one. After a month or two, calculate the distribution of suits and major arcana cards. Do you notice a pattern that reflects your situation? Do certain card(s) show up frequently? Ask yourself why this might be so.

The Environment

Exercise 6.1—Creating a Place To Do Your Readings

Spend some time thinking about where you will do your tarot readings. Consider some of the suggestions in lesson 6 or use your own ideas. Don't feel you have to create a showcase location. Just see what you can do to create a setting that is pleasing and comfortable.

Exercise 6.2—Quest for a Symbol

In this exercise, you will be announcing your intent to find or create an object that will be a personal symbol of your tarot practice. You can buy, find or make this object yourself. Once you have it, place it in your tarot spot as an inspiration for your work.

Read over the description of the Fool. This card often stands for the feeling of joy and freedom that comes from beginning a new adventure. It is in this spirit that you will seek your object. This quest symbolizes the quest for greater understanding you are undertaking by learning the tarot.

Hold the Fool in your hands, and close your eyes. Announce your desire to find or create a tarot symbol. Commit to working until you have it. The value you place on this quest will reinforce the value of your larger quest. Once you have affirmed your intent, let it go. You will find what you are looking for.

This exercise will strengthen your faith and commitment and leave you with a tangible symbol of your purpose. It will also help you learn that hidden within seemingly foolish acts is the experience of life as an adventure.

EXERCISES FOR LESSON 7
Writing a Question

Exercise 7.1—Writing a Tarot Question

You are going to write a question for your first tarot reading. Think about your life for a moment, and choose an area in which you are having some difficulty. (We all have one of these!) Avoid general concerns such as finding a life partner. Pick a specific everyday problem that is troubling you right now in your home or workplace. Choose something that involves you directly and that you care about personally. Follow the recommendations in lesson 7 for writing an effective question. Take notes as you go. We will be using these notes and your question in the next lesson.

Exercise 7.2—Practicing Question Writing

Life will offer you many opportunities to practice writing questions. Any time you face a problem, take a moment to create a question about it. Work on it while you're doing routine activities, such as riding in a car or doing housework.

Writing practice questions helps you learn to analyze a personal problem quickly and recognize what you want in various situations. Also, if you decide to do a reading about the problem, you will have your question ready.

EXERCISE FOR LESSON 8
The Question Reading

Exercise 8.1—Doing a Question Reading

You are going to do a Celtic Cross Question Reading from start to finish. Follow the procedure outlined in lesson 8. (Also refer to the step-by-step outline in appendix F.) You will need a question to be answered. You can use the question you wrote in Exercise 7.1 or write a new one. Interpret the cards as best you can using your intuition and the sections about individual cards and the Celtic Cross.

You may feel a little at sea this first time—not sure whether or not you're doing everything right. Remember there is no one correct interpretation. What you see in the cards is right for you *by definition*, and, no matter what, you will come away with something of value. In future lessons, you will learn some principles of interpretation that will help you feel more confident. At that point, we'll revisit this reading to see what else you can learn from it.

EXERCISES FOR LESSON 9

The Other Reading

Exercise 9.1—Doing a Reading About a News Event

Go through today's newspaper and choose a topic that interests you. Look for one that is intriguing and somewhat controversial. A short-term media event is a good choice because you will get feedback on the situation quickly. Read over the facts that are available, and write a question that covers one aspect of the situation. Do an Other Reading following the procedure described in lesson 9. Write down your interpretation and what you predict the outcome will be.

Later, when the situation has resolved somewhat, go over your reading and relate it to what happened. If your interpretation doesn't seem to fit, look at the cards again to see if you can find something new in them.

Exercise 9.2—Am I Involved?

Think of a problem that is bothering a close friend, relative, or colleague. Choose a person whose concerns are important to you. Write a question about the problem as if you were doing an Other Reading. Deliberately keep yourself out of the question. When you are done, ask yourself these three questions:

1. Do I feel *strong emotions* when I think about this person in this situation?
2. Do I have a vested interest in this situation?
3. Do I desire a particular outcome in this situation?

If you answered yes to any of these questions, rewrite your original question so that it is centered on you. The goal of this exercise is to help you learn to tell when a problem involves you directly and when it doesn't.

Exercise 9.3—Imaginary Situations

You can create a troubling set of circumstances for an imaginary person, and then do an Other Reading about it. You can also borrow a situation from the advice columns in the newspapers. These are great resources for problems of all kinds.

The Open Reading

Exercise 10.1—Doing an Open Reading

During the next few weeks, look for an opportunity to try an Open Reading. I recommend a fairly quiet day when you feel at peace with your life and attuned to the moment. It should be a day when you have the time and inclination to step back a little and look at the larger patterns that are influencing you at this time. If a birthday, anniversary, or other special occasion happens to fall during this period, use it as the basis for your reading. Follow the procedure described in lesson 10.

Interpreting a Single Card

Exercise 11.1—Your Personal Reactions to a Card

Choose any card from the tarot deck. Look at it carefully and then write down your response. It doesn't matter if you are already familiar with this card and know its meanings. Consider whatever comes to mind to be your personal reaction. Some elements to think about are:

What feeling do I sense in the card scene?
What feeling do I sense in myself when I see this card?[1]
Am I attracted, repelled, or neutral about this card?
What aspect of my life comes to mind when I see this card?
Does this card remind me of anyone?
What details seem important in this card, and why?

You may not feel any reaction to the card, or perhaps just a mild one. Try to notice any quick thought, feeling, or image that comes to mind, no matter how slight.

Exercise 11.2—Combining Sources of Meaning

In this exercise, you will practice blending card and position meanings. Choose a card from the tarot deck, and read over its keywords and actions. Try to get a feel for the card's essential meaning.

Imagine that your card has appeared in Position 1 of a Celtic Cross reading. How does being here refine the meaning of this card? How do the card and position meanings work together to create a composite?

---

1. These two feelings may be the same or different.

Write one sentence that sums up your interpretation. Don't try to figure out the right answer because there isn't one. Select a possibility that appeals to you and makes sense. Your sentence doesn't have to relate to your own life in any way as this exercise is simply for practice. For example, the Emperor stands for:

fathering	authority
structure	regulation

Some choices for this card in Position 1 might be:

1. Right now, the *heart of the matter* (Position 1) is that there is too much STRUCTURE (Emperor) in my life.
2. My *present environment* (Position 1) is very REGULATED and CONTROLLED (Emperor).
3. Right now the issue of becoming a FATHER (Emperor) is the *primary factor* in my life (Position 1).

These sentences are all different, but each one blends the meanings of the Emperor and Position 1. In an actual reading, the most appropriate interpretation for you would become clear as you considered other factors.

Next, write a sentence for each of the other nine positions using the same card. If you want extra practice, write more than one sentence for each position, or choose a different card and repeat the exercise.

Exercise 11.3—Interpreting Single Cards in Celtic Cross Readings

Use your ongoing Celtic Cross readings as an opportunity to practice combining the four sources of meaning:

1. personal reaction
2. card meaning
3. position meaning
4. question or situation

Be systematic at first about considering each of these areas so they become second nature to you. Try writing a sentence for each card as described in Exercise 11.2. Of course, you will not have to write these sentences forever. Later you can be more relaxed and simply respond without having to think about where your reaction comes from.

EXERCISES FOR LESSON 12

Major and Minor Arcana Cards

Exercise 12.1—Arcana Cards in the Celtic Cross

In the layouts below, you are given just the distribution of major and minor arcana cards. Write a sentence or two for each one describing what you can sense based just on the positions and Arcana factor. See page 94 for my suggestions.

This exercise is easier if you have something to look at. Take two decks of regular playing cards with different colored backs. One deck will be the major arcana, and one, the minor. (If you don't have playing cards, use squares of colored paper.) Create the layout you are working on by placing the appropriately colored cards *face down* in their assigned positions. In layout one, if blue cards are minor and red cards major, all the cards would be blue except for a red card in Position 10.

Celtic Cross Layouts Showing Major & Minor Arcana Choices

	POSITION NUMBER									
	1	2	3	4	5	6	7	8	9	10
Layout One	Minor	Minor	Minor	Minor	Minor	Minor	Minor	Minor	Minor	**Major**
Layout Two	Minor	Minor	Minor	**Major**	Minor	Minor	Minor	Minor	Minor	Minor
Layout Three	Minor	Minor	Minor	Minor	Minor	Minor	Minor	**Major**	Minor	Minor
Layout Four	Minor	Minor	**Major**	Minor	Minor	Minor	Minor	Minor	Minor	Minor
Layout Five	**Major**	**Major**	Minor	Minor	Minor	Minor	Minor	Minor	Minor	Minor
Layout Six	Minor	Minor	Minor	Minor	**Major**	Minor	**Major**	Minor	Minor	Minor

Exercise 12.2—Comparing the Arcanas Separately

Remove all the major arcana cards from the deck and place them in a pile. Choose a minor arcana card for each one that has a similar meaning. You can choose on your own, or you can use my selections (see page 94.) Put the minor arcana cards you have chosen in a separate pile.

Shuffle and cut the cards in the major arcana pile, and lay out ten in the Celtic Cross. Find the matching minor arcana cards, and form a second Celtic Cross next to the first. Compare your impressions of these two layouts. Ask yourself these questions:

1. What is the overall feeling conveyed by each layout?
2. Is this feeling the same or different?
3. Does one reading seem easier to understand?
4. Does one reading seem more accessible?
5. Does one reading seem more compelling?

You can repeat this exercise with different sets of cards, if you wish.

Exercise 12.3—Readings Using Only Major Arcana Cards

In the next week or so, try doing a reading using just the major arcana cards. I recommend doing an Open Reading as major arcana cards offer the expansive guidance that suits this type of reading.

You may find this technique works well for you. Some people prefer using only the major arcana at all times. Major arcana readings clarify the main, decisive themes at work in your life.

EXERCISES FOR LESSON 13

Aces

Exercise 13.1—The Energy of the Aces

The Aces have a clear energy that is undiluted by situational factors. This exercise will help you experience that energy. Remove the four Aces from your deck and place them in a row in front of you as follows:

Write the four keywords for each Ace on a piece of paper and place it below the card. Now, concentrate on the Aces one at a time until you feel you know them well. Try to get to a point where you can see an Ace and immediately feel its powerful presence. (The first keyword for each Ace includes the word *force!*) Look at the details on the cards, especially the suit icons. Notice how each icon captures the qualities of its Ace.

Exercise 13.2 Visualizing with the Aces

The Aces are excellent images for visualization practice. When you want to feel the qualities of an Ace, picture its image with your inner eye. Simplify the image by visualizing just the hand holding the suit icon. Feel yourself calling down the power of the Ace as a lightning rod calls down the energy of a storm. Some qualities you can tap are:

Ace of Wands—courage, confidence, creativity, enthusiasm
Ace of Cups—love, forgiveness, insight, faith
Ace of Swords—intellect, fortitude, honesty, clarity
Ace of Pentacles—security, prosperity, trust, competence

As you learn more about the Aces, you will know which one is appropriate for any situation and you will have a technique for accessing its energy whenever you wish.

EXERCISES FOR LESSON 14

Court Cards

Exercise 14.1—Reviewing the Court Cards

Remove all 16 court cards from the deck, and place them in a four-by-four square as follows:

Page Wands	Knight Wands	Queen Wands	King Wands
Page Cups	Knight Cups	Queen Cups	King Cups
Page Swords	Knight Swords	Queen Swords	King Swords
Page Pentacles	Knight Pentacles	Queen Pentacles	King Pentacles

Take a moment to look at these royal figures together in one place. They are unique individuals, but they also share commonalities with the other cards in their suit (row) and rank (column). Review the suit qualities in appendix B and the information page for each card. Look for patterns among the cards.

Exercise 14.2—Kings

For each item below, decide on an *action* you might take that reflects the personality of the King. See page 95 for my suggestions. Here's an example:

King of Wands—You've been accused of cheating on an exam, but you know you're innocent.

Possible Action—I would confront my accuser boldly and ask for proof.

1. King of Cups—Your spouse complains that you're never home on weekends.
2. King of Pentacles—A panhandler asks you for one dollar.
3. King of Swords—You find a marijuana cigarette in your daughter's coat pocket.
4. King of Wands—Your roommate keeps borrowing your car without asking.
5. King of Pentacles—Your friend begs you to skip work and go fishing with him.

6. King of Swords—You get an invitation to speak at a conference.
7. King of Cups—A waiter gets your order wrong twice in a row.
8. King of Wands—You're discouraged because your team is playing badly.

Exercise 14.3—Queens

For each item below, decide on a *feeling or thought* that reflects the personality of the Queen. See page 95 for my suggestions. Here's an example:

> Queen of Wands—You've been accused of cheating on an exam, but you know you're innocent.
> Possible Feeling/Thought—I'm confident that I can prove my innocence.

1. Queen of Cups—You find out your cousin has cancer.
2. Queen of Pentacles—You lock your keys in the car.
3. Queen of Swords—You're asked to take over a failing project at work.
4. Queen of Wands—You begin Day One of your new diet.
5. Queen of Pentacles—Your best friend admits to having an affair.
6. Queen of Swords—You interview a promising new employee.
7. Queen of Cups—You decide to take a long walk after lunch.
8. Queen of Wands—You go to a party where you only know the hostess.

Exercise 14.4—Knights

For each scenario, decide which Knight best reflects the situation. Then, give a few phrases that describe that Knight's warning message. See page 95 for my suggestions. Here's an example:

> You've been working 12 hours-a-day for six months. There's so much to do.
> Knight of Pentacles—You're working too hard. You're too compulsive. You never play.

1. You feel depressed and weepy all the time. No one seems to care how you feel.
2. You've bragged that you know lots of important people, but you really don't.
3. The stock market keeps going up. All your money is in a risk-free savings account.
4. You're always yelling at the kids. Their constant fighting is driving you crazy.
5. You told your new assistant that his work is hopelessly sloppy and incomplete.
6. You think your partner is always flirting with others. You don't like it at all.
7. Your son disobeyed you. You won't tolerate that! Your word is law in your house.
8. You refuse to consider retiring even though your spouse wants to discuss it.

Exercise 14.5—Pages

Remove the four Pages from the deck, and place them *face down* in front of you. Mix them together, then turn over one card. Assume this Page represents an opportunity available to you right now, one that reflects the magic of his suit. What do you think it might be? Does this possibility excite you? Is something holding you back? If nothing comes to mind, watch for an inspiration in the next few days.

Exercise 14.6—Court Cards are People

The more you understand your fellow humans, the more you will understand the court cards. Over the next few weeks, observe your relatives, friends, colleagues, and acquaintances. Consider celebrities, historical figures, and characters from books, TV, and films. Ask yourself:

1. What qualities does this person have? Not have?
2. What qualities are helpful to this person? Not helpful?
3. What court card is this person most like? Least like?
4. How is this person unique . . . unlike any type at all?
5. What court card types are common in my life? Uncommon?

Exercise 14.7—Court Card Families

"All the world's a stage, and all the men and women merely players." Shakespeare recognized that each of us is an actor with many roles. Our roles are not who we are—that is a profound mystery. They are the changing personalities we assume as we take part in this show called life.

Create a cast of characters using the personalities of the court cards in four families—the Wands, Cups, Swords, and Pentacles. Each family has a father (King), mother (Queen), teenager (Knight), and young child (Page) of either sex.

Describe these four families so their unique styles are revealed. The members of each family share an approach to life (suit), but have separate positions within the family (rank). What vacation would the Pentacles family take? Would the Knight of Wands drive a Buick or a red Mustang? Here are some props you can use to flesh out your characters:

1. physical characteristics—body type, hair color/style, features
2. home—location, type, furnishings
3. education and occupation
4. possessions—clothes, car, toys
5. free time—vacations, hobbies, sports
6. favorites—foods, movies, songs, books, colors
7. habits—strengths, weaknesses, peculiarities

Exercise 14.8—Court Cards in Action

For each scenario below, write one or two interpretations for the first court card listed. Consider the meaning of the card, the position, and the situation. For extra practice, repeat the exercise using the second court card. Don't consider the court cards together. Simply imagine you drew them in separate readings. See page 95 for my suggestions.

1. You're getting married in three months. Your future father-in-law is critical of the arrangements and wants to change them.
   Knight of Swords—Position 5
   King of Wands—Position 9

2. You're planning to buy a new car. You're not looking forward to haggling with a pushy salesperson.

   Queen of Cups—Position 6
   King of Swords—Position 7

3. Your friend has asked you to watch her kids for a weekend. You want to help, but her children are a handful.

   Queen of Pentacles—Position 1
   Page of Cups—Position 2

4. You've just met someone attractive who has only been divorced for four months. You worry about getting involved in a messy situation.

   Queen of Wands—Position 4
   Knight of Cups—Position 8

5. You've been feeling pain in your chest for several weeks. It's getting worse, but you don't want to go to a doctor.

   Knight of Pentacles—Position 10
   Page of Swords—Position 3

6. You have an idea for an improvement at work that could be very profitable. You suspect your boss will try to take credit for the idea.

   Knight of Wands—Position 2
   King of Pentacles—Position 9

7. For the past year, you've felt restless and dissatisfied. Activities that used to be rewarding now seem pointless.

   Queen of Swords—Position 3
   Page of Wands—Position 7

8. Six months ago a friend borrowed $200 for an emergency. Now he's asking for another $100.

   Page of Pentacles—Position 8
   King of Cups—Position 1

EXERCISES FOR LESSON 15

Card Pairs

Exercise 15.1—Permanent Pairs in the Major Arcana

Below are two scrambled lists of major arcana cards. Match each card in list 1 with the card in list 2 that you feel is its permanent opposing pair. Give a short meaning for each card that shows the balancing relationship. Try this exercise before looking at the card pages. See page 97 for my suggestions. For example:

Magician (Action)   High Priestess (Nonaction)

Scrambled Lists of Major Arcana Permanent Pairs

LIST ONE	LIST TWO
Devil	Death
Sun	Lovers
Chariot	Star
Empress	World
Fool	Hanged Man
Hermit	Moon
Hierophant	Emperor

Exercise 15.2—Other Permanent Pairs

For each minor Arcana card below:

1. Choose one meaning for the card.
2. Think of a meaning that is the opposite.
3. Find another card (major or minor) that suggests this *opposite* meaning.
4. For ideas, scan the keyword summary charts and the opposing cards section of each card.

Two of Wands

Ten of Pentacles

Seven of Swords

Two of Cups

Five of Wands

Five of Swords

Eight of Pentacles

Eight of Wands

Nine of Cups

Exercise 15.3—Court Card Pairs

People both help *and* annoy each other because of their differences. Below are twelve court card pairs. For each one:

1. Choose a personality trait for person A that is typical of that court card.
2. Describe one way A might *help* person B because of that trait.
3. Describe one way A might *annoy* person B because of that trait.

See page 98 for my suggestions and also the charts in Appendices C and D. Here's an example:

Knight of Swords

Trait: direct/blunt.

Helps the Queen of Pentacles to learn to say no.

Annoys the Queen of Pentacles when he is rude to strangers.

Court Card Pairs

	PERSON A	PERSON B
PAIR 1	Knight of Cups	Queen of Wands
PAIR 2	King of Wands	Queen of Cups
PAIR 3	King of Pentacles	Knight of Cups
PAIR 4	Queen of Pentacles	King of Wands
PAIR 5	King of Swords	King of Pentacles
PAIR 6	King of Cups	King of Swords
PAIR 7	Queen of Cups	Queen of Swords
PAIR 8	Knight of Wands	Queen of Pentacles
PAIR 9	Queen of Wands	Knight of Swords
PAIR 10	Knight of Pentacles	King of Cups
PAIR 11	Queen of Swords	Knight of Wands
PAIR 12	Knight of Swords	Knight of Pentacles

Exercise 15.4—Reinforcing Pairs

For each card below:
1. Choose one meaning for the card.
2. Find a card (major or minor) that suggests a *similar* meaning.
3. For ideas, scan the keyword summary charts and the reinforcing cards section of each card.

Three of Wands	Three of Swords	Nine of Pentacles
Four of Pentacles	Five of Cups	Justice
Temperance	Eight of Wands	Six of Cups

Exercise 15.5—Occasional Pairs

For each pair in the chart below, place the two cards side by side in front of you and gaze at them lightly for a few moments. Find some way to interpret the cards so they either *oppose* or *reinforce* each other. See page 99 for my suggestions. Here are two possibilities for the Empress and the Three of Cups:

Empress—a lone woman focused on herself.
Three of Cups—a group of women focused on each other.

Empress—a seated woman who is rather serious and inactive.
Three of Cups—dancing women who are lively and lighthearted.

For extra practice, deal out two cards at random on your own.

Occasional Pairs

	CARD 1	CARD 2
PAIR 1	Hermit	Justice
PAIR 2	Nine of Swords	Four of Swords
PAIR 3	Two of Pentacles	Hanged Man
PAIR 4	Chariot	Death
PAIR 5	Four of Pentacles	Six of Wands
PAIR 6	Lovers	Six of Swords
PAIR 7	Hierophant	Devil
PAIR 8	Nine of Wands	Seven of Pentacles
PAIR 9	Sun	Ten of Swords

Exercise 15.6—Your Balance Issues

Identify a balance issue that is meaningful to you at this time. Here are some possibilities:

1. controlling—letting go
2. being free—being restricted
3. feeling joy—feeling sadness
4. creating peace—creating conflict
5. working—playing
6. playing it safe—risking
7. moving slow—moving fast
8. acting—waiting
9. coming together—moving apart
10. feeling victorious—feeling defeated

Identify two cards that represent the opposite ends of your issue. In the next few weeks, think about these cards from time to time. Are you closer to one of these cards, or in the middle? Watch for these cards to show up in your readings.

Exercises for Lesson 16

Position Pairs in the Celtic Cross

Exercise 16.1—Traditional Position Pairs in the Celtic Cross

Create a Celtic Cross layout using any ten cards from the deck placed *face down*. For each of the six situations below, do the following:

1. Imagine you are doing a Celtic Cross reading, and you have drawn the two cards listed under (A).

2. Find these cards and place them *face up* in the positions indicated. (Remove the cards that are there.)

3. Write a short interpretation of these two cards as a pair. Use the examples in lesson 16 as a model.

4. Turn these cards face down.

5. For extra practice repeat steps 1–4 using the second set of cards (B).

See page 100 for my suggestions.

1. Your 8-year-old has come home from school in tears. His teacher tore up his homework because he didn't follow directions and his handwriting was sloppy.
(A) Page of Cups (Position 1) and Knight of Pentacles (Position 2)
(B) Two of Pentacles (Position 1) and Judgement (Position 2)

2. You're afraid your partner is having an affair. You want to believe it isn't true, but you're suspicious.
(A) Six of Cups (Position 3) and Moon (Position 5)
(B) Seven of Cups (Position 3) and King of Swords (Position 5)

3. One member of your work team is not pulling his weight. You've let the problem go in the past, but now his laziness is really hurting the group.
(A) Two of Swords (Position 4) and Three of Wands (Position 6)
(B) Ten of Wands (Position 4) and Strength (Position 6)

4. For seven years, you've owned and operated a store with a partner. Now, she wants to leave with her share. You will have to sell the store to buy her out.
(A) Ten of Pentacles (Position 7) and Death (Position 8)
(B) Queen of Cups (Position 7) and Queen of Pentacles (Position 8)

5. You've fallen in love with someone that your parents would not find acceptable. So far, you've kept your relationship secret, but you can't continue hiding forever.
(A) Three of Swords (Position 5) and World (Position 10)
(B) Wheel of Fortune (Position 5) and Fool (Position 10)

6. You've done an Other Reading about a public figure who is being investigated for financial improprieties. (Note the different positions for the second card of each set).
(A) Two of Wands (Position 9) and Seven of Swords (Position 4)
(B) Eight of Wands (Position 9) and Emperor (Position 8)

Exercise 16.2—Other Pairings in the Celtic Cross

Below are some new Celtic Cross pairings. For each one, write a brief description of what you could learn from that pair. See page 101 for my suggestions. For example: Position 1—Position 4 = how something from the past (4) is influencing the present (1).

Position 1—Position 6	Position 3—Position 10
Position 1—Position 7	Position 4—Position 8
Position 2—Position 5	Position 5—Position 7
Position 2—Position 8	Position 6—Position 10
Position 3—Position 4	

Exercise 16.3—Reexamining Your Celtic Cross Readings for Pairs

Reexamine the reading you did in exercise 8.1 in light of your new understanding of pairs in the Celtic Cross. Can you discover any new insights? Check the obvious pair positions, but look for others as well. You may be surprised at what you find . . . or you may not notice anything new at all. Review other readings in this way for extra practice.

EXERCISES FOR LESSON 17

Reversed Cards

Exercise 17.1—The Energy of a Card

Shuffle the cards so there is a mixture of upright and reversed cards (see appendix E). Hold the deck face down in one hand. Turn over the first card, and lay it in front of you. Answer these questions:

1. What is the energy of this card for me at this moment? Listen for a word or phrase to pop into your mind. Don't try to remember an official meaning; simply wait for an idea to enter awareness. Let the energy of the card present itself to you on its own.
2. What is the level of this energy as shown by the card's orientation? An upright card represents high energy; a reversed card represents low energy.
3. How am I experiencing this energy at this level? Again, let an idea come to mind on its own.

Here are two examples:

Nine of Wands—upright
1. perseverance
2. high level
3. I'm determined to get good grades at school.

Queen of Swords—reversed
1. sitting in judgment (based on the image)
2. low level
3. I'm trying not to judge my sister very much.

Continue this exercise by turning over new cards one by one. Stop if you feel any strain or restlessness. You want to feel relaxed and pleasantly engaged. There are no right answers, so feel free to accept whatever comes.

Exercise 17.2—Interpreting Reversed Cards

For each scenario below, imagine that you have drawn the given reversed card. Write a brief interpretation. Show how the usual energy of the card is either at a low level or *needs to be* at a low level. See page 102 for my suggestions. Here are two examples. The card's meaning is in SMALL CAPITALS, and the reversal effect is in *italics*.

Situation: I've hurt my back in an accident. I'm in a lot of pain.
Card: Queen of Wands—reversed
Interpretation. I've *lost* much of my ROBUST GOOD HEALTH because of this accident.

Situation: I'll never finish this assignment on time even if I work all night.
Card: Nine of Pentacles—reversed
Interpretation: I should *stop trying* to HANDLE EVERYTHING MYSELF.

1. I wonder why my love life has been stalled for so long.
   Three of Wands—reversed
2. I finally got my promotion, but my family doesn't want to move.
   Chariot—reversed
3. My friend wants me to join her protest against the new landfill.
   Ace of Swords—reversed
4. I've been making one sale after another! I've got the golden touch right now.
   Tower—reversed
5. My cousin wants me to invest in his new company, but I'm hesitating.
   Knight of Swords—reversed
6. I don't want to see my boyfriend anymore. I'm not sure why.
   Four of Cups—reversed
7. My daughter is divorcing and wants to live with me for a while.
   Six of Pentacles—reversed
8. I love my new baby, but I'm so worn out from lack of sleep.
   Page of Cups—reversed
9. I can't stand school. I want to quit when the semester's over.
   Temperance—reversed
10. My meditations are getting more powerful. It scares me a little.
    Death—reversed

Exercise 17.3—Upside-down Meanings

For each card in the list below write a brief interpretation that reverses the regular meaning in some way. Use ideas based on twisting, flipping, changing, rejecting, denying, and the like. The interpretation doesn't have to relate to your life; any possibility will do. Look at the reversed card while you work for inspiration. See page 103 for my suggestions. Here are some examples with the upside-down meanings in italics

World—reversed
1. My whole world has been *turned upside-down.*
2. She's *rejecting* the outside world. She wants to stay *isolated in her own circle.* (See image.)

King of Cups—reversed
1. I don't trust her. Something's *not on the up-and-up.*
2. I'm *tired* of being diplomatic! I want to say what I think.

1. Justice—reversed
2. Page of Swords—reversed
3. Hanged Man—reversed
4. Four of Wands—reversed
5. Ace of Pentacles—reversed

6. Knight of Cups—reversed
7. Six of Swords—reversed
8. Hierophant—reversed
9. Three of Pentacles—reversed

EXERCISES FOR LESSON 18

Creating the Story

Exercise 18.1—Stream-of-Consciousness Talking

You can practice stream-of-consciousness talking anytime you feel comfortable speaking your thoughts out loud. (For most of us, this means being alone!) Say every thought as it occurs to you. The idea is to "hear" a thought inwardly and then vocalize it. As you finish speaking one thought, listen for the next one.

In the next few weeks, try this exercise whenever you can. Work toward being able to speak naturally with no sense of urgency. Try to get to the point where thoughts about the process don't intrude too much. This is not an easy state to achieve, but it is well worth the effort.

Exercise 18.2—Tarot Improvisation

In theater improvisation, members of the audience call out the names of a few objects, and the actors must assemble a skit based on those elements. In this exercise, the cards are the elements, and you are the actor who must bring them together on the fly.

Shuffle and cut the cards in the usual way. Hold the deck face down in one hand. Turn over the first three cards, and lay them in a row. Now, create a story around the cards. Don't struggle to come up with a clever scenario. Just allow any tale to unfold. In *The Castle of Crossed Destinies* by Italo Calvino,[1] the characters tell their tales to each other using only tarot card images.

When you are through, set the first three cards aside and deal out three more for a new story. Or, if you like, keep the first three cards and lay out a fourth. Incorporate this card into the original tale. Continue developing the story by laying out new cards one at a time. The spirit of this exercise is spontaneous play. Stop if you feel any pressure or strain.

Exercise 18.3—The Structure of the Celtic Cross

Lay out any ten cards in the usual Celtic Cross format. Read the interpretation procedure for this spread in the Celtic Cross section. Create a story following these steps. How well does this approach work for you? What changes would you make?

---

1. Italo Calvino, *The Castle of Crossed Destinies* (New York: Harcourt Brace Jovanovich, 1969).

Next, lay out a new set of ten cards. Experiment with different story structures. Try starting with the outcome card (10) and working backward or building a story around a striking card pair. Explore new approaches with different sets of cards. For your readings, you will probably settle on a favorite approach, but it helps to know of other possibilities that you can draw on as needed.

Exercise for Lesson 19

Some Final Thoughts

Exercise 19.1—Return of What Do I Believe?

In exercise 1.1, I asked you to write down briefly what you do and do not believe about the tarot and to assign a percentage to those beliefs where:

0% = "I am totally skeptical about using the tarot for anything but fun."

100% = "I am absolutely convinced that the tarot can give me specific, personal guidance."

Repeat this exercise now *before rereading what you wrote earlier.* When you're done, go back and look at your original answer. Pause to reflect on all that you have learned and experienced since you began this course of study.

III

SUGGESTIONS
FOR EXERCISES

Suggestions for Exercises—Lesson 3

Exercise 3.1—What are the Suit Qualities?

1. Cups—negative
2. Pentacles—negative
3. Swords—positive
4. Swords—negative
5. Wands—positive
6. Pentacles—positive
7. Cups—positive
8. Swords—positive
9. Wands—negative
10. Pentacles—positive
11. Swords—negative
12. Wands—positive
13. Cups—negative
14. Cups—positive
15. Wands—negative
16. Cups—negative
17. Pentacles—negative
18. Swords—positive
19. Pentacles—positive
20. Swords—negative
21. Cups—positive
22. Wands—negative
23. Wands—positive
24. Pentacles—negative

Exercise 3.2—Suit Qualities: Clear-Cut Examples

1. Pentacles—negative
   compulsive, overorganized, rigid
2. Wands—negative
   imprudent, irresponsible, unprepared
3. Pentacles—positive
   dependable, reliable, responsible
4. Swords—positive
   logical, mental, analytical
5. Cups—positive
   intuitive, spiritual, quiet
6. Wands—positive
   enthusiastic, exuberant, wholehearted
7. Cups—positive
   caring, kind, sympathetic, concerned
8. Swords—negative
   biting, critical, insensitive
9. Pentacles—negative
   stubborn, obstinate, unbending
10. Swords—negative
    arrogant, condescending, high-handed, patronizing
11. Pentacles—positive
    dogged, tenacious, thorough, persistent
12. Cups—negative
    hypersensitive, sulky, temperamental, touchy
13. Wands—positive
    brave, heroic, self-confident, valiant
14. Wands—negative
    hasty, rash, hot-tempered, impulsive
15. Swords—positive
    objective, equitable, impartial, just, discerning
16. Cups—negative
    overrefined, frail, fragile, lazy

Suggestions for Exercises—Lesson 12

Exercise 12.1—Arcana Cards in the Celtic Cross

1. All cards are minor except the outcome (Position 10). This situation is a temporary personal drama, but its impact will be powerful and significant in some way.
2. The only major arcana card is in the Past (Position 4). The circumstances of the moment are the result of some major event from the past, or what was once of major significance is now fading.
3. Position 8—the environment—is the only major arcana card. This situation may be part of a larger undertaking, or the outside influence may be especially strong.
4. Since Position 3 is the only major arcana card, the hidden, underlying energy here is strong. Things may be minor on the surface, but the force sustaining them is powerful.
5. Two major arcana cards are at the center of the reading (Positions 1 and 2). Two powerful forces are coming together for better or worse. The minor factors circling around are an offshoot of this core dynamic.
6. Someone *thinks* (Position 5) that his *role* (Position 7) in the situation is major, but the actual circumstances do not bear this out.

Exercise 12.2—Comparing the Arcanas

Fool—Three of Wands (going into unexplored territory)
Magician—Two of Wands (having personal power)
High Priestess—Four of Swords (resting quietly)
Empress—Ten of Pentacles (affluence, luxury)
Emperor—Four of Pentacles (control)
Hierophant—Eight of Pentacles (learning, studying)
Lovers—Nine of Cups (sexual pleasure)
Chariot—Nine of Pentacles (self-control, discipline)
Strength—Nine of Wands (stamina, endurance, heart)
Hermit—Seven of Swords (being alone)
Wheel of Fortune—Eight of Wands (rapid pace, quick developments)
Justice—Ten of Wands (accepting responsibility)
Hanged Man—Ten of Swords (martyrdom, sacrifice)
Death—Five of Cups (loss, good-byes)
Temperance—Two of Pentacles (balance)
Devil—Nine of Swords (despair, lack of joy)
Tower—Five of Pentacles (hard times)
Star—Six of Cups (good will, sharing)
Moon—Two of Swords (self-deception)
Sun—Six of Wands (acclaim, prominence)
Judgement—Seven of Pentacles (decision point)
World—Ten of Cups (happiness, fulfillment)

Suggestions for Exercises—Lesson 14

Exercise 14.2—Kings

King of Cups: I would sit down with my spouse to discuss his/her concerns. (CARING)

King of Pentacles: I would give him five dollars. He probably needs it more than I do. (SUPPORTING)

King of Swords: I would ask my daughter for her story before making any judgments. (JUST)

King of Wands: I would booby trap my car so an alarm goes off if my roommate starts it. (CREATIVE)

King of Pentacles: I would tell my friend, "Sorry, they need me at work." (RELIABLE)

King of Swords: I would accept the invitation because I'm an excellent public speaker. (ARTICULATE)

King of Cups: I would smile and give my order a third time. (PATIENT)

King of Wands: I would call a huddle and get everyone fired up again. (INSPIRING)

Exercise 14.3—Queens

Queen of Cups: My cousin is going to need extra love and support. (LOVING)

Queen of Pentacles: I can figure out a way to get the keys if I put my mind to it. (RESOURCEFUL)

Queen of Swords: What's the *real* reason I was given this hopeless project? (ASTUTE)

Queen of Wands: I'll have extra energy when I lose weight. (ENERGETIC)

Queen of Pentacles: I'll keep this secret since my friend entrusted me with it. (TRUSTWORTHY)

Queen of Swords: I'll be open and honest in this interview so there are no misunderstandings. (HONEST)

Queen of Cups: I can use this time to meditate and recenter myself. (SPIRITUAL)

Queen of Wands: I know I can make new friends easily. (SELF-ASSURED)

Exercise 14.4—Knights

Knight of Cups: You're too sulky. You're oversensitive. Your emotions are ruling you.

Knight of Wands: You're boasting. Bragging doesn't impress. You're too focused on appearances.

Knight of Pentacles: You're too cautious. You're settling for less. You're afraid to risk.

Knight of Wands: You act without thinking. You're too angry. You're adding to the fighting.

Knight of Swords: You're too blunt. You're too critical. People have feelings.

Knight of Cups: You're too jealous. You're overemotional. You're imagining things.

Knight of Swords: You're too domineering. You're insensitive. Your son isn't your slave.

Knight of Pentacles: You're too stubborn. You won't compromise. You're afraid to change.

Exercise 14.8—Court Cards in Action

Two possible interpretations are given for each card. Phrases in SMALL CAPITALS are card meanings. *Italic* phrases are position meanings.

1. Knight of Swords—Position 5
   a. My father-in-law is TOO CRITICAL AND OVERBEARING. He's *all I can think about right now.*
   b. My *preference* is to tell my father-in-law EXACTLY WHAT I THINK of his interference . . . to REALLY TELL HIM OFF!

   King of Wands—Position 9
   a. The *key* is to recognize that my father-in-law is used to BEING THE CENTER OF ATTENTION.
   b. The *best way for me to proceed* is to PROJECT MY OWN AUTHORITY NATURALLY.

2. Queen of Cups—Position 6
   a. A salesperson who is *patient and caring* may show up IN THE NEAR FUTURE.
   b. The purchase may *go more smoothly in the future* if I LET MY INTUITION GUIDE ME.

   King of Swords—Position 7
   a. I can be successful if I *follow the model* of the King of Swords—RESEARCH THE FACTS SO I KNOW WHAT I'M TALKING ABOUT.
   b. *If I take a stance* that is HONEST, the car dealership may do likewise.

3. Queen of Pentacles—Position 1
   a. This situation *revolves around* the talents of the Queen of Pentacles: to GIVE LOVE AND CARE TO CHILDREN.
   b. The *heart of the matter* is that I need to be LOYAL AND TRUSTWORTHY.

   Page of Cups—Position 2
   a. A *secondary factor* is that this situation is an OPPORTUNITY to make a LOVING, THOUGHTFUL GESTURE for a friend.
   b. The KIDS (Pages) may *surprise me* by BEING SWEET AND LOVING.

4. Queen of Wands—Position 4
   a. I've met SOMEONE WHO IS SEXY AND ATTRACTIVE, but I *need to stop focusing on that right now.*
   b. This situation is risky, but *in the past,* I've always BEEN ABLE TO HANDLE JUST ABOUT ANYTHING.

   Knight of Cups—Position 8
   a. I must be careful because I'm caught up in an *atmosphere* of ROMANCE that may overwhelm my better judgment.
   b. This *person* has been through an EMOTIONAL breakup and will be EXTRA VULNERABLE AND NEEDY.

5. Knight of Pentacles—Position 10
   a. My body is telling me that *I am going to have to be* EXTRA CAUTIOUS.
   b. Even if I avoid this problem now, I will *eventually* have to BE REALISTIC ABOUT IT.

   Page of Swords—Position 3
   a. The *source of the problem* is that I need to FACE THE TRUTH about my health.

b. *Fundamentally,* this situation is a CHALLENGE that I must meet with FORTITUDE AND RESOLVE.

6. Knight of Wands—Position 2
   a. I must keep an eye on my boss who is BRASH AND NERVY; he could *oppose* me in this situation.
   b. I need to *reinforce myself* with an EXTRA DOSE OF CONFIDENCE.

   King of Pentacles—Position 9
   a. My *hope* is that my idea WILL WORK AND MAKE MONEY for the company.
   b. I need to find *someone I can turn to* for RELIABLE information on handling this situation COMPETENTLY.

7. Queen of Swords—Position 3
   a. I probably have *an unrecognized need;* I must FACE WHAT NEEDS TO BE FACED, EVEN IF UNPLEASANT.
   b. The *deeper reason* why I'm dissatisfied is that I'm beginning to SEE THROUGH THE FALSE PROMISES of my old way of life.

   Page of Wands—Position 7
   a. I've lost my SENSE OF ADVENTURE; *I* want to feel PASSIONATE ABOUT LIFE again.
   b. My HIGH-ENERGY, CREATIVE *persona* may not be serving me any longer.

8. Page of Pentacles—Position 8
   a. *My friend expects me* to be the one he can ALWAYS COUNT ON.
   b. The *context of this situation* is a PRACTICAL, MONEY MATTER.

   King of Cups—Position 1
   a. The *most important consideration* is TO HELP A FRIEND WHO IS IN NEED.
   b. It's *crucial* that I make a WISE decision about what to do.

Suggestions for Exercises—Lesson 15

Exercise 15.1—Permanent Pairs in the Major Arcana

Devil (hopelessness)—Star (hope)
Sun (enlightenment)—Moon (bewilderment)
Chariot (control)—Hanged Man (letting go)
Empress (mothering)—Emperor (fathering)
Fool (beginning)—Death (ending)
Hermit (disengaging)—World (engaging)
Hierophant (group beliefs)—Lovers (personal beliefs)

Exercise 15.3—Court Card Pairs

1. Knight of Cups
   trait: introspective/introverted
   helps the Queen of Wands care more about her inner life
   annoys the Queen of Wands because he obsesses about his feelings

2. King of Wands
   trait: forceful
   helps the Queen of Cups be more assertive
   annoys the Queen of Cups because he assumes she will follow him

3. King of Pentacles
   trait: steady
   helps the Knight of Cups be calm under pressure
   annoys the Knight of Cups because he (KgP) is so consistent

4. Queen of Pentacles
   trait: down-to-earth
   helps the King of Wands enjoy the simple things of life
   annoys the King of Wands when she rejects anything showy

5. King of Swords
   trait: intellectual
   helps the King of Pentacles by explaining issues well
   annoys the King of Pentacles when he (KgS) is too theoretical

6. King of Cups
   trait: tolerant
   helps the King of Swords temper justice with mercy
   annoys the King of Swords when he (KgC) forgives unjust behavior

7. Queen of Cups
   trait: loving
   helps the Queen of Swords be more sensitive
   annoys the Queen of Swords because she (QnC) is not tough enough

8. Knight of Wands
   trait: adventurous/restless
   helps the Queen of Pentacles go a little crazy sometimes
   annoys the Queen of Pentacles when he's constantly on the go

9. Queen of Wands
   trait: cheerful
   helps the Knight of Swords be warm and outgoing
   annoys the Knight of Swords when she is unfazed by incompetence

10. Knight of Pentacles
    trait: hard-working/grinding

helps the Knight of Swords be warm and outgoing

annoys the Knight of Swords when she is unfazed by incompetence

10. Knight of Pentacles

trait: hard-working/grinding

helps the King of Cups to focus on the task as well as people

annoys the King of Cups when he (KnP) drives people too hard

11. Queen of Swords

trait: honest

helps the Knight of Wands be up-front with everyone

annoys the Knight of Wands by seeing through his charm

12. Knight of Swords

trait: incisive/cutting

helps the Knight of Pentacles get to the point

annoys the Knight of Pentacles by refusing to discuss details

Exercise 15.5—Occasional Pairs

1. Hermit: someone hiding from the law
    Justice: a representative of the law

2. Nine of Swords: not being able to rest
    Four of Swords: being able to rest peacefully

3. Two of Pentacles/Hanged Man: both figures have a bent leg ... perhaps a knee problem?

4. Chariot/Death: both cards show powerful figures ready to crush anything in their paths

5. Four of Pentacles: someone who is alone and loves money
    Six of Wands: someone who loves people and is surrounded by them

6. Lovers: enjoying the delights of paradise
    Six of Swords: cast out of paradise to suffer and toil

7. Hierophant: good
    Devil: evil

8. Nine of Wands/Seven of Pentacles: two workers who have stopped their labors to rest

9. Sun: sunrise
    Ten of Swords: sunset

Suggestions for Exercises—Lesson 16

Exercise 16.1—Traditional Position Pairs in the Celtic Cross

Phrases in SMALL CAPITALS refer to card meanings. *Italic* phrases refer to position meanings.

1. Position 1—Position 2
   A. Page of Cups—Knight of Pentacles
   My son is a SWEET, SENSITIVE guy who TAKES EVERYTHING TO HEART. *His teacher* is too INFLEXIBLE and GRIM. She's DRIVING MY SON TOO HARD by insisting on an UNREASONABLE LEVEL OF PERFECTION.

   B. Two of Pentacles—Judgement
   The *central conflict* is that school should be FUN and ENJOYABLE, not a place for harsh, public JUDGMENT. I can help my son learn to COPE better and be more RESILIENT at school. I must make sure my own JUDGMENTS are fair.

2. Position 3—Position 5
   A. Six of Cups—Moon
   On the surface, I'm beset by FEARS and DOUBTS. Perhaps I'm DELUDING myself. The *deeper truth* may be that there is GOOD WILL. My partner is probably INNOCENT.

   B. Seven of Cups—King of Swords
   The *source of the problem* is that I'm letting my IMAGINATION RUN WILD. I CAN'T SEPARATE FACT FROM FICTION. I must find out the FACTS. Be FAIR and HONEST. Refuse to let emotion cloud my REASON. On the other hand, have I forgotten to be loving in my CONCERN WITH THE TRUTH?

3. Position 4—Position 6
   A. Two of Swords—Three of Wands
   I've IGNORED THE WARNING SIGNS of trouble in the *past.* I've AVOIDED the problem because DEALING WITH IT WOULD BE UNPLEASANT. I'm *going to* have to demonstrate LEADERSHIP. My team is counting on me to TAKE CHARGE and PROVIDE DIRECTION.

   B. Ten of Wands—Strength
   I've *been* COVERING for this employee. It's been HARD on everyone having to SHOULDER HIS SHARE of the load, but if I'M PATIENT, he may yet become an asset. It will take EXTRA RESOLVE on my part.

4. Position 7—Position 8
   A. Ten of Pentacles—Death
   I want to CONTINUE AS I AM. The store is SUCCESSFUL and WELL-ESTABLISHED, and *I feel* SECURE and happy there. *My partner wants to* END our collaboration and MOVE ON to something else.

   B. Queen of Cups—Queen of Pentacles
   To me the store is more than just a job. I have PUT MY HEART INTO IT. I FEEL the same way about my partner, but she has a more PRACTICAL, MATTER-OF-FACT point of view. *To her,* a business is a business. Moving on is NOT A BIG, EMOTIONAL DEAL.

5. Position 5—Position 10
    A. Three of Swords—World
       I'm WORRIED there will be a HORRIBLE SCENE that might lead to a BREAK-UP. In fact, my fears may be groundless. We may ALL COME TOGETHER *in the end.* I may yet ACHIEVE MY HEART'S DESIRE.
    B. Wheel of Fortune—Fool
       Both cards suggest there is a MYSTERIOUS ELEMENT to this love that I must honor. *I think* this relationship is a major TURNING POINT, one that is DESTINED to be. If I have FAITH in my choice and TRUST MY HEART, all *will be* well. It *will be* a new BEGINNING for me.
6. Position 9—Position 4 and Position 9—Position 8
    A. Two of Wands—Seven of Swords
       This politician was involved in something SHADY in the *past.* There is some HIDDEN DISHONOR. The *key* appears to be his desire for PERSONAL POWER and INFLUENCE. This politician is BOLD and DIRECT in going after what he wants.
    B. Eight of Wands—Emperor
       The investigation will likely move into HIGH GEAR soon as NEW INFORMATION comes to light. This politician is *running up against* the power and authority of the JUSTICE SYSTEM.

Exercise 16.2—Other Pairings in the Celtic Cross

Position 1—Position 6
how the current situation (1) is drawing people or events to you (6)
how the present (1) will evolve in the near future (6)

Position 1—Position 7
how an aspect of you (7) is influencing the current situation (1)
how an ideal aspect of you (7) could alter the present environment (1)

Position 2—Position 5
how a factor for change (2) is affecting your point of view (5)
how an opposing force (2) could cause an alternate outcome (5)

Position 2—Position 8
two sources of information about an opposing factor (2) in the environment (8)
how another's point of view (8) might act as a supporting element (2)

Position 3—Position 4
how something from the past (4) is the root cause of the situation (3)
how something that needs to be discarded (4) is still an unacknowledged goal (3)

Position 3—Position 10
how an unconscious influence (3) is impacting the projected outcome (10)
how some hidden agenda (3) is dictating the projected outcome (10)

Position 4—Position 8
how a person from the past (4) is still part of the environment (8)

how others (8) are still expecting you to be the way you were in the past (4)

Position 5—Position 7

how your self-image (7) is affecting your attitudes (5)

how the role you've given yourself (7) is shaping your expectations for the future (5)

Position 6—Position 10

what the future will hold in the short-term (6) and long-term (10)

what could eventually happen (10) if you embrace a certain way of being (6)

Suggestions for Exercises—Lesson 17

Exercise 17.2—Interpreting Reversed Cards

Phrases in SMALL CAPITALS refer to card meanings. *Italic* phrases refer to the effect of the reversal.

Three of Wands—reversed

> I'm in a rut. I *rarely* BREAK OUT OF MY NORMAL ROUTINE to seek new experiences.

Chariot—reversed

> My DESIRE TO GET MY OWN WAY is being *thwarted,* but MY WIN at work will *mean little* if my family is unhappy.

Ace of Swords—reversed

> I *don't feel like getting too involved* in this CAUSE.

Tower—reversed

> There is a *small chance* my run of good fortune could END SUDDENLY.

Knights of Swords—reversed

> My cousin is a GREAT TALKER, but he's *not* that KNOWLEDGEABLE about the technical aspects of this field.

Four of Cups—reversed

> I'm *beginning* to LOSE INTEREST in this relationship. I feel a *small, but growing* urge to WITHDRAW.

Six of Pentacles—reversed

> I'm *not sure I have enough* PHYSICAL AND EMOTIONAL RESOURCES to support my daughter through this crisis in my home.

Page of Cups—reversed

> My feelings of LOVE and TENDERNESS for my baby are being *drowned out* by my need for sleep!

Temperance—reversed

> I'm *pretty low* on PATIENCE right now. I'm tempted to take *drastic action.*

Death—reversed

> An IMPORTANT INNER CHANGE is *struggling to happen,* but my fears are *blocking* it.

Exercise 17.3—Upside-Down Meanings

The effect of the reversal is in *italics*.

Justice—reversed

> This verdict is crazy! Justice has been *turned on its head*.
> This decision has *tipped the scales* against me. (See image.)

Page of Swords—reversed

> This child is so *contrary*. She *defies me at every turn!*
> These results are illogical—the *opposite of what we expected*.

Hanged Man—reversed

> I *don't know if I'm up or down*. Nothing is the way it seems.
> I sacrificed everything, but look at me now! I'm *back on my feet*. (See image.)

Four of Wands—reversed

> The celebration wasn't what I expected. It *turned sour* on me.
> I *mustn't get too excited*. I've got to play it cool.

Ace of Pentacles—reversed

> I *can't* seem to *hold onto* my money. It just *slips through my fingers*. (See image.)
> I don't feel stable. The *ground keeps shifting* under me.

Knight of Cups—reversed

> One day *I'm up*, the next day *I'm down*. These mood swings are difficult.
> I *pretend* I don't have strong feelings, but I do.

Six of Swords—reversed

> This "boat" is going to *capsize*. (See image.)
> I *refuse* to stay depressed. I'm going to have some fun.

Hierophant—reversed

> I'm *dropping out* of school.
> I *don't see my religion the same way* anymore.

Three of Pentacles—reversed

> The team's *reversed direction*.
> I'm *not going to plan*. I'm just going to be spontaneous.

IV

CARD DESCRIPTIONS

Introduction to the Card Descriptions

Here are the features you will find on the card pages:

Name and Picture

The name of the card with a small picture of its image from the Universal Waite deck.

Keywords

Keywords are 3–5 words or phrases that capture the main themes of a card. They are listed at the top of the page. Three keyword summary charts are included in this section for reference.

Actions

Actions are phrases describing how the energy of each keyword manifests. Two sample actions for the High Priestess are "looking beyond the obvious" and "sensing the secret and hidden." These are ways to experience *mystery*. The active form is used to emphasize how a card represents dynamic energy.

Opposing Cards

An opposing pair consists of two cards with meanings that can be opposites. Some cards are listed that might form an opposing pair with the given card under some circumstances. These are only some of the possibilities. See lesson 15 and Appendices C (suits) and D (ranks) for more on opposing cards.

Reinforcing Cards

A reinforcing pair consists of two cards with meanings that can be similar. Some cards are listed that might form a reinforcing pair with the given card under some circumstances. These are only some of the possibilities. See lesson 15 for more on reinforcing cards.

Court Card Pairs

Court cards form natural pairs because of their distinctive personalities. Compare the ranks and suits of the two cards to understand the interaction. See lesson 15 and Appendices C (suits) and D (ranks) for more on court card pairs.

Ace-Ace Pairs

An Ace-Ace pair does not show an opposition, but a unique chance to grow in a new direction that taps the energy of both suits.

Description

The description consists of a few paragraphs of extra information about a card and what it implies in a reading. The major arcana descriptions tend to be general and philosophical. The minor arcana descriptions are more concrete and everyday.

Reversed?

There are no separate explanations for reversed cards. The meaning of a reversed card depends on what the card would mean if upright. A reversed card shows that a card's energy is present, but at a lower level. For some reason, the energy cannot express freely, normally, or completely. It may be:

    still in its early stages
    losing force and power
    blocked or restricted
    incomplete
    inappropriate
    being denied
    only present in appearance

See lesson 17 for more information on reversed cards.

Part 1

Major Arcana

Tarot Keywords Major Arcana

FOOL (0)	MAGICIAN (1)	HIGH PRIESTESS (2)	EMPRESS (3)
Beginning Spontaneity Faith Apparent Folly	Action Conscious Awareness Concentration Power	Nonaction Unconscious Awareness Potential Mystery	Mothering Abundance Senses Nature
EMPEROR (4)	**HIEROPHANT (5)**	**LOVERS (6)**	**CHARIOT (7)**
Fathering Structure Authority Regulation	Education Belief Systems Conformity Group Identification	Relationship Sexuality Personal Beliefs Values	Victory Will Self-Assertion Hard Control
STRENGTH (8)	**HERMIT (9)**	**WHEEL OF FORTUNE (10)**	**JUSTICE (11)**
Strength Patience Compassion Soft Control	Introspection Searching Guidance Solitude	Destiny Turning Point Movement Personal Vision	Justice Responsibility Decision Cause and Effect
HANGED MAN (12)	**DEATH (13)**	**TEMPERANCE (14)**	**DEVIL (15)**
Letting Go Reversal Suspension Sacrifice	Ending Transition Elimination Inexorable Forces	Temperance Balance Health Combination	Bondage Materialism Ignorance Hopelessness
TOWER (16)	**STAR (17)**	**MOON (18)**	**SUN (19)**
Sudden Change Release Downfall Revelation	Hope Inspiration Generosity Serenity	Fear Illusion Imagination Bewilderment	Enlightenment Greatness Vitality Assurance
	JUDGEMENT (20)	**WORLD (21)**	
	Judgment Rebirth Inner Calling Absolution	Integration Accomplishment Involvement Fulfillment	

0

The Fool

- BEGINNING
- SPONTANEITY

- FAITH
- APPARENT FOLLY

Actions

BEGINNING

   entering a new phase

   striking out on a new path

   expanding horizons

   starting something new

   beginning an adventure

   going on a journey

   heading into the unknown

being SPONTANEOUS

   living in the moment

   letting go of expectations

   doing the unexpected

   acting on impulse

   feeling uninhibited

   surprising someone

   feeling carefree

having FAITH

   trusting the flow

   staying open

   letting go of worry and fear

   feeling protected and loved

   living in joy

   recapturing innocence

   believing

embracing FOLLY

   accepting your choices

   taking the "foolish" path

   pursuing a pipe dream

   being true to yourself

   taking a "crazy" chance

   trusting your heart's desire

Opposing Cards: Some Possibilities

Hierophant—following convention, routine

Death—ending, closing down

Devil—feeling cynical, lacking faith

Two of Swords—blocking off experience, feeling tense, holding back

Four of Pentacles—order and regularity

Reinforcing Cards: Some Possibilities

Hanged Man—having faith in what is, going with the flow

Star—innocence, faith, trust

Judgement—rebirth, new starts

Three of Wands—expanding horizons, going into unexplored territory

Description

THE FOOL.

As Card 0, the Fool lies at the beginning of the major arcana, but also somewhat apart from the other cards. In medieval courts, the court jester was someone who was not expected to follow the same rules as others. He could observe and then poke fun. This makes the Fool unpredictable and full of surprises. He reminds us of the unlimited potential and spontaneity inherent in every moment. There is a sense with this card that anything goes—nothing is certain or regular. The Fool adds the new and unfamiliar to a situation.

The Fool also represents the complete faith that life is good and worthy of trust. Some might call the Fool too innocent, but his innocence sustains him and brings him joy. In readings, the Fool can signal a new beginning or change of direction—one that will guide you onto a path of adventure, wonder, and personal growth. He also reminds you to keep your faith and trust your natural responses. If you are facing a decision or moment of doubt, the Fool tells you to believe in yourself and follow your heart no matter how crazy or foolish your impulses may seem.

1

The Magician

- ACTION
- CONSCIOUS AWARENESS
- CONCENTRATION
- POWER

Actions

taking ACTION
  doing what needs to be done
  realizing your potential
  making what's possible real
  practicing what you preach
  carrying out plans
  producing magical results
  using your talents

acting CONSCIOUSLY
  knowing what you are doing and why
  acknowledging your motivations
  understanding your intentions
  examining the known situation

CONCENTRATING
  having singleness of purpose
  being totally committed
  applying the force of your will
  feeling centered
  setting aside distractions
  focusing on a goal

experiencing POWER
  making a strong impact
  having vitality
  creating miracles
  becoming energized
  feeling vigorous
  being creative

Opposing Cards: Some Possibilities

High Priestess—nonaction, intuition, accessing the unconscious
Hanged Man—suspending action, not doing
Seven of Cups—lacking focus and commitment
Four of Swords—resting quietly, storing energy
Eight of Swords—confused and uncertain, powerless

Reinforcing Cards: Some Possibilities

Chariot—focusing, concentrating, being forceful
Two of Wands—personal power, wielding a strong force
Eight of Wands—quick action, making your move
Eight of Pentacles—focus and concentration

Description

The Magician is the archetype of the active, masculine principle—the ultimate achiever. He symbolizes the power to tap universal forces and use them for creative purposes. Note his stance in the picture. He acts as a lightning rod—one arm extended up into the Divine for inspiration, the other pointing toward Earth to ground this potent energy.[1] His abilities appear magical at times because his will helps him achieve what seem to be miracles.

What makes the Magician so powerful? First, he is not afraid to act. He believes in himself and is willing to put that belief on the line. He also knows what he intends to do and why. He doesn't hesitate because he understands his situation exactly. The Magician can focus with single-minded determination. As long as he remembers the divine source of his power, the Magician remains the perfect conduit for miracles.

In a reading, the Magician implies that the primal forces of creativity are yours if you can claim your power and act with awareness and concentration. This card is a signal to act and act now, provided you understand exactly what you want and are committed to getting it.

1. Rachel Pollack, *Seventy-Eight Degrees of Wisdom: A Book of Tarot. Part 1: The Major Arcana* (London: Aquarian, 1980), p. 30.

2

The High Priestess

- NONACTION
- UNCONSCIOUS AWARENESS
- POTENTIAL
- MYSTERY

Actions

staying NONACTIVE
  withdrawing from involvement
  allowing events to proceed without
    intervention
  being receptive to influence
  becoming calm
  being passive
  waiting patiently

accessing the UNCONSCIOUS
  using your intuition
  seeking guidance from within
  trusting your inner voice
  opening to dreams and the imagination
  being aware of a larger reality

seeing the POTENTIAL
  understanding the possibilities
  opening to what could be
  seeing your hidden talents
  allowing development
  letting what is there flower

sensing the MYSTERY
  looking beyond the obvious
  approaching a closed off area
  opening to the unknown
  remembering something important
  sensing the secret and hidden
  seeking what is concealed
  acknowledging the Shadow

Opposing Cards: Some Possibilities

Magician—acting consciously, thinking, the known and obvious
Two of Wands—acting boldly
Seven of Wands—being aggressive
Eight of Wands—putting plans into action

Reinforcing Cards: Some Possibilities

Hermit—looking inward, withdrawing, seeking guidance
Hanged Man—suspending activity, waiting
Four of Swords—resting quietly, contemplating

Description

The High Priestess is the guardian of the unconscious. She sits in front of the thin veil of unawareness which is all that separates us from our inner landscape. She contains within herself the secret of these realms and offers us the silent invitation, "Be still and know that I am God."

THE HIGH PRIESTESS

The High Priestess is the feminine principle that balances the masculine force of the Magician. The feminine archetype in the tarot is split between the High Priestess and the Empress. The High Priestess is the mysterious unknown that women often represent, especially in cultures that focus on the tangible and known. The Empress represents woman's role as the crucible of life.

In readings, the High Priestess poses a challenge to you to go deeper—to look beyond the obvious, surface situation to what is hidden and obscure. She also asks you to recall the vastness of your potential and to remember the unlimited possibilities you hold within yourself. The High Priestess can represent a time of waiting and allowing. It is not always necessary to act to achieve your goals. Sometimes they can be realized through a stillness that gives desire a chance to flower within the fullness of time.

3

The Empress

- MOTHERING
- ABUNDANCE
- SENSES
- NATURE

Actions

MOTHERING
   giving birth
   nourishing life
   nurturing and caring for others
   cherishing the world
   expressing tenderness
   working with children

welcoming ABUNDANCE
   enjoying extravagance
   receiving lavish reward
   luxuriating in plenty
   having more than enough
   feeling rich

experiencing the SENSES
   giving and receiving pleasure
   focusing on the body
   appreciating beauty
   feeling vibrantly healthy
   being earthy
   doing physical activity

responding to NATURE
   relating to plants and animals
   embracing the natural
   feeling connected to the Earth
   going outdoors
   harmonizing with natural rhythms

Opposing Cards: Some Possibilities

Emperor—fathering, order and discipline, regularity
Death—principle of death
Four of Pentacles—miserly possessiveness
Nine of Pentacles—refinement, sophistication

Reinforcing Cards: Some Possibilities

Lovers—sexual fulfillment, pleasure
Star—generosity, free-flowing love
Nine of Cups—enjoying the senses
Seven of Pentacles—material reward
Ten of Pentacles—affluence, luxury, physical comfort

Description

The Empress and the High Priestess are the two halves of the female archetype in the major arcana. The Empress represents the fertile, life-giving Mother who reigns over the bounty of nature and the rhythms of the Earth. From her comes all the pleasures and joys of the senses and the abundance of new life in all its forms. The Empress encourages you to strengthen your connections with the natural world which is the ground of our being. Too often false sophistications and pleasures take us far from our roots. Let the Empress remind you to keep your feet firmly planted in the Earth.

In readings the Empress can refer to any aspect of Motherhood. She can be an individual mother, but as a major arcana card, she also goes beyond the specifics of mothering to its essence—the creation of life and its sustenance through loving care and attention.

The Empress can also represent lavish abundance of all kinds. She offers a cornucopia of delights, especially those of the senses—food, pleasure, and beauty. She can suggest material reward, but only with the understanding that riches go with a generous and open spirit. The Empress asks you to embrace the principle of life and enjoy its bountiful goodness.

4

The Emperor

- FATHERING
- STRUCTURE

- AUTHORITY
- REGULATION

Actions

FATHERING
  establishing a family line
  setting direction and tone
  protecting and defending
  guiding growth
  bringing security and comfort
  offering explanations

emphasizing STRUCTURE
  creating order out of chaos
  categorizing
  being systematic
  providing shape and form
  being organized
  applying reason
  coordinating
  sticking to a plan

exercising AUTHORITY
  taking a leadership role
  commanding
  exerting control
  representing the establishment
  being in a position of strength
  coming in contact with officials
  setting direction

REGULATING
  establishing law and order
  operating from sound principles
  applying rules or guidelines
  working within the legal system
  setting standards of behavior
  following a regimen

Opposing Cards: Some Possibilities

Empress—mothering, free-flowing abundance
Seven of Cups—dissipation, lack of order
Five of Swords—bending the rules, breaking the law

Reinforcing Cards: Some Possibilities

Hierophant—conforming to rules
Justice—concerns of justice and legality
Two of Wands—having authority
Three of Wands—assuming leadership
Four of Pentacles—control, structure, order

Description

The figure of the Emperor says much about the essential qualities of this card. We see a stern, commanding figure seated on a stone-slab throne. His back is straight, and his eyes meet ours directly. He is confident of his complete authority to rule.

The Emperor represents structure, order, and regulation—forces to balance the free-flowing, lavish abundance of the Empress. He advocates a four-square world where trains are on time, games are played by rules, and commanding officers are respected. In chaotic situations, the Emperor can indicate the need for organization. Loose ends should be tied up, and wayward elements, harnessed. In situations that are already over-controlled, he suggests the confining effect of those constraints.

The Emperor can represent an encounter with authority or the assumption of power and control. As the regulator, he is often associated with legal matters, disciplinary actions, and officialdom in all its forms. He can also stand for an individual father or archetypal Father in his role as guide, protector, and provider.

5

The Hierophant

- EDUCATION
- BELIEF SYSTEMS

- CONFORMITY
- GROUP IDENTIFICATION

Actions

getting an EDUCATION
  pursuing knowledge
  becoming informed
  increasing understanding
  studying and learning
  seeking a deeper meaning
  finding out more

having a BELIEF SYSTEM
  sharing a cultural heritage
  learning a religious tradition
  honoring ritual and ceremony
  identifying a world view
  following a discipline
  knowing where to put your faith

CONFORMING
  following the rules
  taking an orthodox approach
  staying within conventional bounds
  adapting to the system
  fitting in
  going along with the program
  doing what's expected
  being part of the Establishment

identifying with a GROUP
  being committed to a cause
  devoting energy to a group
  joining an organization
  working as part of a team
  feeling loyal to others
  being in an institutionalized setting

Opposing Cards: Some Possibilities

Fool—being "crazy" and unorthodox
Lovers—*personal* beliefs
Two of Wands—diverging from the crowd, being a pioneer
Seven of Swords—being a lone wolf
Two of Pentacles—being flexible, changing with the times

Reinforcing Cards: Some Possibilities

Emperor—following rules
Three of Cups—focusing on the group
Three of Pentacles—working in a team or group
Eight of Pentacles—learning, studying
Ten of Pentacles—conforming, following rules, conservative

Description

Except in rare cases, every human grows and develops within a culture. We learn by living with others. The Hierophant represents such official learning, especially in groups. A Hierophant is someone who interprets secret knowledge. On Card 5 we see a religious figure in a formal church setting. He is wearing the elaborate vestments of his office. His task is to bring the two initiates into the church so they can take up their appointed roles.

Besides churches, there are schools, clubs, teams, companies, and societies. The Hierophant represents all of these because his realm is structured groups with rules and assigned roles. Such environments emphasize belief systems—facts, rules, procedures, and ritual. Members are rewarded for following conventions. They develop a group identity. The Hierophant is one of three cards that focuses on the group. (The Three of Cups and the Three of Pentacles are the others.)

In readings, the Hierophant often represents learning with experts or knowledgeable teachers. This card also stands for institutions and their values. The Hierophant is a symbol of the need to conform to rules or fixed situations. His appearance in a reading can show that you are struggling with a force that is not innovative, free-spirited, or individual. Groups can be enriching or stifling, depending on circumstances. Sometimes we need to follow a program or embrace tradition; other times we need to trust ourselves.

6

The Lovers

- RELATIONSHIP
- SEXUALITY

- PERSONAL BELIEFS
- VALUES

Actions

RELATING to others
  establishing bonds
  feeling love
  forming a union or marriage
  acknowledging kinship
  sympathizing with another
  getting closer
  making a connection
  being intimate

being SEXUAL
  seeking union
  experiencing desire
  making love
  opening to another
  responding with passion
  feeling a physical attraction
  tapping inner energy

establishing PERSONAL BELIEFS
  questioning received opinions
  figuring out where you stand
  staying true to yourself
  setting your own philosophy
  going by your own standards
  making up your own mind

determining VALUES
  struggling with temptation
  choosing between right and wrong
  facing an ethical or moral choice
  refusing to let ends justify means
  finding out what you care about

Opposing Cards: Some Possibilities

Hierophant—established beliefs
Hermit—being alone, not relating, less sexuality
Five of Cups—loss in relationships
Three of Swords—rejection, separation

Reinforcing Cards: Some Possibilities

Empress—sexual fulfillment, pleasure
Two of Cups—union, marriage, connection
Nine of Cups—sexual pleasure
Ten of Cups—family relationships, bonding
Ten of Pentacles—permanent unions, family ties

Description

The Lovers is one card that is easy to remember. Love and sex are riveting subjects, and, as you'd expect, this card represents both. The urge for union is powerful and, in its highest form, takes us beyond ourselves. That is why an angel is blessing the bond between the man and woman on this card.

In readings, Card 6 often refers to a relationship that is based on deep love—the strongest force of all. The relationship may not be sexual, although it often is or could be. More generally, the Lovers can represent the attractive force that draws any two entities together in a relationship—whether people, ideas, events, movements, or groups.

Card 6 can also stand for tough value choices and the questioning that goes with them. In some decks,[1] the Lovers shows a man torn between two women—a virgin and a temptress. This rather old-fashioned triangle symbolizes the larger dilemmas we face when we are tempted between right and wrong.

The Lovers can indicate a moral or ethical crossroads—a decision point where you must choose between the high road or the low road. This card can also represent your personal beliefs because to make such a decision you must know where you stand. Following your own path can mean going against those who are urging you in a direction that is wrong for you.

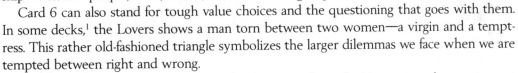

1. For example, *Tarot of Marseilles* (Turnhout, Belgium: Carta Mundi, 1996). Distributed by U.S. Games.

7

The Chariot

- •VICTORY
- • WILL

- • SELF-ASSERTION
- • HARD CONTROL

Actions

achieving VICTORY
  reaching your goal
  winning
  being successful
  dominating
  coming out on top
  beating the competition

using your WILL
  being determined to succeed
  focusing your intent
  rising above temptation
  letting nothing distract you
  sustaining an effort
  concentrating your energies
  fixing on a goal

ASSERTING yourself
  being ego-focused
  establishing an identity
  knowing who you are
  feeling self-confident
  having faith in yourself
  looking out for your interests

achieving HARD CONTROL
  mastering emotions
  curbing impulses
  maintaining discipline
  holding in anger
  getting your own way
  assuming the reins of power
  showing authority

Opposing Cards: Some Possibilities

Strength—soft control
Hanged Man—accepting God's will, putting others first
Tower—defeat, humbling experience
Eight of Swords—confusion, self-doubt
Ten of Swords—powerless, in the pits, putting others first

Reinforcing Cards: Some Possibilities

Magician—using your will, concentrating
Two of Wands—being in authority, dominating
Six of Wands—triumph, self-confidence
Four of Pentacles—control
Nine of Pentacles—self-control, discipline

Description

Picture Julius Caesar riding his chariot triumphantly into Rome. He has defeated his enemies and conquered vast, new lands. This is the spirit of the Chariot. Card 7 represents the victories that are possible through willpower and self-mastery. A military image is appropriate for the Chariot because this card stands for the strengths associated with combat—discipline, grit, determination, and assertiveness.

The Chariot represents the positive aspects of the ego. A healthy ego is one that is strong and self-assured. It knows what it wants and how to get it. We can get annoyed with someone whose ego is *too* healthy, but we often turn to that person to lead us through difficult moments. We know he or she won't be wishy-washy.

In readings, the Chariot often appears when hard control is or could be in evidence. At its best, hard control is not brutal, but firm and direct. It is backed by a strong will and great confidence. The Chariot can mean self-control or control of the environment. This card also represents victory. There are many types of wins; the Chariot's is of the win-lose type. Your success comes from beating the competition to become number one. Such moments are glorious in the right circumstances.

8

Strength

- STRENGTH
- PATIENCE

- COMPASSION
- SOFT CONTROL

Actions

showing STRENGTH
    knowing you can endure
    having a gallant spirit
    feeling an unshakable resolve
    taking heart despite setbacks
    having stamina
    being a rock

being PATIENT
    dealing calmly with frustration
    accepting others
    taking time
    maintaining composure
    refusing to get angry
    showing forbearance

being COMPASSIONATE
    giving others lots of space
    tolerating
    understanding what others are feeling
    accepting
    forgiving imperfection
    being kind

achieving SOFT CONTROL
    persuading
    working with
    guiding indirectly
    being able to influence
    tempering force with benevolence
    demonstrating the strength of love

Opposing Cards: Some Possibilities

Chariot—hard control
Eight of Cups—weariness, lack of strength
Six of Swords—being listless, lacking heart
Five of Pentacles—ill health, weakness

Reinforcing Cards: Some Possibilities

Hanged Man—taking time, patience
Nine of Wands—stamina, strength to endure

Description

Usually we think of strength in physical terms—big arms, powerful legs—but there is also inner strength. Inner strength comes from an exercise of the heart muscle. It is perseverance, courage, resolve, and composure—qualities that help us endure when times are tough. In the past, a person with inner strength was said to have character; he or she could be counted on in the darkest moments. Card 8 represents this energy of quiet determination. Strength is not a flashy card, but one that is solid and reliable.

Card 8 also represents patience and compassion. Getting angry is easy when events turn sour, but dealing calmly with frustration takes great strength. So does accepting others and forgiving mistakes. We need strength to mold situations softly. The Chariot controls through mastery and authority. Card 8 is more subtle, even loving. Notice how the lion (itself a symbol of strength) is being guided and tamed by the woman's gentle hands.

Card 8 will appear in a reading when its qualities are needed. It can be a reminder not to despair or give up. You have the inner strength to endure and triumph. If you are pushing too hard, you need to withdraw for the moment and be patient. If other people or circumstances are driving you crazy, remember the strength that comes with love and forbearance. These will see you through the hardest moments.

9

The Hermit

- INTROSPECTION
- SEARCHING

- GUIDANCE
- SOLITUDE

Actions

being INTROSPECTIVE
thinking things over
focusing inward
concentrating less on the senses
quieting yourself
looking for answers within
needing to understand

SEARCHING
seeking greater understanding
looking for something
wanting the truth at all costs
going on a personal quest
needing more
desiring a new direction

receiving/giving GUIDANCE
going to/being a mentor
accepting/offering wise counsel
learning from/being a guru
turning to/being a trusted teacher
being helped/helping

seeking SOLITUDE
needing to be alone
desiring stillness
withdrawing from the world
experiencing seclusion
giving up distractions
retreating into a private world

Opposing Cards: Some Possibilities

Lovers—being in a relationship, sexuality
World—involvement with the world
Two of Cups—making connections, partnerships
Three of Cups—being in a group, being with others
Nine of Cups—sensual pleasure

Reinforcing Cards: Some Possibilities

High Priestess—looking inward, withdrawing
Four of Cups—withdrawing, being introverted
Eight of Cups—searching for deeper meaning
Four of Swords—contemplating, being quiet
Seven of Swords—being alone, staying away from others

Description

The traditional hermit is a crusty, bearded character who has withdrawn from the company of men to live a life of seclusion and hardship. Card 9 supports this understanding. The Hermit represents the desire to turn away from the getting and spending of society to focus on the inner world. He seeks answers within and knows that they will come only with quiet and solitude.

There comes a point in life when we begin to question the obvious. We sense there is a deeper reality and begin to search for it. This is mainly a solitary quest because answers do not lie in the external world, but in ourselves. The hermit on Card 9 reminds us of Diogenes, the Greek ascetic who is said to have gone out with a lantern in hand to search for an honest man. Diogenes is a symbol of the search for truth that the Hermit hopes to find by stripping away all diversions.

In readings, the Hermit often suggests a need for time alone—a period of reflection when distractions are limited. In times of action and high energy, he stands for the still center that must be created for balance. He can also indicate that withdrawal or retreat is advised for the moment. In addition, the Hermit can imply seeking of all kinds, especially for deeper under-standing or the truth of a situation. "Seek, and ye shall find," we have been told, and so the Hermit stands for guidance as well. We can receive help from wise teachers, and, in turn, help others as we progress.

10

The Wheel of Fortune

- DESTINY
- TURNING POINT

- MOVEMENT
- PERSONAL VISION

Actions

feeling a sense of DESTINY
  using what chance offers
  seeing life's threads weave together
  finding opportunity in an accident
  opening to luck
  sensing the action of fate
  witnessing miracles

being at a TURNING POINT
  reversing
  moving in a different direction
  turning things around
  having a change in fortune
  altering the present course
  being surprised at a turn of events

feeling MOVEMENT
  experiencing change
  feeling the tempo of life speed up
  being swept up in new developments
  rejoining the world of activity
  getting involved

having a PERSONAL VISION
  seeing how everything connects
  becoming more aware
  uncovering patterns and cycles
  expanding your outlook
  gaining greater perspective
  discovering your role and purpose

Opposing Cards: Some Possibilities

Two of Swords—being stuck, at an impasse
Four of Swords—rest, quiet, slow pace
Four of Pentacles—blocked change, no movement
Seven of Pentacles—assessment before direction change

Reinforcing Cards: Some Possibilities

Eight of Wands—rapid pace, quick developments

Description

In Greek mythology, there are three women known as the Fates. They are responsible for spinning the destiny of each person at his or her birth. It is not surprising that the Fates are spinners because the wheel of fortune is an apt image for the elusive turns of a man's fate. This is the theme of Card 10.

WHEEL of FORTUNE.

The Wheel of Fortune is one of the few cards in the major arcana that does not have a human figure as a focal point. This is because its center is above the realm of man—in the higher levels (clouds) where the destinies of all are woven together in the tapestry of life. The tarot recognizes that each person sets his own path in life, but is also subject to the larger cycles that include him. We experience chance events that appear to be accidents although they are part of the great plan.

In readings, the Wheel of Fortune can indicate a vision or realization that stikes with great force. If you've been struggling with a problem or tough situation, this card can signal that you will find the answer if you stand back and view everything from a larger perspective.

The Wheel of Fortune also represents unexpected encounters and twists of fate. You can't predict surprises; you can only be aware when one is circling around. Indeed, Card 10 often suggests wheel-like actions—changes in direction, repeating cycles, and rapid movement. When the energy of the Wheel arrives, you will feel life speed up. You are caught in a cyclone that may deposit you anywhere. "Round and round and round she goes, and where she stops, nobody knows."

11

Justice

• JUSTICE
• RESPONSIBILITY

• DECISION
• CAUSE AND EFFECT

Actions

respecting JUSTICE
    insisting on fairness
    acting on ethical principles
    being involved in legal concerns
    committing to honesty
    seeking equality
    being impartial
    trying to do what is right

assuming RESPONSIBILITY
    settling old accounts and debts
    being accountable
    acknowledging the truth
    admitting involvement
    handling the situation
    doing what has to be done

preparing for a DECISION
    weighing all sides of an issue
    setting a course for the future
    balancing all factors
    determining right action
    choosing with full awareness

understanding CAUSE AND EFFECT
    accepting the results you created
    seeing how you chose your situation
    recognizing the action of karma
    knowing that what is makes sense
    making connections between events

Opposing Cards: Some Possibilities

Two of Swords—avoiding the truth, disavowing your role
Five of Swords—lack of integrity, not doing what is right
Seven of Swords—shirking responsibility

Reinforcing Cards: Some Possibilities

Emperor—justice, regulations, legal issues
Judgement—deciding, accepting past actions/mistakes
Ten of Wands—accepting responsibility, being accountable
Nine of Swords—guilt over the past, acknowledging mistakes
Seven of Pentacles—assessing where you are, deciding a future course

Description

On Card 11 we see the familiar figure of Justice. She has the scales of equality and impartial judgment in one hand, and the sword of decision in the other. In the tarot, Justice represents the understanding that life is ultimately fair and just. Even though the vagaries of day-to-day life can make us doubt this fact, Justice reminds us that there is divine balance. Notice the similarity between the Emperor and Justice. Both cards stand for universal order; the Emperor in its underlying structure, Justice in the action of karma—cause and effect.

There is a serious feel to Card 11—the tone of the courtroom. This card refers to legal matters of all kinds, but is not restricted to them. The courts are where judgments are made and decisions rendered. Our legal system is the official arena in which we explore the principles of Justice—fairness, impartiality, and the quest for truth.

In readings, Justice often appears when you are concerned with doing what is right or making sure you receive your due. This card can also appear when you are feeling the impact of a past mistake or good deed. The *cause* you set in motion is now returning to you as an *effect*.

Sometimes Justice is a signal to do what needs to be done. A time comes when responsibilities must be accepted, and accounts settled. The past will continue to haunt you if you do not recognize your mistakes and make amends for them. You will need to weigh matters carefully and perhaps make important decisions about your future course.

12

The Hanged Man

- LETTING GO
- REVERSAL
- SUSPENSION
- SACRIFICE

Actions

LETTING GO
  having an emotional release
  accepting what is
  surrendering to experience
  ending the struggle
  being vulnerable and open
  giving up control
  accepting God's will

REVERSING
  turning the world around
  changing your mind
  overturning old priorities
  seeing from a new angle
  upending the old order
  doing an about-face

SUSPENDING action
  pausing to reflect
  feeling outside of time
  taking time to just be
  giving up urgency
  living in the moment
  waiting for the best opportunity

SACRIFICING
  being a martyr
  renouncing a claim
  putting self-interest aside
  going one step back to go two steps forward
  giving up for a higher cause
  putting others first

Opposing Cards: Some Possibilities

Magician—acting, doing
Chariot—self-assertion
Seven of Wands—defiance, struggling against
Ten of Wands—struggle
Four of Pentacles—holding on, control

Reinforcing Cards: Some Possibilities

Fool—faith in what is, going with the flow
High Priestess—suspending activity, waiting
Strength—patience, taking time
Four of Swords—rest, suspended activity
Ten of Swords—sacrifice, martyrdom

Description

The Hanged Man is one of the most mysterious cards in the tarot deck. It is simple, but complex. It attracts, but also disturbs. It contradicts itself in countless ways. The Hanged Man is unsettling because it symbolizes the action of paradox in our lives. A paradox is something that appears contradictory, and yet is true. The Hanged Man presents to us certain truths, but they are hidden in their opposites.

The main lesson of the Hanged Man is that we "control" by letting go—we "win" by surrendering. The figure on Card 12 has made the ultimate surrender—to die on the cross of his own travails—yet he shines with the glory of divine understanding. He has sacrificed himself, but he emerges the victor. The Hanged Man also tells us that we can "move forward" by standing still. By suspending time, we can have all the time in the world.

In readings, the Hanged Man reminds us that the best approach to a problem is not always the most obvious. When we most want to force our will on someone, that is when we should release. When we most want to have our own way, that is when we should sacrifice. When we most want to act, that is when we should wait. The irony is that by making these contradictory moves, we find what we are looking for.

13

Death

- ENDING
- TRANSITION
- ELIMINATION
- INEXORABLE FORCES

Actions

ENDING

closing one door to open another
bringing something to a close
completing a chapter
concluding unfinished business
putting the past behind you
having a parting of the ways

going through TRANSITION

changing status
moving from the known to the unknown
being cast adrift
waiting in an in-between state
being in the middle

ELIMINATING excess

cutting out what isn't necessary
shedding old attitudes
getting down to bare bones
concentrating on essentials
getting back to basics

experiencing INEXORABLE FORCES

being in the path of sweeping change
being caught in the inescapable
going through what cannot be avoided
being part of a powerful movement
riding your fate
accepting the inevitable

Opposing Cards: Some Possibilities

Fool—beginning
Empress—birth
Judgement—rebirth, fresh start

Reinforcing Cards: Some Possibilities

Tower—sweeping impact, powerful forces
Eight of Wands—conclusion, ending
Five of Cups—loss, good-byes
Eight of Cups—moving on, finishing up

Description

Death! A powerful energy indeed. Who can look at the dark, skeletal figure on Card 13 and not feel uneasy? Here we see the face of our deepest fear—our greatest unknown. We recoil from Death because we think of it as annihilation. In the tarot (and in life I would suggest) Death is not a permanent end, but a transition into a new state. Life is eternal in its essence, if not in its form. To grow, to move, to live—we must "die" to the old to give birth to the new.

It is a truism in tarot work that Card 13 *rarely* has anything to do with physical death. A responsible card reader never interprets Card 13 in this way because this view is too limiting. Death is not something that

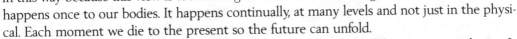

happens once to our bodies. It happens continually, at many levels and not just in the physical. Each moment we die to the present so the future can unfold.

In readings, Death often represents an important ending that will initiate great change. It signals the end of an era, a moment when a door is closing. At such times, there may be sadness and reluctance, but also relief and a sense of completion. Death also suggests getting down to basics. Dying has a way of making you concentrate on what's important. This card reminds you to cut out the unnecessary. Death can also mean you will experience an inexorable force. Death is inevitable, and sometimes there are events that are inescapable as well. When these moments occur, the best approach is to ride your fate and see where it takes you.

14

Temperance

- TEMPERANCE
- BALANCE

- HEALTH
- COMBINATION

Actions

being TEMPERATE
  finding the middle ground
  showing moderation
  avoiding excess
  mitigating a harsh position
  looking for the golden mean
  reaching a compromise
  offsetting an extreme

maintaining BALANCE
  experiencing harmony
  achieving equilibrium
  bringing together opposites
  recognizing all sides
  fostering cooperation
  feeling centered and secure

experiencing HEALTH
  renewing energy and vigor
  healing
  enjoying well-being
  recovering
  flourishing

COMBINING forces
  gathering together what is needed
  joining with others
  consolidating
  finding the right mix
  creating synthesis
  getting it all together

Opposing Cards: Some Possibilities

Tower—extremes, exploding apart
Five of Wands—disagreement, competition, imbalance
Seven of Cups—excess, overindulgence
Five of Swords—discord, lack of harmony
Five of Pentacles—ill health

Reinforcing Cards: Some Possibilities

World—integration, synthesis, combination
Two of Cups—connection, working together
Three of Cups—joining forces, working together
Two of Pentacles—balance, finding the right mix
Three of Pentacles—teamwork, combining

Description

There are certain people who exude a kind of quiet composure. They may not say much, but they go about their business with an air of calm deliberation. Their presence is comforting because they are so centered. For me, this is the energy of Temperance.

To be temperate is to show moderation and self-restraint. In a world full of enticing indulgences, it is often necessary to find the middle ground. Sensible, maybe, but also a bit boring? The energy of Temperance may seem unexciting on the surface, but it is the calm of a hurricane's eye. All around are swirling winds, but in the center is a still point that brings everything into balance.

In readings, Temperance can represent a need for moderation, especially when extreme cards are present (such as the Knights). This card can also indicate a need for balance. In conflict situations, Temperance suggests that compromise and cooperation are vital. Look for any opportunity to bring opposing parties together. In fact, to *temper* can mean to modify by adding a new component. By combining and recombining, we come up with the ideal mixture or solution. Temperance is the card of good health in all areas—physical, mental, and emotional. When illness or dis-ease is a concern, Temperance holds out the promise of vitality and well-being.

15

The Devil

- BONDAGE
- MATERIALISM

- IGNORANCE
- HOPELESSNESS

Actions

experiencing BONDAGE
    accepting an unwanted situation
    being obsessed
    feeling tied down against your will
    losing independence
    allowing yourself to be controlled
    being addicted and enslaved
    submitting to another

focusing on the MATERIAL
    being caught up in appearances
    believing only in the physical
    forgetting the spiritual
    getting and spending
    overindulging the senses

staying in IGNORANCE
    being unaware
    operating within a narrow range
    experiencing limitation
    choosing to stay in the dark
    fearing the unknown
    being taken in by appearances

feeling HOPELESS
    believing the worst
    despairing
    lacking faith
    seeing a cold world
    thinking negatively
    foreseeing a bleak future
    doubting

Opposing Cards: Some Possibilities

Fool—having faith, believing
Star—hope, faith, optimism
Four of Wands—freedom, release
Six of Cups—good will, innocence, simple joys
Ten of Cups—joy, peace, blessings

Reinforcing Cards: Some Possibilities

Seven of Cups—overindulgence, dissipation
Eight of Swords—confusion, restriction
Nine of Swords—despair, lack of joy

Description

Lucifer. Mephistopheles. Satan. The Prince of Darkness. No matter what we call him, the Devil is our symbol for what is bad and undesirable. From our human perspective, we see the world as a struggle between light and dark. We want to vanquish the bad so the good can prevail. In fact, good and bad cannot be separated, just as you cannot separate a shadow from its source. Darkness is simply the absence of light, and it is caused by errors that hide the truth. Card 15 shows us these errors.

First is ignorance—not knowing the truth and not realizing we do not know. Second is materialism—the belief that there is nothing but the physical. As spiritual beings, we long for the Divine, but we lose contact with this source of truth if we trust only our senses. There is also hopelessness, which robs us of our joy and movement toward the light.

Traditionally the Devil stands for evil, but it does not have this rather frightening meaning in a reading. This card lets you know that you are caught in an unhealthy, unproductive situation. You may be in the dark about something—ignorant of the truth and its implications. You may be obsessed by a person, idea, substance, or pattern that you know is bad for you (or maybe you don't!). Sometimes this card reflects back the negativity that has made you doubt yourself and your future. We are prone to many errors in life. Card 15 lets us know when they are serious enough to require attention. When you see the Devil, examine your assumptions carefully. Make sure you are not working from a false picture of yourself and the situation. Hold fast to the highest vision of who you are.

16

The Tower

• SUDDEN CHANGE
• RELEASE

• DOWNFALL
• REVELATION

Actions

going through SUDDEN CHANGE
    experiencing upheaval
    having plans disrupted
    being surprised
    undergoing a crisis
    having routines shaken up
    being in chaos

RELEASING
    exploding
    having an emotional outburst
    erupting in anger
    crashing through ego defenses
    breaking through pretense
    letting everything go

FALLING DOWN
    being humbled
    experiencing a crash
    toppling from the heights
    having a downturn in fortune
    suffering a blow to the ego

having a REVELATION
    suddenly realizing the truth
    exposing what was hidden
    having a burst of insight
    seeing through illusions
    getting the answer
    seeing everything in a flash

Opposing Cards: Some Possibilities

Chariot—victory, control
Temperance—middle ground, staying together, contained
Star—serenity, calm
Six of Wands—acclaim, pride
Ten of Cups—peace, serenity

Reinforcing Cards: Some Possibilities

Death—sweeping impact, powerful forces
Sun—enlightenment, revelation
Five of Pentacles—hard times

Description

THE TOWER.

The Tower is an unsettling card. Fire, lightning, falling on jagged rocks— definitely looks like trouble! Card 16 will not be welcomed by those who dislike change. It represents a sudden, dramatic upheaval or reversal in fortune. Usually change is gradual, giving us time to adapt, but sometimes it is quick and explosive. This is the action of the Tower.

In films, the hero sometimes slaps someone who is groggy or babbling. Having tried everything else, he finally resorts to a sharp sting to snap him out of it. Sudden crises are life's way of telling you to wake up. Something's wrong, and you're not responding. Are you too full of pride? Expect a blow to the ego. Are you holding back your anger? Expect the dam to burst. Are you stuck in a rut? Expect a surprise.

How you respond to the Tower's change makes all the difference in how uncomfortable the experience will be. Recognize that the disruption occurred because it was needed. Perhaps embracing the change is too much to ask, but try to find the positive in it. In fact, you may feel tremendous release that you have finally been forced in a new direction. You may have a burst of insight about your situation and reach a new level of understanding about it.

17

The Star

- HOPE
- INSPIRATION
- GENEROSITY
- SERENITY

Actions

regaining HOPE
    having faith in the future
    thinking positively
    believing
    counting your blessings
    seeing the light at the end of the tunnel
    feeling great expectation
    looking forward to success

being INSPIRED
    regaining motivation
    realizing an inner strength
    seeing the way clear
    being stimulated to a higher level
    creating
    receiving the answer

being GENEROUS
    wanting to give or share
    spreading the wealth
    opening your heart
    giving back what you have received
    letting love flow freely
    offering with no reservations
    holding nothing back

feeling SERENE
    experiencing peace of mind
    relaxing
    finding your still center
    remaining untroubled
    savoring perfect calm
    being tranquil amid trouble
    enjoying harmony

Opposing Cards: Some Possibilities

Devil—hopelessness, lack of faith, pessimism
Tower—upheaval, chaos
Moon—being troubled, disturbed, anxious
Two of Swords—blocked flow of feelings
Nine of Swords—guilt, anguish

Reinforcing Cards: Some Possibilities

Fool—innocence, faith, trust
Empress—generosity, free-flowing love
Six of Cups—good will, sharing
Ten of Cups—joy, positive feelings, blessings

Description

People have always looked to the stars as a source of inspiration and hope. There is something about their twinkling light that draws us out of ourselves and up into a higher plane. When we turn our eyes heavenward, we no longer feel the distress of Earth. The Star reminds me of the clear, high voice of a soprano. There is something otherworldly about it. All the harshness and density of everyday life has been refined away leaving only the purest essence. After being exposed to the Star, we feel uplifted and blessed.

In readings, the Star is most welcome when grief and despair have overwhelmed us. In our darkest moments, we need to know that there is hope, that there is light at the end of the tunnel. The Star is the opposite of the Devil who strips us of our faith in the future. Card 17 holds out the promise that we can eventually find peace of mind. The Star also reminds us to open our heart and release our fears and doubt. If you have been holding back in any way, now is the time to give generously.

It is important to remember that the Star is inspiring, but it is not a card of practical solutions or final answers. Without hope we can accomplish nothing, but hope is only a beginning. When you see Card 17, know that you are on the right track. Your goals and your aspirations are blessed, but to realize them, you must take positive action. Use the light of the Star to guide you in your efforts.

18

The Moon

- FEAR
- ILLUSION

- IMAGINATION
- BEWILDERMENT

Actions

feeling FEAR
 releasing inner demons
 feeling a nameless apprehension
 suffering from phobias
 giving in to the shadow self
 lacking courage
 being overcome by anxieties

believing ILLUSIONS
 accepting a false picture
 deceiving yourself
 having unrealistic ideas
 misapprehending the truth
 experiencing distortions
 chasing after a fantasy

stimulating the IMAGINATION
 having vivid dreams or visions
 opening to fantasy
 plumbing the unconscious
 entertaining unusual thoughts
 being outlandish and bizarre

feeling BEWILDERED
 losing direction and purpose
 having trouble thinking clearly
 becoming confused
 being easily distracted
 feeling disoriented
 wandering aimlessly

Opposing Cards: Some Possibilities

Star—being serene, untroubled, at peace
Sun—assurance, clarity, enlightenment

Reinforcing Cards: Some Possibilities

Seven of Cups—illusions, unrealistic ideas, fantasy
Two of Swords—self-deception, not seeing the truth
Eight of Swords—confusion, lack of clarity

Description

If you look around the room right now, you will (probably!) see people and objects that are comforting in their familiarity. Everything is exactly as you expect it to be. You *know* that if you closed your eyes and opened them, the room would be the same. But . . . have you ever lost the familiar to find, in its place, a world so extraordinary you can't even grasp it? This is the experience of the Moon.

THE MOON.

Most of the time we live in a tiny pocket of normality that we wrap around us like a security blanket. We turn our backs on the mysterious universe that waits outside. From time to time we may sneak a peek with our imagination, or venture out through fantasy or expanded awareness. We can be thrust out there unprepared through drugs, madness, or intense experiences such as battle.

The Moon is the light of this realm—the world of shadow and night. Although this place is awesome, it does not have to be frightening. In the right circumstances, the Moon inspires and enchants. It holds out the promise that all you imagine can be yours. The Moon guides you to the unknown so you can allow the unusual into your life.

Sadly, we are usually afraid of the Moon. In readings, this card often stands for fears and anxieties—the ones that come in the darkest part of the night. Card 18 also stands for illusions. It is easy to lose our way in the moonlight. Be careful not to let deceptions and false ideas lead you astray. Sometimes the Moon is a signal that you are lost and wandering aimlessly. You must find your way back to the path and your clarity of purpose.

19

The Sun

- ENLIGHTENMENT
- GREATNESS

- VITALITY
- ASSURANCE

Actions

becoming ENLIGHTENED
 understanding
 finding the sense behind the chaos
 attaining a new level of insight
 having an intellectual breakthrough
 getting to the heart of the matter
 realizing the truth

experiencing GREATNESS
 achieving prominence
 being singled out for notice
 having a personal moment of glory
 setting an outstanding example
 shining forth brilliantly
 demonstrating distinction
 becoming the center of attention

feeling VITALITY
 becoming radiantly energized
 bursting with enthusiasm
 experiencing joy
 feeling invigorated
 getting charged up
 enjoying great health

having ASSURANCE
 feeling free and expansive
 honoring your true self
 knowing you can succeed
 being confident
 believing in your worth
 trusting your abilities
 forgiving yourself

Opposing Cards: Some Possibilities

Moon—confusion, disorientation, illusion
Eight of Cups—weariness
Six of Swords—depressed, listless
Five of Pentacles—being rundown, tired

Reinforcing Cards: Some Possibilities

Tower—enlightenment, revelation
World—accomplishment, great achievement
Two of Wands—personal power, vitality, brilliance
Six of Wands—acclaim, prominence

Description

Brilliant. Radiant. Sparkling. So many of our words reflect (!) the power and glory of light. When we turn on the light in a room, we *illuminate* it so all the dark corners are visible. When we turn on the light in our minds, we are *enlightened*. We see clearly and understand the truth. Both within and without, the energy of light expands our limits and makes us shine.

Throughout history, people have honored the Sun as the source of light and warmth. In the myths of many cultures, the Sun is a prominent god—full of vigor and courage. He is the vital energy center that makes life on Earth possible. In the tarot the Sun also symbolizes vitality and splendor. The Sun is definitely not a meek and retiring card.

In readings, you will understand Card 19 if you imagine yourself to be a sun god. How do you think and feel? You have total confidence in yourself. You are not cocky, but profoundly sure of your power. You have unlimited energy and glow with health. You have a greatness about you and stand out brilliantly. Finally, you see and understand all that is happening within your sphere. When you see this card, know that you will be successful at all you undertake. Now is the time to let your light shine.

20

Judgement

- JUDGMENT
- REBIRTH

- INNER CALLING
- ABSOLUTION

Actions

making a JUDGMENT
    having a day of reckoning
    separating the wheat from the chaff
    making an honest appraisal
    getting off the fence
    using critical faculties
    taking a stand
    making hard choices

feeling REBORN
    awakening to possibilities
    transforming
    enjoying renewed hope
    making a fresh start
    seeing everything in a new light
    discovering joy

hearing a CALL
    recognizing your true vocation
    feeling inner conviction
    feeling an impulse to act
    deciding to make a difference
    feeling drawn in a new direction
    knowing what you must do
    answering a need

finding ABSOLUTION
    feeling cleansed and refreshed
    releasing guilts and sorrows
    forgiving yourself and others
    atoning for past mistakes
    unburdening yourself
    feeling sins washed away

Opposing Cards: Some Possibilities

Death—death, endings
Five of Cups—regret, mistakes
Nine of Swords—guilt, blame, feelings of sinfulness

Reinforcing Cards: Some Possibilities

Fool—rebirth, new starts
Justice—deciding, accepting past mistakes/actions
Seven of Pentacles—decision point

Description

On Card 20, we see people rising up at the call of an angel. It is Judgment Day, when the faithful are brought to heaven, but what about those who are not saved? Have they been judged and found wanting? For their sins, will they be denied the presence of God? It is this aspect of judgment that is unsettling. How can judgment be reconciled with forgiveness?

In fact, judgment comes in two forms. The hurtful kind says, "What you did is wrong, and you are bad and worthless for having done it." This type of judgment separates and leaves no room for redemption. It is possible to judge without condemning. We assess the matter, weigh all sides and try to discern the truth. We recognize the need to choose and hope for the courage to do so wisely—but without blame.

In readings, Card 20 can be a reminder that judgments are necessary; sometimes you *must* decide. At such moments, it is best to consider the matter carefully and then commit yourself without censure. If you are being judged yourself, learn from the process. Take what is of value, correct what needs correcting, but never lose sight of your worth.

Card 20 also stands for the feelings that come with salvation. When the angel calls, you are reborn—cleansed of all guilts and burdens. The past and its mistakes are behind you, and you are ready to begin anew. You may feel a calling—a personal conviction of what you are meant to do. If you are in a low period, in need of hope and absolution, Judgement can show that renewal is at hand.

21

The World

- INTEGRATION
- ACCOMPLISHMENT

- INVOLVEMENT
- FULFILLMENT

Actions

INTEGRATING

experiencing wholeness
bringing parts together
achieving dynamic balance
combining
creating synthesis
joining together
working in unison

ACCOMPLISHING

realizing your goals
prospering
achieving your heart's desire
seeing dreams come true
flourishing
finding a beautiful solution

becoming INVOLVED

contributing
healing
rendering a service
using a gift or talent
sharing what you have
giving of yourself
feeling engaged
being active

feeling FULFILLED

savoring the present
taking pleasure in life
enjoying peace of mind
getting satisfaction
finding contentment
counting your blessings

Opposing Cards: Some Possibilities

Hermit—isolation
Four of Cups—lack of involvement, apathy, withdrawal
Five of Wands—working at cross-purposes, lack of integration

Reinforcing Cards: Some Possibilities

Temperance—integration, synthesis, combination
Sun—accomplishment, achievements
Nine of Cups—achieving your heart's desire
Ten of Cups—happiness, emotional fulfillment
Ten of Pentacles—affluence, material fulfillment

Description

It's Thanksgiving Day. You've just finished a delicious meal, and there's a hot mug of coffee in your hand. Friends and family are arguing about the latest fiasco, the baby's cooing at you from across the table, and your feet are rubbing the belly of a devoted mutt. You're happy, fulfilled, and truly thankful (at least until you have to start the dishes!). For this moment, the World and everything in it is yours.

We all recognize this feeling. It can come at any time or place and is always welcome. We can feel it at home raking the leaves or on the world stage accepting the Nobel Prize. It can seem quiet and simple, or wild and glorious. What is this feeling, and where does it come from? Card 21 can help us find out.

A major element of happiness is wholeness—the sense that everything is working together in harmony. Not in a static way, but with dynamic balance. Involvement is also important. To be happy, we must feel connected—engaged with what is around us. There is also accomplishment—knowing that we have goals and are moving toward them successfully. When all these elements come together, we feel fulfilled and blessed.

The World represents these moments and all that goes into them. In readings, it is a very positive sign that you are in a position to realize your heart's desire. What that is for you depends on the situation, but it will always feel great. Remember, though, that Card 21 is a symbol of active contribution and service. To hold the World in our hands, we must give of ourselves to it. That is the source of true happiness.

Part 2

Minor Arcana

Tarot Keywords Minor Arcana—Ace–Ten

	WANDS	CUPS	SWORDS	PENTACLES
ACE	Creative Force Enthusiam Confidence Courage	Emotional Force Intuition Intimacy Love	Mental Force Truth Justice Fortitude	Material Force Prosperity Practicality Trust
TWO	Personal Power Boldness Originality	Connection Truce Attraction	Blocked Emotions Avoidance Stalemate	Juggling Flexibility Fun
THREE	Exploration Foresight Leadership	Exuberance Friendship Community	Heartbreak Loneliness Betrayal	Teamwork Planning Competence
FOUR	Celebration Freedom Excitement	Self-Absorption Apathy Going Within	Rest Contemplation Quiet Preparation	Possessiveness Control Blocked Change
FIVE	Disagreement Competition Hassles	Loss Bereavement Regret	Self-Interest Discord Open Dishonor	Hard Times Ill Health Rejection
SIX	Triumph Acclaim Pride	Good Will Innocence Childhood	The Blues Recovery Travel	Having/Not Having: Resources Knowledge Power
SEVEN	Aggression Defiance Conviction	Wishful Thinking Options Dissipation	Running Away Lone-Wolf Style Hidden Dishonor	Assessment Reward Direction Change
EIGHT	Quick Action Conclusion News	Deeper Meaning Moving On Weariness	Restriction Confusion Powerlessness	Diligence Knowledge Detail
NINE	Defensiveness Perseverance Stamina	Wish Fulfillment Satisfaction Sensual Pleasure	Worry Guilt Anguish	Discipline Self-Reliance Refinement
TEN	Overextending Burdens Struggle	Joy Peace Family	Bottoming Out Victim Mentality Martyrdom	Affluence Permanence Convention

Tarot Keywords Minor Arcana—Court Cards

	WANDS	CUPS	SWORDS	PENTACLES
PAGE	Be Creative Be Enthusiastic Be Confident Be Courageous	Be Emotional Be Intuitive Be Intimate Be Loving	Use Your Mind Be Truthful Be Just Have Fortitude	Have an Effect Be Practical Be Prosperous Be Trusting/ Trustworthy
KNIGHT Positive	Charming Self-Confident Daring Adventurous Passionate	Romantic Imaginative Sensitive Refined Introspective	Direct Authoritative Incisive Knowledgeable Logical	Unwavering Cautious Thorough Realistic Hardworking
KNIGHT Negative	Superficial Cocky Foolhardy Restless Hot-Tempered	Overemotional Fanciful Tempermental Overrefined Introverted	Blunt Overbearing Cutting Opinionated Unfeeling	Stubborn Unadventurous Obsessive Pessimistic Grinding
QUEEN	Attractive Wholehearted Energetic Cheerful Self-Assured	Loving Tenderhearted Intuitive Psychic Spiritual	Honest Astute Forthright Witty Experienced	Nurturing Bighearted Down-to-Earth Resourceful Trustworthy
KING	Creative Inspiring Forceful Charismatic Bold	Wise Calm Diplomatic Caring Tolerant	Intellectual Analytical Articulate Just Ethical	Enterprising Adept Reliable Supporting Steady

Ace of Wands

- CREATIVE FORCE
- ENTHUSIASM
- CONFIDENCE
- COURAGE

Actions

using CREATIVE FORCE
  inventing a better way
  expanding your potential
  opening to greater possibilities
  conceiving a dream
  expressing yourself
  stimulating your imagination
  allowing a talent to unfold
  coming up with a solution

showing ENTHUSIASM
  feeling fired up and eager
  creating an aura of excitement
  being ready to tackle the world
  inspiring others
  sustaining optimism
  giving 110 percent

having CONFIDENCE
  believing in yourself
  feeling assured of your abilities
  being sure of success
  having high self-esteem
  having faith in your path
  knowing things will work out

proceeding with COURAGE
  tackling a challenging task
  going beyond your limits
  being true to your beliefs
  daring to take a stand
  facing your fears
  going for it

Ace-Ace Pairs

An Ace-Ace pair shows that a new spirit is entering your life. It draws on the energy of the Ace of Wands—creativity, excitement, adventure, courage, personal power—plus one of these:

Ace of Cups—deep feelings, intimacy, attunement, compassion, love
Ace of Swords—intelligence, reason, justice, truth, clarity, perseverance
Ace of Pentacles—prosperity, abundance, trust, security, groundedness

Description

The Ace of Wands is a symbol of possibility in the area of creativity, excitement, adventure, courage, and personal power. In readings, it shows that a seed of bold enthusiasm has been planted in your life although you may not yet recognize it. When the seed sprouts, it could take almost any form. It might be a creative idea, surge of optimism, or need to act boldly. On the outside, it could be an offer, gift, opportunity, encounter, or synchronistic event.

When you see this Ace, examine your life to see how its potent, confident energy could work for you. Be daring and brave. Sometimes you have to risk to get what you want. Look for the path that will excite you and push you beyond your limits. Seize the initiative, and let your enthusiasm take you to new heights. Wands are the suit of individual power and fulfillment. This Ace tells you that a time of passion is beginning. You will be able to assert your best for all to see.

The Ace of Wands is also the card of creativity. Under its influence, you can become a conduit for inspiration and invention. Forget tired, worn-out solutions. You have the chance to be original. Trust your own creative potential, and there will be no end to what you can achieve.

Two of Wands

- PERSONAL POWER
- BOLDNESS

- ORIGINALITY

Actions

having PERSONAL POWER
  commanding attention and respect
  directing those around you
  holding the world in your hands
  wielding influence
  calling the shots
  having authority
  swaying others to your position
  being able to achieve your goals

being BOLD
  daring to do what you want
  taking a risk
  gambling events will go your way
  confronting the situation head-on
  taking the initiative
  speaking your mind
  facing fear directly
  taking the bull by the horns
  seizing the day

showing ORIGINALITY
  doing what no one else has done
  creating your own style
  being a pioneer
  taking a different approach
  inventing something new
  diverging from the crowd
  marching to a different drummer

Opposing Cards: Some Possibilities

High Priestess—being passive, staying in the background
Hierophant—conforming, going along with the group
Eight of Swords—powerlessness, fear of action
Ten of Swords—victim mentality, powerlessness
Ten of Pentacles—going by the rules, being conventional

Reinforcing Cards: Some Possibilities

Magician—personal power, wielding a strong force
Emperor—authority
Chariot—personal power, command
Sun—vitality, brilliance, greatness

Description

The Two of Wands glorifies individual courage and greatness. This card taps the same energy as the Magician, but with one important difference. The Magician represents the archetype of power—the impersonal energy of creativity and strength. The Two of Wands stands for that power brought down to Earth and made personal. Personal power is an invigorating force that fills you up and lends you the courage to be great. A powerful person is like a magnet that attracts all those within a certain area.

True power always comes from the Divine. It passes through us and then flows out into the world. When we understand this relationship, we are blessed because this flow brings with it a tremendous feeling of expansion and fulfillment. We feel as if we can accomplish anything. Problems develop when we forget that we are not the *source* of power, only its conduit. We must be careful not to let the intoxicating feelings that come with power overwhelm our good sense and blind us to our true desires and intentions.

In readings, the Two of Wands indicates that power is a major issue in the situation. You or someone else has it or wants it. When you see this card, look carefully at your goals and activities to make sure you are using power wisely. Don't support power for its own sake, but enjoy it when it serves your worthwhile purposes. Take this gift and use it to mold your environment in positive ways.

The Two of Wands can also stand for an extra dose of daring and inventiveness. When you see this card, trust that the time is right for the bold, creative move that will knock their socks off. Forget subtlety and old, tired approaches. Allow yourself free rein and you'll be amazed at the results.

Three of Wands

- EXPLORATION
- FORESIGHT

- LEADERSHIP

Actions

EXPLORING the unknown
seeking out uncharted areas
going in quest of new adventure
expanding horizons
leaving the secure behind
tackling something different

having FORESIGHT
being visionary
looking for greater possibilities
planning ahead
knowing what to expect
getting a premonition
anticipating obstacles
taking the long view

demonstrating LEADERSHIP
showing others the way
taking the main role
providing needed direction
rallying the group behind you
assuming a responsible position
setting an example
serving as a representative

Opposing Cards: Some Possibilities

Two of Swords—avoiding the facts, staying stuck
Ten of Pentacles—being conservative, focusing on security

Reinforcing Cards: Some Possibilities

Fool—expanding horizons, going into unexplored territory
Emperor—leadership, providing direction
Eight of Cups—going on a trip, starting a journey
Three of Pentacles—planning, preparing for the future

Description

On the Three of Wands, we see a figure standing on a cliff looking out over the sea to distant mountains. From this height, he sees all that lies ahead. This is a card of vision and foresight. When we want to see farther, we climb higher. By going up, we increase our range and remove ourselves from the immediate situation. We detach and gain perspective.

In readings, the Three of Wands can tell you to take the long view. Don't react to the heat of the moment, but step back and reconsider. See how the present fits into the greater picture. This card asks you to be a visionary—to dream beyond current limitations. It can indicate premonitions or other intuitions about what is to come.

Taking the long view is an aspect of leadership—another meaning of the Three of Wands. When we see far, we have the knowledge to guide others to their best future. Someone who knows the way can show it to those who follow. When you see the Three of Wands, know that now is the time to accept your vision and be confident that you can lead others to it.

A leader not only sees far, but he is willing to go there first, if necessary. The Three of Wands is a card of exploration. Compare this figure to the Fool who is also on a cliff edge. The Fool steps out in innocence, not realizing he is going to fall to his fate. The adventurer on the Three of Wands is also willing to step out, but with full awareness of what he is doing. His courage is more informed, if less spontaneous. The Three of Wands encourages you to move fearlessly into new areas. Let the ships on your horizon take you far out into unknown seas.

Four of Wands

- CELEBRATION
- FREEDOM

- EXCITEMENT

Actions

CELEBRATING

rejoicing over a happy event

recognizing a success

observing an anniversary, milestone, or
special time

congratulating on a job well done

reflecting on accomplishments

enjoying some well-deserved rewards

taking part in a ceremony or rite

seeking FREEDOM

getting out of an oppressive situation

breaking free of bonds

cutting loose

opening to new possibilities

escaping unhappy circumstances

claiming self-determination

letting go of limitations

feeling EXCITED

bubbling over with delight

feeling thrilled

look forward expectantly

getting caught up in the moment

feeling jubilant

relishing the moment

being surprised

Opposing Cards: Some Possibilities

Devil—bondage, lack of freedom
Ten of Wands—burdens, being in an oppressive situation
Four of Cups—apathy, lack of excitement, flat feeling
Six of Swords—mild depression, little to celebrate
Eight of Swords—restriction, lack of freedom

Reinforcing Cards: Some Possibilities

Three of Cups—excitement, high spirits, celebration
Two of Pentacles—fun, excitement, parties

Description

Do you remember the thrill you felt as a child seeing your birthday cake alight with candles? Or waiting to get on a roller coaster? Or slow dancing with your first love? This bubbly, high-as-a-kite feeling lies at the heart of the Four of Wands. As a toddler, my son expressed it through his "happy dance." He'd run in place faster and faster, barely able to control his delight. Of course, as mature(!) adults, we contain this feeling, but it never leaves completely. Each of us still has an excited, little kid inside waiting to come out.

In readings, the Four of Wands often represents the events and experiences that generate excitement. These vary from person to person, but the stirring feelings are the same. Sometimes such times arrive unexpectedly. The Four of Wands can signal a surprise or spontaneous thrill. Other times this card represents planned celebrations, such as weddings, anniversaries, birthdays, and victory parties. These events have their solemn side, but they are also a chance to feel the joy of living.

The Four of Wands often means freedom. Freedom can take many forms, but it always brings with it an exhilarating feeling. When we break the bonds that bind us, whether physical, mental, or emotional, we feel triumphant and able to move on to a new period of growth and happiness. If you feel trapped or restricted right now, use the energy of the Four of Wands to launch you into freedom. Do not be afraid to claim the open vistas that are rightfully yours.

Five of Wands

- DISAGREEMENT
- COMPETITION

- HASSLES

Actions

DISAGREEING
> feeling everyone is at cross-purposes
> being torn by dissension
> quarreling, arguing, and bickering
> becoming embroiled in a debate
> being at odds with others
> quibbling over details

experiencing COMPETITION
> feeling the thrill of the contest
> going against an opponent
> rising to the challenge
> being involved in a game or sport
> trying to outdo yourself
> going for the gold
> looking for a fight
> having a rival
> being challenged by an upstart

experiencing HASSLES
> getting annoyed by demands
> having minor setbacks
> needing to take care of details
> suffering from irritations
> being bothered by trivialities

Opposing Cards: Some Possibilities

Temperance—balance, agreement, working together
World—integration, working together
Two of Cups—truce, agreement, coming together
Two of Pentacles—working smoothly, getting people together
Three of Pentacles—teamwork, cooperation

Reinforcing Cards: Some Possibilities

Seven of Wands—opposition, fighting
Ten of Wands—struggle, hassles, meeting resistance
Five of Swords—discord, people set against each other

Description

You wake up and stub your toe going to the bathroom. You're in the shower and find out there's no soap. At breakfast, you get juice on your shirt. When you get to the car, your battery is dead. It's going to be a terrible, horrible, no good, very bad day.[1] You're beset by hassles—those petty annoyances that are infuriating *because* they are so minor.

The Five of Wands stands for times when your environment seems to be fighting you. Nothing flows smoothly; everyone is working at cross-purposes. The figures on this card are all batting at each other. There is no coordinated effort, no agreement. When this card shows up, be prepared for a bumpy ride. You're going to need extra patience and perseverance to get to the point where you can accomplish something. The Five of Wands does not represent major blockages, just many small, irritating ones.

This card also stands for competition. In the right circumstances, competition is useful. It fosters extra effort, generates excitement, and encourages the best. When the Five of Wands appears in a reading, check for competitive elements. You may be involved in a contest, race, or game. You may discover you have rivals who are opposing you or challenging your position. You may feel disheartened (or invigorated!) by the dog-eat-dog environment you find yourself in. At its heart, competition is divisive. Make sure it is helping you and others reach your true goals. Otherwise, work toward cooperation.

---

1. Phrase from Judith Viorst, *Alexander and the Terrible, Horrible, No Good, Very Bad Day* (New York: Atheneum, 1972).

Six of Wands

- TRIUMPH
- ACCLAIM

- PRIDE

Actions

TRIUMPHING
  having your day in the sun
  being vindicated
  walking away with the prize
  prevailing against all comers
  coming out on top
  achieving success

receiving ACCLAIM
  being acknowledged
  getting a pat on the back
  receiving an award or citation
  getting praise or a compliment
  earning applause
  achieving recognition

feeling PRIDE
  enjoying healthy self-esteem
  strutting your stuff
  holding your head up high
  feeling worthy of notice
  having a high opinion of yourself
  putting yourself above others
  being arrogant
  condescending
  feeling self-important

Opposing Cards: Some Possibilities

Tower—humility, loss of acclaim
Five of Cups—loss, defeat
Ten of Swords—self-deprecating, in the pits
Five of Pentacles—rejection, lack of recognition

Reinforcing Cards: Some Possibilities

Chariot—triumph, self-confidence
Sun—acclaim, prominence
Nine of Cups—self-satisfaction, achieving what you want

Description

The Six of Wands is the minor arcana counterpart of the Chariot. Both of these cards represent moments of victory and triumph. Sometimes in life, all we want to do is win—to be number one. You can see this dream in the faces of athletes, politicians, and other champions as they step into the winner's circle. It's all been worthwhile. I'm the best. I've won!

In readings, the Six of Wands appears when you have been working hard toward a goal, and success is finally within reach. The recognition you have sought so long is yours. You can receive the acclaim, honor, and reward you deserve. If you do not feel close to victory now, know that it is on its way provided you are doing all you can to make it happen. The victory of this card does not have to involve beating someone else. You can triumph over yourself, the environment, or the odds.

The Six of Wands also represents a healthy self-esteem. Feeling good about your accomplishments is an important part of success, but too much pride can lead to arrogance and self-inflation. When you see this card, check that you are not feeling superior to others. It is easy to forget that individual achievement is not really individual at all. Our talents begin in the Divine, develop with the love and support of others, and only in the end express *through* us. How can we indulge in excess pride?

In the *Purgatorio* Dante considers pride the first and greatest sin that must be overcome by souls reaching toward heaven. When the Six of Wands appears, enjoy your triumph, feel good about yourself, but remember Dante's words:

O gifted men, vainglorious for first place,
how short a time the laurel crown stays green

. . . .

A breath of wind is all there is to fame
here upon earth: it blows this way and that,
and when it changes quarter it changes name.[1]

---

1. Dante Alighieri, *The Purgatorio*, John Ciardi, trans. (New York: New American Library, 1957), p. 123.

Seven of Wands

- AGGRESSION
- DEFIANCE

- CONVICTION

Actions

being AGGRESSIVE
  going after what you want
  asserting yourself
  taking the offensive
  firing the first shot
  fighting
  making your point forcefully
  seizing the advantage

being DEFIANT
  holding out against pressure
  defending your position
  opposing all challengers
  combating criticism
  refusing to yield
  saying "no!"
  resisting authority

showing CONVICTION
  being sure
  having a fixed position
  demonstrating strong character
  standing up for what you believe
  knowing you are right
  acting resolutely
  being firm

Opposing Cards: Some Possibilities

High Priestess—being passive, holding back
Hanged Man—waiting, letting go
Three of Pentacles—teamwork

Reinforcing Cards: Some Possibilities

Five of Wands—opposition, fighting
Nine of Wands—defending your position, refusing to yield
Five of Swords—conflict, "me-against-them" mentality

Description

The Seven of Wands is about taking a stand. Taking a stand is a forceful act that changes the energy flow of the world for good or ill. Most of the time we flow with our lives as if on a river. Events and feelings carry us forward with little effort. Sometimes, though, we are not content to drift. We want to resist the flow, or change its course entirely!

The figure on the Seven of Wands appears to be in a battle. He's either attacking or under attack, probably both. When we decide to take a stand, we set in motion an energy of resistance. When we take up a firm position, others do the same. The Seven of Wands stands for aggression *and* defiance because they are two sides of the same coin. You attack; your opponent defends. He counterattacks; you defend.

Some battles are worth fighting, others just cause trouble. If you are involved in a conflict, ask yourself if it's worth the struggle. Is it important? Does it have value? Will the outcome serve you or others? If so, be bold and aggressive. Defend your position. Refuse to yield! If not, then consider letting the conflict go. Be honest with yourself about this. You will be tempted to hold onto your position, especially if you have invested much time and energy into it. Don't let battle lines be drawn unless the war is worth fighting.

The Seven of Wands can also indicate strong convictions. In order to take a firm stand, you must believe in your position and yourself. You'll need integrity and strength of character to see you through. If your cause is just, use the energy of the Seven of Wands to make a difference.

Eight of Wands

- QUICK ACTION
- CONCLUSION

- NEWS

Actions

taking QUICK ACTION
    making your move
    striking while the iron is hot
    declaring yourself openly
    putting plans into action
    rushing into a new area
    moving into high gear
    getting caught up in change

coming to a CONCLUSION
    culminating an effort
    having all elements come together
    closing out an activity
    experiencing a grand finale
    finding a successful resolution
    completing unfinished business

receiving NEWS
    getting an important message
    obtaining a needed bit of information
    finding the missing puzzle piece
    discovering the truth
    having a meaningful conversation
    learning more

Opposing Cards: Some Possibilities

High Priestess—waiting, holding off
Four of Swords—not rushing in, preparing
Seven of Pentacles—assessment, taking stock before action

Reinforcing Cards: Some Possibilities

Magician—taking action, carrying out plans
Wheel of Fortune—rapid pace, quick developments
Death—conclusion, endings
Eight of Cups—finishing up, ending a chapter

Description

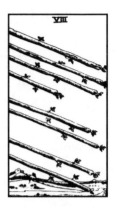

In the film *The Ten Commandments*, Moses touches his staff to water to set a plague in motion. His staff is the agent of power that initiates events. Moses' staff reminds me of the wands on this card. They are a symbol of the onset of action and its effects. Before acting, we think, imagine, speculate, talk, and dream. This is the realm of air—the sky. Then, finally, we make our move. We bring our ideas down to Earth and put them into action.

In readings, the Eight of Wands is often a sign that *now* is the time to declare yourself. All the elements are ready and will work for you as long as you don't hesitate. The iron is hot—so strike! If events are in motion, they will proceed rapidly. You may feel caught in a whirlwind, but soon the dust will settle, and you will see how your plans have fared.

The Eight of Wands also stands for the arrival of news or information. You may see or hear something important. The news could show up in a disguised form, so stay alert. Pay attention to everything that comes your way for a while.

This card also signifies endings. Sooner or later, all activities run their course. The eight wands on this card not only symbolize putting events into motion, but also bringing them to a close. They appear to be ending their flight by coming down to Earth. If you see the Eight of Wands in a reading, it may be time to conclude whatever you have been doing. Celebrate the past, but prepare to move on to something new.

Nine of Wands

- DEFENSIVENENSS
- PERSERVERANCE

- STAMINA

Actions

DEFENDING yourself
    assuming ill will
    expecting the worst
    taking extra precautions
    being paranoid
    feeling wary and guarded
    protecting others
    remembering past attacks

PERSEVERING
    persisting despite all setbacks
    refusing to take "no" for an answer
    seeing something through to the end
    getting knocked down, then standing up
    keeping your resolve
    trying repeatedly

showing STAMINA
    continuing despite fatigue
    holding fast
    drawing on hidden reserves
    holding together through force of will
    demonstrating physical strength
    keeping up the pace

Opposing Cards: Some Possibilities

Three of Cups—friendship, trusting someone
Six of Cups—innocence, believing the best
Eight of Cups—weariness, fatigue

Reinforcing Cards: Some Possibilities

Strength—endurance, resolve, heart
Seven of Wands—defending a position, holding out
Two of Swords—being defensive, closing yourself off
Eight of Pentacles—persistence

Description

The figure on the Nine of Wands has definitely been through tough times. His head and arm are bandaged, and he's leaning on a "crutch." This fighter has seen some battles, but he's still standing! He's hurt, but he's not down. When we have had a bad experience, we feel weary and battle-scarred. Even if we aren't hurt physically, our psyches are wounded. Our openness, innocence, and trust are gone, replaced by wary defensiveness.

In readings, the Nine of Wands can be a warning that you must proceed carefully. Keep a watchful eye because there is the possibility that you will be hurt. If you have already been burned, you know what this man is feeling. Life's lessons can be hard sometimes, especially when hopes have been dashed. It is natural to feel defensive at such times, but try to avoid becoming bitter. Your experience has wounded you, but it has strengthened you as well.

Strength is the other aspect of the Nine of Wands. This fighter is tough! He has the physical stamina and the inner drive to persist despite all setbacks. In *The Terminator*, Arnold Schwarzenegger plays an android from the future who never gives up. In the end he is nothing but a wire framework with glowing eyes, but he still keeps coming—dragging himself along the floor to his goal. This is the spirit of the Nine of Wands. This card tells you to keep going no matter what. Even if everyone and everything seems to be against you right now, don't give up. Within you are the hidden reserves you need to prevail.

Ten of Wands

- OVEREXTENDING
- BURDENS

- STRUGGLE

Actions

OVEREXTENDING
  trying to do too much
  refusing to say "no"
  taking all the blame
  assuming another's debt
  doing the lion's share
  having to work overtime
  shouldering all the work
  being saddled with an extra load

feeling BURDENED
  never having time to relax
  feeling tied to a treadmill
  being taxed to the limit
  assuming responsibility
  being held accountable
  carrying out an unpleasant duty
  cleaning up a messy situation
  being left holding the bag

STRUGGLING
  fighting uphill
  doing everything the hard way
  experiencing resistance
  pushing against the current
  having to work for every gain
  finding that nothing comes easily
  laboring

Opposing Cards: Some Possibilities

Fool—carefree, living in the moment
Hanged Man—letting go
Four of Wands—free of burdens, escaping oppression
Four of Swords—relaxing, resting
Seven of Swords—avoiding responsibility

Reinforcing Cards: Some Possibilities

Justice—accepting responsibility, being accountable
Five of Wands—struggle, hassles, resistance
Six of Swords—getting by, struggling along
Nine of Swords—worrying
Five of Pentacles—struggling, hard times

Description

On the Ten of Wands, we see a bent figure trying to carry ten heavy poles. They are ranged so closely in front of him that he can't even see where he's going. Nothing exists for this man except his burdens and responsibilities. How true this is for so many today! We take on so much, trying to do all the things that need to be done. We think that if we can hang on until the weekend (or vacation, or end of the semester) then we can finally relax. The weekend comes, and the overload continues.

In readings, the Ten of Wands can be a sign that you are pushing yourself too hard. If your days are an endless round of duties and tasks, you need to lighten up for the sake of your health and well-being. Cut back, and take on only those activities that give you pleasure. If you love your work, but it's all-consuming, you may be too narrowly focused in one area. Balance your life with other interests.

The Ten of Wands can also stand for times when you have to assume the lion's share of responsibility. You may be blamed or left holding the bag. On the other hand, you may have to step forward and take charge because you are the only one capable enough. Rightly or wrongly, the cleanup will fall to you.

The Ten of Wands indicates that your life is going to be tougher than usual for a time. You will have to fight uphill for every little gain. Each step will feel like a struggle. When you see this card, be kind to yourself. Lighten the load wherever you can, and let others help you. You don't have to handle everything yourself.

Page of Wands

- BE CREATIVE
- BE ENTHUSIASTIC

- BE CONFIDENT
- BE COURAGEOUS

Actions

BE CREATIVE

take a novel approach
be original
invent
find a new area of self-expression
use your art
come up with a solution
go in a new direction

BE ENTHUSIASTIC

jump in wholeheartedly
get excited
show optimism
be the first to volunteer
be passionate
get your blood flowing

BE CONFIDENT

tackle a challenge
say "yes, I can"
believe in yourself
stretch your envelope
move beyond doubts
focus on success
know that where there's a will, there's a way

BE COURAGEOUS

take a risk
be daring
have an adventure
avoid the sure thing
take assertive action
be a leader
overcome a fear

Court Card Pairs

The Page of Wands can form a pair with any other court card. Compare the ranks and suits of the two cards to see what such a pair might mean.

Description

The Page of Wands is a messenger bringing you opportunities for passion. He delivers real chances to experience creativity, courage, charm, and inspiration—the wonders of the Wands suit. In readings, this Page suggests that an opening may appear that excites you, feeds your talents, or dares you to be great. When you see such a chance, act on it!

The Page of Wands can also stand for a child or young-at-heart adult whose interactions with you involve independence, high energy, risky behavior, or shared enthusiasms. Sometimes the Page of Wands implies that your entire situation is suffused with the spirit of excitement and adventure. At such times, feel free to express your individuality and power with light-hearted abandon.

Knight of Wands

- CHARMING/SUPERFICIAL
- SELF-CONFIDENT/COCKY
- DARING/FOOLHARDY
- ADVENTUROUS/RESTLESS
- PASSIONATE/HOT-TEMPERED

Actions

CHARMING/SUPERFICIAL

is physically attractive/focuses on style and appearance
disarms opposition with a smile/can be thoughtless and insensitive
is sexy and seductive/pursues sexual conquests
generates glamour and excitement/avoids deep or serious matters
is honey-tongued/may say or do what's expedient

SELF-CONFIDENT/COCKY

totally lacks self-doubt/overestimates abilities
has a can-do attitude/may boast and brag
is convinced of his or her talent/exaggerates accomplishments
is self-assured at all times/is brash and nervy
doesn't sweat the small stuff/is sometimes presumptuous

DARING/FOOLHARDY

will risk anything without fear/is reckless and rash
will tackle what others avoid/will endanger self and others
is the first to volunteer for danger/doesn't give danger due respect
loves being a hero/is impetuous
boldly goes where no one has gone before/is a daredevil

ADVENTUROUS/RESTLESS

loves travel and new experiences/is never content to be still
seeks novelty and change/can't set down roots or make ties
makes things happen/lacks inner peace and serenity
rises to every challenge/won't stop to smell the roses
is footloose and fancy-free/must have constant stimulation

PASSIONATE/HOT-TEMPERED

is easily roused to action/angers easily
feels strong loyalties/is too ready for a fight
feels everything powerfully/lashes out when riled
takes a vocal stand/often acts without thinking
jumps in with both feet/may have a chip on his or her shoulder

Court Card Pairs

The Knight of Wands can form a pair with any other court card. Compare the ranks and suits of the two cards to see what such a pair might mean.

Description

On the positive side, the Knight of Wands is full of energy and life. He's never afraid to try something new and will reach for all the gusto he can. Others may shake their heads at his crazy stunts, but they still admire his courage and passion. He's sexy and irresistible . . . always the charmer. On the negative side, this Knight is a little too sure of himself and his abilities. He tends to be shallow and thoughtless. Don't expect a deep commitment from him. He's also reckless and irresponsible. He acts without thinking and constantly gets in trouble because of his temper.

In readings, a Knight of Wands shows that his confident, passionate style is involved in the situation as an aspect of you, someone else, or the atmosphere in general. You need to ask yourself, "Is this Knight's energy helping or hurting?"

If his style is evident, then balance is needed. Is your confidence really cockiness? Are you angry and impatient all the time? Are you crazy about someone whom you know is going to break your heart? Is your company rushing into something risky with no preparation? It may be time for a change.

If this Knight's energy is missing, a dose of passion and daring may be called for. Are you in a rut? Try something new. Are you always planning every last detail? Wing it next time. Are you working too hard? Go out and have some fun. Let the Knight of Wands introduce you to his world of adventure, excitement, and risk.

Queen of Wands

- ATTRACTIVE
- WHOLEHEARTED
- ENERGETIC

- CHEERFUL
- SELF-ASSURED

Actions

ATTRACTIVE

    is appealing and popular
    creates a powerful first impression
    makes friends easily
    has great sex appeal
    is warm and outgoing

WHOLEHEARTED

    is loaded with enthusiasm
    tackles a task with total dedication
    gives the utmost in any situation
    is open and sincere
    doesn't hold anything back

ENERGETIC

    leads a busy and active life
    is vigorous and strong
    radiates health and vitality
    has an inner vibrancy
    is a natural athlete

CHEERFUL

    is optimistic and upbeat
    has an encouraging word for all
    brightens whatever room he/she is in
    has a warm and sunny disposition
    can shake off the blues easily

SELF-ASSURED

    quietly demonstrates self-confidence
    handles any situation with aplomb
    can't be easily rattled or provoked
    is spontaneous and gracious in defeat
    has faith in his/her abilities

Court Card Pairs

The Queen of Wands can form a pair with any other court card. Compare the ranks and suits of the two cards to see what such a pair might mean.

Description

The personality of the Queen of Wands combines the positive fire energy of the Wands suit with the inward focus of a Queen. She is the one voted most popular in her class. She is always attractive and often good-looking. Her warm smile and easygoing manner bring her lots of friends and admirers. Her energy is contagious, and her enthusiasm, total. No matter what the task, she tackles it with wholehearted dedication and commitment. Nothing gets her down. She is always upbeat and cheerful—ready to look for the positive in the situation. Her life is full and busy, and she prefers it that way. She loves to be going and doing. She keeps up this pace because she is radiantly healthy and fit. She is often a good athlete, being naturally strong and coordinated. Although she's never arrogant, the Queen of Wands has a deep faith in her own abilities. Her quiet self-assurance comes from the knowledge that she can accomplish whatever she sets her mind to.

In readings, The Queen of Wands asks you to *think and feel* as she does. For example: Do you feel attractive? Do you believe in yourself? Are you full of energy? Can you shake off the blues? Are you gung ho about life?

This Queen can also represent a man or woman who is like her, or an atmosphere of cheerful and confident enthusiasm. In a reading, she tells you that her special energy has meaning for you at this time. Let yourself be inspired by this Queen in whatever form she appears in your life.

King of Wands

- CREATIVE
- INSPIRING
- FORCEFUL

- CHARISMATIC
- BOLD

Actions

CREATIVE

develops innovative projects and ideas
opens up new areas of experience
has natural artistic ability
uses self-expression for useful purposes
masterminds new strategies
is original and inventive

INSPIRING

communicates enthusiasm
creates an atmosphere of excitement
sets an example others want to follow
instills confidence
is a powerful, natural leader

FORCEFUL

seems to dominate the environment
has a commanding presence
is assertive when necessary
earns respect and willing compliance
carries authority naturally

CHARISMATIC

is often showy and theatrical
enjoys making the gesture with flair
naturally becomes the focus of attention
magnetically attracts others
is watched, imitated, and talked about

BOLD

is intrepid
is willing to take chances when the stakes
    are high
confronts opposition directly
dares to stand and be different
is unconcerned with what others think
has the courage of his/her convictions

Court Card Pairs

The King of Wands can form a pair with any other court card. Compare the ranks and suits of the two cards to see what such a pair might mean.

Description

The personality of the King of Wands is a combination of the positive fire energy of the Wands suit and the active, outward focus of a King. He is creative and never settles for old, tired approaches. He trusts his originality and allows his inspirations to take form. He's enthusiastic. He steps forward and takes the lead if the opportunity presents itself. Others follow when he shows them the way with confidence. He's forceful in pursuing his goals. He's not a quiet, passive observer unless that suits his purposes. He jumps in and creates results. He's dramatic and exciting. This King is never a wallflower; more often the center of attention. He's bold and daring. He avoids the safe, easy route because he has the energy and assurance to take risks and win. The King of Wands has the courage of his convictions and always believes in himself.

In readings, the King of Wands asks you to take the kinds of *actions* he might take. For example: creating a masterpiece, leading the way, taking a risk, or making a splash. This King can also represent a man or woman who is acting as he does, or an atmosphere of excitement, daring, and drama. In a reading, he tells you that his special energy has meaning for you at this time. Let yourself be inspired by this King in whatever form he appears in your life.

Ace of Cups

- EMOTIONAL FORCE
- INTUITION
- INTIMACY
- LOVE

Actions

using EMOTIONAL FORCE
   getting in touch with your feelings
   letting your heart lead the way
   empathizing with others
   expressing deep feelings
   responding viscerally

developing INTUITION
   trusting your inner voice
   responding to messages from within
   experiencing direct knowing
   enhancing your psychic awareness
   getting in tune with yourself
   going with your gut reaction

experiencing INTIMACY
   feeling an attraction grow
   falling in love
   establishing a bond with another
   developing a relationship
   getting close to someone
   going to a deeper level

proceeding with LOVE
   expressing affection
   opening yourself to others
   responding sympathetically
   letting your love light shine
   giving to those in need
   getting rid of negativity
   forgiving and forgetting

Ace-Ace Pairs

An Ace-Ace pair shows that a new spirit is entering your life. It draws on the energy of the Ace of Cups—deep feelings, intimacy, attunement, compassion, love—plus one of these:

   Ace of Wands—creativity, excitement, adventure, courage, personal power
   Ace of Swords—intelligence, reason, justice, truth, clarity, perseverance
   Ace of Pentacles—prosperity, abundance, trust, security, groundedness

Description

The Ace of Cups is a symbol of possibility in the area of deep feelings, intimacy, attunement, compassion, and love. In readings, it shows that a seed of emotional awareness has been planted in your life although you may not yet recognize it. When the seed sprouts, it could take almost any form. It might be an attraction, strong feeling, intuitive knowing, or sympathetic reaction. On the outside, it could be an offer, gift, opportunity, encounter, or synchronistic event.

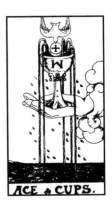

When you see this Ace, examine your life to see how its loving energy could work for you. This card often means that love is the essence of the situation. It may or may not be romantic love. Look for ways in which you can begin to connect with others. Do you have someone to forgive, or do you want to ask for forgiveness? Can you set aside your anger and find peace? Would you like to drop your reserve and let your feelings show? The Ace of Cups tells you that this is the time.

This card also suggests inner attunement and spirituality. Cups are the suit of the heart, and this Ace stands for the direct knowing that comes from the heart. Trust what your feelings are telling you. Seek out ways to explore your consciousness and your connections with Spirit. Allow the power of your emotions to guide you in a new direction. Embrace the love that is the Ace of Cups.

Two of Cups

- CONNECTION
- TRUCE

- ATTRACTION

Actions

making a CONNECTION
    joining with another
    celebrating a marriage or union
    cementing a friendship
    establishing a partnership
    working together
    sharing
    helping and being helped
    seeing commonalities

calling a TRUCE
    healing a severed relationship
    bringing together opposites
    letting bygones be bygones
    coming to a satisfactory agreement
    declaring peace
    forgiving and forgetting

acknowledging an ATTRACTION
    recognizing a bond that is developing
    accepting your preferences
    letting yourself be drawn in
    moving toward
    feeling a positive response

Opposing Cards: Some Possibilities

Hermit—needing to be alone, solitude
Five of Wands—disagreement, staying apart, no peace
Four of Cups—self-absorbed, being alone
Five of Cups—broken relationship

Reinforcing Cards: Some Possibilities

Lovers—union, marriage, connection
Temperance—connection, working together
Ten of Cups—kinship, family ties, connections

Description

To understand the Two of Cups, all you have to do is look at its image. A man and a woman are gazing at each other, ready to share their cups (emotions). Here is the very picture of romantic and sexual attraction. The energy between these two is almost palpable. The Two of Cups shows the beauty and power that is created when two come together. This is the card that lovers want to see, and, in fact, the Two of Cups is the minor arcana equivalent of the Lovers in many ways.

The Two of Cups has a deeper meaning as well. Whenever two forces are drawn together, there is the potential for bonding. This card can stand for the union of any two entities—people, groups, ideas, or talents. In readings, the Two of Cups tells you to look for connections in your life, especially those that are one-on-one. Now is *not* the time to separate or stay apart. It is the time to join with another and work as a partnership. If you are in conflict, look for truce and the chance to forgive and be forgiven. If you are struggling with two choices or tendencies within yourself, seek to reconcile them.

Usually, the Two of Cups is welcome in a reading, but it can also sound a note of warning. The energy of Two can be very compelling. If you have ever stood next to two people in love, you know what I'm talking about. They create between themselves a world of their own that can feel exclusionary to others. "Two's company, three's a crowd." Make sure that the tendency to pair off is not creating disharmony in your situation.

Three of Cups

- EXUBERANCE
- FRIENDSHIP
- COMMUNITY

Actions

feeling EXUBERANT
bursting with energy
being in the flow
celebrating
overflowing with high spirits
feeling on top of the world
dancing and singing
putting yourself out there

enjoying FRIENDSHIP
getting together with people you like
experiencing camaraderie
extending/receiving hospitality
sharing
finding companions
trusting others
relying on outside help

valuing COMMUNITY
taking part in a support group
developing a team spirit
working together
uniting with others
forming a group bond
helping each other
discovering a common goal
being neighborly

Opposing Cards: Some Possibilities

Hermit—being solitary, withdrawing from the group
Nine of Wands—lack of trust, wariness
Three of Swords—lonely, isolated, hurting
Six of Swords—sad, depressed
Nine of Swords—anguished, joyless

Reinforcing Cards: Some Possibilities

Hierophant—focusing on the group
Temperance—joining forces, working together
Four of Wands—excitement, high spirits, celebration
Three of Pentacles—working in a group

Description

There are three cards in the tarot that focus on the group—each from a different point of view. For the Hierophant, it's the formal approach. For the Three of Pentacles it's teamwork, and for the Three of Cups, it's emotions. What does it feel like to join with others? What is friendship and community? These are the questions answered by the Three of Cups.

On this card, we see three women dancing together in a circle. Their arms reach out to each other to connect their feelings (Cups). In many settings, women create and nurture the social glue that bonds people together. These dancing women are a symbol of coming together in love. (Of course, these feelings do not only relate to women.)

In readings, the Three of Cups can signify a friend or the feelings associated with friendship. This card can represent community—the network of support created when we interact with others. It can be a group in which the members feel a bond. When you see the Three of Cups, examine your attachments to the groups in your life from an emotional point of view. Consider reaching out to give or receive help. This card stands for all forms of support, including formal aid such as counseling and other social services.

The women on the Three of Cups also express joy and high spirits. Such feelings are not limited to groups, but can be especially strong there. Celebrations spontaneously arise when people feel connected, loved, and secure. The Three of Cups can stand for a mood or experience that makes you feel like dancing and singing.

Four of Cups

- SELF-ABSORPTION
- APATHY

- GOING WITHIN

Actions

being SELF-ABSORBED
concentrating on your own feelings
wanting for yourself
being unaware of others
giving out little
withholding affection
seeing only your point of view
ignoring gifts and blessings

feeling APATHETIC
passively accepting
losing interest
feeling disengaged
making little effort
finding life stale and flat
lacking motivation
feeling little desire

GOING WITHIN
being introspective
meditating
dreaming
contemplating
pausing to reflect
getting lost in reverie
withdrawing from involvement
losing outer awareness

Opposing Cards: Some Possibilities

World—involvement, caring, taking part
Four of Wands—excitement, high energy, optimism
Two of Cups—connection, sharing with others
Eight of Pentacles—making an effort, working hard

Reinforcing Cards: Some Possibilities

Hermit—withdrawing, being introverted
Four of Swords—contemplating, taking time alone
Six of Swords—listless, depressed

Description

Those who enjoy kayaking and other river sports know that there are areas of the river where the water flows in a dangerous circular motion. Instead of moving forward, it turns back on itself. In the same way, we can get stuck in *emotional* hydraulics. The Four of Cups represents such periods of self-absorption.

If you are self-absorbed, you tend to refer everything back to yourself—your own interests and desires. On this card, we see a man who is unaware of the cup being offered to him. He misses this gift because he's turned within. In readings, the Four of Cups can indicate that you are wrapped up for the moment in your own world.

In some situations, you *must* focus on yourself. When life is too stressful, you need to devote time and energy to yourself or you will feel swamped. The Four of Cups can represent a positive period of self-reflection and renewal. By taking the time to go within to dream, muse, and reflect, you restore your emotional balance.

The Four of Cups is sometimes a sign of apathy. You don't really care much about anything. Your life seems stale and flat because you've lost interest in the activities that used to bring you pleasure. You're not motivated to make much of an effort in any direction. At such times, the Four of Cups can show that you're stuck emotionally. You need something to focus on that will so engage your mind and heart that your path down river becomes clear again. Open yourself to your surroundings. Soon you will be on your way again.

Five of Cups

- LOSS
- BEREAVEMENT

- REGRET

Actions

suffering a LOSS
   letting go of a hope
   giving up the win
   experiencing a setback
   being defeated
   having a possession taken away
   saying good-bye

feeling BEREFT
   breaking up a relationship
   feeling deprived of love
   longing to be reunited
   grieving
   feeling sorrow

feeling REGRET
   being disappointed by events
   crying over spilt milk
   wanting to turn back the clock
   wishing for what might have been
   believing you made the wrong choice
   acknowledging mistakes

Opposing Cards: Some Possibilities

Lovers—establishing a relationship
Judgement—absolving yourself, releasing regret
Six of Wands—triumph, winning
Two of Cups—relationship
Nine of Cups—contentment, satisfaction

Reinforcing Cards: Some Possibilities

Death—loss, good-byes
Three of Swords—separation, loss of love, heartache
Six of Swords—sadness
Five of Pentacles—rejection, lack of support, loss of approval

Description

The Five of Cups is about loss. On this card, we see a figure draped in black and covered in grief. He so dominates the card that it is hard to look beyond him. The Five of Cups refers to that time when the pain of a loss is most acute. This man is looking only at the overturned cups in front of him. For now, he cannot acknowledge the two cups that are still standing. Later, when he has healed somewhat, he will be able to see all that remains.

In readings, the Five of Cups can alert you to the possibility of a loss and its associated emotions—sorrow, regret, denial. The loss could be great or small. It could be tangible (money, possession, relationship, work), or intangible (dream, opportunity, prospect, reputation). You may already know what this card represents, but if not, use it as a warning to help you avoid a loss or reduce its toll.

You may feel discouraged by this card, but it does have a positive side. Every loss opens new possibilities for growth because every loss initiates change. Loss hurts because it is our emotional resistance to change. No matter how much we accept intellectually that we must go with the flow, if that flow separates us from what we love, our feelings say, "No!"

In a story from *Zen Flesh, Zen Bones*,[1] the master Hakuin is falsely accused of fathering a child. He's ruined, but he accepts his loss and takes tender care of the child for a year. Suddenly, the real father appears, and just as willingly, Hakuin yields the child to its parents, accepting *loss* again. We who are not Zen masters may not flow quite so lightly with events, but we can learn from this story. The more we struggle to keep what is gone, the more we suffer.

---

1. Paul Reps, compilator, *Zen Flesh, Zen Bones: A Collection of Zen and Pre-Zen Writings* (Tokyo: Tuttle, 1957), pp. 7–8.

Six of Cups

- GOOD WILL
- INNOCENCE

- CHILDHOOD

Actions

experiencing GOOD WILL
   acting kindly or charitably
   doing a good turn for another
   sharing what you have
   having a noble impulse
   receiving a gift
   feeling blessed
   being well-intentioned

focusing on CHILDHOOD
   being with a child or young person
   feeling carefree
   being taken care of
   feeling nostalgic
   indulging in play
   enjoying youthful activities
   having a baby

enjoying INNOCENCE
   feeling simple contentment
   surrounding yourself with goodness
   being blissfully unaware
   having a clear conscience
   shunning corruption
   being acquitted
   appreciating simple joys

Opposing Cards: Some Possibilities

Devil—negativity, corruption, coveting
Nine of Wands—lack of innocence, believing the worst
Five of Swords—cynical, hostile, selfish
Seven of Swords—deceiving, manipulating
Nine of Swords—guilty

Reinforcing Cards: Some Possibilities

Star—good will, sharing
Ten of Cups—feeling blessed, happy, joyful

Description

In the film *Parenthood* there is a scene in which all the members of a large family come together to witness a birth. As the camera moves from person to person, we see as if for the first time the uniqueness of each one. The people talk and laugh, but suddenly their actions seem anything but ordinary. There is a sweetness in the air that builds until we see its very embodiment—the new baby. This is the spirit of the Six of Cups.

It is a truism that there is violence, anger, and mean-spiritedness in the world. Certainly there is enough of this, but there is also much good will and caring. A mother hands a drink to her child. A friend lends his car for the weekend. A worker fills in for a sick colleague. Small gestures, barely noticed, but so important. The Six of Cups is a card of simple goodness. It encourages you to be kind, generous, and forgiving.

The Six of Cups also represents innocence—a word with many shades of meaning. You can be innocent in the strictly legal sense of lack of guilt. You can be innocent of the truth—unaware of some secret. You can be lacking in deceit or corruption—innocent of ulterior motive. Finally, you can be virtuous or chaste. These are all possibilities that can apply to the Six of Cups, depending on the situation.

Notice that the two figures on the Six of Cups appear to be children. Often this card represents a baby or young child. In a larger sense, it embraces all of childhood and the feelings we associate with youth (ideally!)—being carefree, playful, secure, and loved. Children are our treasure, and the special sweetness of the Six of Cups is a quality to be treasured as well.

Seven of Cups

- WISHFUL THINKING
- OPTIONS

- DISSIPATION

Actions

indulging in WISHFUL THINKING
    creating fantasies
    dreaming
    getting caught up in illusions
    letting your imagination run wild
    kidding yourself about the facts
    building castles in the air
    waiting for your ship to come in
    lacking focus and commitment
    avoiding putting ideas to the test

having many OPTIONS
    being offered many alternatives
    facing an array of choices
    believing in limitless possibilities
    looking at a wide open field
    getting to pick and choose

falling into DISSIPATION
    overindulging
    letting everything go
    becoming disorganized
    eating/drinking/partying to excess
    neglecting your health
    entering into addictive patterns
    being inclined toward indolence
    being lazy
    procrastinating

Opposing Cards: Some Possibilities

Magician—focus and commitment
Emperor—discipline, structure
Temperance—balance, moderation
Four of Pentacles—order, control
Eight of Pentacles—working hard, applying yourself
Nine of Pentacles—discipline, restraint, refinement

Reinforcing Cards: Some Possibilities

Devil—overindulgence, dissipation
Moon—illusions, unrealistic ideas, fantasy
Nine of Cups—sensual excess

Description

As I gaze around the room right now, taking in the casual disarray, I know the Seven of Cups speaks to me—for better or worse. It says, "Yes, order and hard work are nice, but . . . isn't it more fun to just let everything go?" Letting everything go is what the Seven of Cups is all about.

It's easy to worship the gods of efficiency and neatness. We like trim lawns, alphabetized filing systems, and time management—the world of the Emperor. We admire order in all its forms and want everything to be just right. The Seven of Cups provides the balance. This card stands for all that is sloppy, impractical, and lax.

When the Seven of Cups appears in a reading, it is important to look carefully at how disordered your situation is. Is everything too controlled and regular? Perhaps you need to let things fall apart a little. When a rigid system breaks up, there can be a tremendous release of creativity. The man on the Seven of Cups is amazed by all the options he has.

On the other hand, if you are in a chaotic situation, some tightening may be necessary. No one is happy and productive in a crazy environment. Regularity gives structure to life. Taken to an extreme, the looseness of the Seven of Cups can lead to harmful patterns of decadence, addiction, and self-indulgence.

Sometimes the laziness applies to your thoughts and dreams. It is easy to wish for something, but not so easy to make that wish come true. When you see this card, make sure that you are backing up your plans with work and effort. Tighten up your life and commit to doing what it takes to reach your goals . . . even if it means (sigh) cleaning house.

Eight of Cups

- DEEPER MEANING
- MOVING ON

- WEARINESS

Actions

seeking DEEPER MEANING
   focusing on personal truth
   leaving the rat race
   looking for answers
   concentrating on what is important
   starting on a journey of discovery
   finding out the facts
   devoting more time to the spiritual

MOVING ON
   realizing the current cycle is over
   abandoning a hopeless situation
   disentangling yourself
   starting on a trip of unknown length
   letting go
   finishing up and walking away

growing WEARY
   feeling drained by demands
   dragging through the day
   feeling tired and listless
   lacking energy
   losing hope
   getting weighed down by worries
   becoming burned out

Opposing Cards: Some Possibilities

Strength—endurance, strength
Sun—vitality, high energy
Nine of Wands—hanging on, persevering

Reinforcing Cards: Some Possibilities

Hermit—searching for deeper meaning
Death—moving on, leaving
Three of Wands—going on a trip, going into new territory
Eight of Wands—finishing up, ending a chapter
Six of Swords—moving on, going on a trip

Description

A psychologist friend once told me that when a group is ready to break up, the members give off subtle signs to that effect. They display a certain restlessness. They arrive late to meetings, communicate less, and seem distracted. At some level the participants know it is time to move on, but they need a while to work up to that final step.

This process applies in many situations where an ending is approaching. Nothing is permanent in life. Sooner or later, everything slips away . . . or we slip away from it. The Eight of Cups stands for those moments when we realize, once and for all, that the past is gone. What was true is no longer true. The signs of change are in our face, and we must accept them. It is time to move on.

Moving on can mean a physical change such as leaving a job, location, or relationship. It can also mean an inner change—releasing old patterns, especially those that have dominated our thoughts and emotions. On the Eight of Cups, we see a man leaving on a journey. He has turned away from his old feelings (cups/river) to strike out on a new path. Sometimes moving on can mean searching for a deeper truth or reality. One day we wake up and realize that we have been asleep in our own lives—living a dream that no longer satisfies.

Some changes can be wearying. Endings are not always easy. One of the signs of a readiness to leave is lack of energy. When you feel tired and dispirited, you know that something is wrong, and it's time for a new direction. Reexamine your life and your priorities. You will find where in your life you need to move on.

Nine of Cups

- WISH FULFILLMENT
- SATISFACTION

- SENSUAL PLEASURE

Actions

having your WISH FULFILLED
  achieving what you desire
  obtaining your goal
  getting what you *think* you want
  having your dream come true

feeling SATISFIED
  indulging in a little smugness
  enjoying the situation just as it is
  feeling pleased as punch
  getting the results you hoped for
  feeling all's well with the world
  being contented

enjoying SENSUAL PLEASURE
  experiencing luxury
  savoring a delicious meal
  appreciating the arts
  making love
  relaxing
  experiencing beauty
  enjoying physical exertion

Opposing Cards: Some Possibilities

Hermit—focusing less on the senses
Five of Cups—regret

Reinforcing Cards: Some Possibilities

Empress—enjoying the senses
Lovers—sexual pleasure
World—achieving your heart's desire
Six of Wands—pride in self, achieving what you want
Seven of Cups—sensual excess

Description

The man on the Nine of Cups reminds me of "the cat who ate the canary." Now, a canary is a pet strictly off limits to hungry felines. Any cat who manages to catch one is going to feel pretty smug about it. This is the feeling tone of the Nine of Cups—pure indulgence and self-satisfaction.

At the physical level, the Nine of Cups is a sign of delight in all the senses. Sights, sounds, tastes, feelings. This card encourages you to seek pleasure and enjoy your body in every way. You can commune with the natural world as well—the body of Mother Earth. She, too, delights in sharing her abundance.

At the personal level, the Nine of Cups indicates contentment with the way things are. Notice how the man is seated confidently with his arms folded and a smile on his face. He has everything he wants and couldn't be happier about it. "See all my cups!" he seems to say. "Aren't they great?"

Sometimes it's wonderful to sit back and revel in the knowledge that all's right with the world. But a word of caution. You may be tempted to indulge yourself at the cost of someone else (like our mischievous cat!). This may feel great at the time, but sooner or later the feathers around your mouth will be discovered, and regret will set in. Pursuit of pleasure without regard to consequences is never satisfying in the long run.

In many tarot traditions, the Nine of Cups is known as the Wish Card. It shows your wish will come true. A wonderful prospect, but remember your fairy tale lessons. You must be sure you know what you really want and accept the responsibilities that go with your wish. If that is the case, then enjoy your good fortune!

Ten of Cups

- JOY
- PEACE

- FAMILY

Actions

feeling JOY
  embracing happiness
  having a sense of well-being
  radiating love
  delighting in good fortune
  counting your blessings
  expressing delight

enjoying PEACE
  experiencing serenity
  doing away with hostilities
  restoring harmony
  reducing stress and tension
  feeling contented and at ease
  calling a truce
  relaxing

looking to the FAMILY
  working for peace in the home
  going on a family event
  reaffirming a family commitment
  supporting a relative in need
  bonding with family members
  forgiving someone in the family

Opposing Cards: Some Possibilities

Devil—lack of joy or peace
Tower—upheaval, chaos
Three of Swords—heartbreak, loneliness
Nine of Swords—anguish, sorrow, despair
Ten of Swords—in the pits, feeling victimized

Reinforcing Cards: Some Possibilities

Lovers—family relationships, bonding
Star—joy, positive feelings, blessings
World—happiness, emotional fulfillment
Six of Cups—feeling blessed, happy, joyful

Description

On the Ten of Cups we see a loving couple with their carefree children. The family home is in the background, surrounded by trees and water. A rainbow of cups is overhead blessing the scene. A cynic might scoff at this romantic picture, but I see it as a symbol of what our emotional life could be at its best. The feelings represented here are an ideal that is within the reach of each of us.

First, there is joy. Joy goes beyond happiness, contentment, enjoyment. It is the feeling that comes when we know at the deepest level that we are one with all that is, and it is good. Unfortunately, this is not exactly a common feeling! Too often we are blinded by the trials of life and overwhelmed by their challenges. Joy exists, though, and is our birthright.

Peace is another aspect of the Ten of Cups—the serenity that comes when all elements are in harmony. There is inner peace and outer peace, which are reflections of each other. When you are in harmony with yourself, you *experience* harmony in your environment. When you see the Ten of Cups, know that an end to hostility is possible. If there is fighting around you, it may cease. If you are at war with yourself, you may find peace.

In readings, this card often signals a time of abundant blessings. It tells you that you can reach for the fulfillment you deserve, and it will come to you. Look for ways to realize joy and create peace. You may find the key to happiness in your family. Your family is the group of people you are attached to emotionally— for better or worse! If there is trouble in your family right now, work to restore harmony. The time is right for greater closeness.

Page of Cups

- BE EMOTIONAL
- BE INTUITIVE

- BE INTIMATE
- BE LOVING

Actions

BE EMOTIONAL

    be moved or touched
    let your feelings show
    respond to beauty
    be sentimental or romantic
    shed your detachment
    let your heart lead the way

BE INTUITIVE

    receive guidance from within
    act on a hunch
    remember your dreams
    have a psychic experience
    experience direct knowing
    trust your gut reaction

BE INTIMATE

    start or renew a love affair
    meet someone you're attracted to
    get closer to someone
    go beyond formalities
    have a special moment of togetherness
    solidify a friendship
    share something personal

BE LOVING

    make a thoughtful gesture
    express sympathy and understanding
    forgive yourself
    forgive someone who has hurt you
    apologize to someone you have hurt
    reach out and touch someone
    mend a broken relationship
    brighten someone's day
    respond with caring rather than anger
    refuse to judge or condemn

Court Card Pairs

The Page of Cups can form a pair with any other court card. Compare the ranks and suits of the two cards to see what such a pair might mean.

Description

The Page of Cups is Cupid bringing you opportunities for love. He delivers real chances to experience romance, deep feelings, and the inner life—the wonders of the Cups suit. In readings, this Page suggests that an opening may appear that stirs your emotions, pulls at your heartstrings, or brings you great joy. When you see such a chance, act on it!

The Page of Cups can also stand for a child or young-at-heart adult whose interactions with you involve emotional needs, moodiness, love, intimacy, or spirituality. Sometimes the Page of Cups implies that your entire situation is suffused with the spirit of love and emotion. At such times, feel free to express and enjoy your feelings with light-hearted abandon.

PAGE of CUPS.

Knight of Cups

- ROMANTIC/OVEREMOTIONAL
- IMAGINATIVE/FANCIFUL
- SENSITIVE/TEMPERAMENTAL
- REFINED/OVERREFINED
- INTROSPECTIVE/INTROVERTED

Actions

ROMANTIC/OVEREMOTIONAL

idealizes love/lacks self-restraint
emphasizes feelings/is often jealous
concentrates on the poetry of life/tends to be gushy and melodramatic
remembers special occasions/blows hot and cold in affections
expresses sentiments beautifully/brings flowers, but forgets to put gas in the car

IMAGINATIVE/FANCIFUL

can tap the fertile unconscious/indulges in idle daydreams
looks beyond the obvious/has big ideas that come to nothing
never takes the mundane path/has an unrealistic approach
spins marvelous tales/has an overactive imagination
is visionary/can shade the truth

SENSITIVE/TEMPERAMENTAL

is aware of moods and feelings/is prone to mood swings
helps others open up/can be petulant and sulky
responds deeply to life/gels melancholy and depressed
understands the pains of others/broods excessively
is tactful and diplomatic/takes offense easily

REFINED/OVERREFINED

appreciates beauty in all forms/leaves dirty work to others
seeks the finest/can't face unpleasantness
creates a pleasing environment/lacks robust good health
understands subtlety/emphasizes style over substance
is suave and gracious/gets overwhelmed by pressure

INTROSPECTIVE/INTROVERTED

values the inner life/focuses inward to excess
tries to understand why/may avoid active participation
questions motivations/is driven to self-examination
seeks self-improvement/exaggerates personal failings
sees below the surface/can't relax around others

Court Card Pairs

The Knight of Cups can form a pair with any other court card. Compare the ranks and suits of the two cards to see what such a pair might mean.

Description

On the positive side, the Knight of Cups is a sensitive soul. He is a poet—a lover of all things romantic and refined. He uses his imagination in wondrous ways and taps the deepest levels of emotion. He knows how to create beauty and share it with others. On the negative side, this Knight is prone to flights of fancy and illusion. His melodramatic moods are legendary, and his emotions often get the better of him. He's too temperamental and takes offense easily. He can't stand unpleasantness and will always let others deal with it.

In readings, a Knight of Cups shows that his sensitive style is involved in the situation in some way—as an aspect of you, someone else, or the atmosphere in general. You need to ask yourself, "Is this Knight's energy helping or hurting?"

If his style is evident, then balance is needed. Are your feelings appropriate or excessive? Are your daydreams unrealistic? Is someone's moodiness driving you crazy? Is your home life ruled by emotion rather than common sense? It may be time for a change.

If this Knight's energy is missing, a dose of poetry may be called for. Are you too restrained? Express your feelings. Do you always make the most practical choice? Go for the extravagant one instead. Do you avoid introspection? Take some time to look within and think about your life. Let the Knight of Cups introduce you to his world of romance and beauty.

Queen of Cups

- LOVING
- TENDERHEARTED
- INTUITIVE

- PSYCHIC
- SPIRITUAL

Actions

LOVING

    turns away wrath with caring
    is unconditionally accepting
    is sensitive to the feelings of others
    dispels anger and hate
    has infinite patience

TENDERHEARTED

    is easily moved by another's pain
    reacts with sensitivity and compassion
    is kind and gentle with all creatures
    can never turn away someone in need
    feels what others are feeling

INTUITIVE

    is always tuned to emotional under-
      currents
    senses the climate of a situation
    is guided by the heart
    trusts an inner sense of what is true
    understands without having to ask

PSYCHIC

    is open to the unconscious
    has a well-developed sixth sense
    can have a telepathic bond with another
    has a finely tuned sensibility
    is a natural medium

SPIRITUAL

    feels oneness with God and the universe
    has reverence for all life
    finds joy in communion
    appreciates the deeper meanings of life
    sees the world as a holy place

Court Card Pairs

The Queen of Cups can form a pair with any other court card. Compare the ranks and suits of the two cards to see what such a pair might mean.

Description

The personality of the Queen of Cups combines the positive water energy of the Cups suit with the inward focus of a Queen. Because she has a sweet, loving, and sensitive nature, the Queen of Cups has a kind word for everyone, and never reacts with anger or impatience. There is a gentleness about her that soothes and calms. Compassion is her watchword. Her reactions to the world are guided by her feelings. In all matters, she lets her heart lead the way. She senses emotional currents and knows what others are experiencing without having to ask. She is never moody, but understands moods and their influence. She trusts her intuition and so is more open to knowledge that comes from within herself and beyond. She is often moved by the beauty and tragedy of life. The Queen of Cups feels deeply and has a reverence for all aspects of God's creation. Her love includes and embraces everyone and everything.

In readings, the Queen of Cups asks you to *think and feel* as she does. For example: Are you aware of the emotional climate? Are you feeling loving? Do you trust your heart? Have you received an intuitive message? Have you been moved by another's pain?

This Queen can also represent a man or woman who is like her, or an atmosphere of gentle love, acceptance, and respect for feelings. In a reading, she tells you that her special energy has meaning for you at this time. Let yourself be inspired by this Queen in whatever form she appears in your life.

King of Cups

- WISE
- CALM
- DIPLOMATIC

- CARING
- TOLERANT

Actions

WISE

gives good advice
has a deep grasp of human nature
teaches through loving attention
knows what others need for growth
sees right to the heart of the matter
understands many levels of experience

CALM

maintains his/her composure
has a quieting influence on others
is emotionally stable and secure
keeps his/her head in a crisis
never seems nervous or tense

DIPLOMATIC

can balance the needs of many people
keeps everyone working together happily
can diffuse a tense situation
achieves goals through subtle influence
says just the right word at the right time

CARING

responds to emotional needs
is a natural healer and therapist
takes action to help those in need
feels compassion for the less fortunate
does volunteer and charity work

TOLERANT

has open and broad-minded views
accepts the limitations of others
is comfortable with all types of people
allows others their freedom
is patient in trying circumstances

Court Card Pairs

The King of Cups can form a pair with any other court card. Compare the ranks and suits of the two cards to see what such a pair might mean.

Description

The personality of the King of Cups is a combination of the positive water energy of the Cups suit and the active, outward focus of a King. He is wise and understanding, with a deep knowledge of the world that comes from the heart. He is a teacher and way-shower who guides his students with loving attention. He cares about others sincerely and always responds to their needs with compassion. He heals with a gentle touch and a quiet word. He is calm and relaxed in all situations, seeming to know intuitively what is called for at any moment. Others turn to him for advice because they know he will listen attentively. There is always a peacefulness around him that others respond to. He is tolerant of all points of view and shows patience in the most trying circumstances. He gives others freedom to grow and develop in their own ways without asking anything in return.

In readings, the King of Cups asks you to take the kinds of *actions* he might take. For example: responding calmly in a crisis, using diplomacy rather than force, reaching out to help, or accepting a different point of view. This King can also represent a man or woman who acts as he does, or an atmosphere of caring, tolerance, and understanding. In a reading, he tells you that his special energy has meaning for you at this time. Let yourself be inspired by this King in whatever form he appears in your life.

Ace of Swords

- MENTAL FORCE
- FORTITUDE

- JUSTICE
- TRUTH

Actions

using MENTAL FORCE
    being objective
    thinking your way through
    finding out the facts
    analyzing the situation
    using your intellect
    applying logic and reason

having FORTITUDE
    overcoming adversity
    facing problems
    resolving a situation
    finding the strength to overcome
    surmounting obstacles
    being undaunted by setbacks

seeking JUSTICE
    righting a wrong
    championing a cause
    doing what is right
    establishing the truth
    accepting responsibility
    wanting what is fair

proceeding with TRUTH
    dispelling doubts
    cutting through confusion
    seeing through illusions
    having clear understanding
    being honest
    finding out what is real

Ace-Ace Pairs

An Ace-Ace pair shows that a new spirit is entering your life. It draws on the energy of the Ace of Swords:—intelligence, reason, justice, truth, clarity, perseverance—plus one of these:

    Ace of Wands—creativity, excitement, adventure, courage, personal power
    Ace of Cups—deep feelings, intimacy, attunement, compassion, love
    Ace of Pentacles—prosperity, abundance, trust, security, groundedness

Description

The Ace of Swords is a symbol of possibility in the area of intelligence, reason, justice, truth, clarity, and fortitude. In readings, it shows that a seed of clear understanding has been planted in your life although you may not yet recognize it. When the seed sprouts, it could take almost any form. It might be a compelling idea, desire for the truth, call to justice, or a need to be honest. On the outside, it could be an offer, gift, opportunity, encounter, or synchronistic event.

Sometimes this Ace stands for a challenge that will test you in some way. Life never goes smoothly for long. Sooner or later a hurdle shows up, and the Ace of Swords can tell you when one is coming. This card is also a reminder to you to face your challenge, whatever it is, with courage, honesty, and a firm resolve. In every challenge, there is opportunity.

When you see the Ace of Swords, examine your life to see how its clean, sharp energy could work for you. Think about your problem objectively. Look for situations that are unjust or confusing and resolve to set them right. Above all else, commit to being honest and ethical. This card tells you that you do have the inner resources to overcome all obstacles and find the truth of your situation. That is the promise of the Ace of Swords.

Two of Swords

- BLOCKED EMOTIONS
- AVOIDANCE

- STALEMATE

Actions

BLOCKING EMOTIONS
   denying true feelings
   stifling a natural response
   keeping another at arm's length
   hiding distress
   turning a deaf ear
   being defensive
   maintaining your cool

AVOIDING the truth
   refusing to look at facts
   pretending everything's fine
   ignoring the warning signs
   closing your eyes to what's going on
   avoiding an unpleasantness
   choosing not to know

being at a STALEMATE
   feeling afraid to act
   reaching an impasse
   staying stuck
   refusing to decide
   being unwilling to rock the boat
   staying on the fence

Opposing Cards: Some Possibilities

Fool—opening up, uninhibited
Wheel of Fortune—moving, getting things going
Justice—accepting the truth, accepting responsibility
Star—free flow of positive feelings
Three of Wands—moving forward, looking at the facts

Reinforcing Cards: Some Possibilities

Moon—self-deception, not seeing the truth
Nine of Wands—being defensive, closing yourself off
Seven of Swords—running away from the truth
Four of Pentacles—stalemate, blockage

Description

On the Two of Swords, we see a young woman who has put a barrier of swords across her heart. Her rigid posture tells us of her struggle to keep her feelings under control. She is fending off any approach from the outside. "Nothing comes in, and nothing goes out," she seems to say.

The Two of Swords is about the barriers we put up between ourselves and others and those we create within ourselves. Internally, we block off emotions and refuse to feel them. We avoid looking at the truth and pretend that everything's OK. We think one way, but feel another. In countless ways, we divide off parts of ourselves and try to maintain them even when we know they need to be reconciled.

In readings, the Two of Swords often appears when you are not willing to accept some truth about yourself or the situation. What are you really feeling? Are you resisting tender feelings because you might be hurt? Are you furious even though you're smiling? What are you refusing to look at? Notice the blindfold on this woman. She can't look at the truth or even acknowledge that there is trouble.

The most common barrier is a closed heart. When we cut ourselves off emotionally, we *sever* the connection that allows our love to flow outward. Sometimes this action is necessary, but it always comes at a great price. Every time we close off our heart, we find it more difficult to open again.

Another barrier between people is a deadlocked situation. When two parties are set in their positions—*cut off* from each other—there is a stalemate. To break it, the "opponents" must come out from behind their swords and listen to each other. The lesson of the Two of Swords is that barriers are not the answer. We must stay open if we are to find peace and wholeness.

Three of Swords

- HEARTBREAK
- LONELINESS

- BETRAYAL

Actions

feeling HEARTBREAK
 causing heartbreak
 suffering emotional pain
 hurting inside
 being disappointed
 getting some unsettling news
 having your feelings hurt
 huring someone's feelings
 receiving little solace

feeling LONELY
 being separated
 wandering far from home
 being spurned or rejected
 feeling isolated from those you love
 being deserted in time of need
 feeling lost

experiencing BETRAYAL
 discovering a painful truth
 finding your trust misplaced
 being let down
 letting someone down
 getting stabbed in the back
 turning against someone
 breaking your word
 acting against

Opposing Cards: Some Possibilities

Lovers—intimacy, feeling love
Three of Cups—companionship, trust
Ten of Cups—joy, love, peace, togetherness

Reinforcing Cards: Some Possibilities

Five of Cups—separation, loss of love, heartache
Nine of Swords—anguish, heartbreak
Five of Pentacles—rejection, separation, lack of support

Description

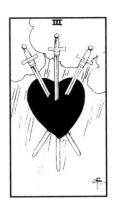

You open the door to find your partner in the arms of someone else. You overhear your best friend laughing at you behind your back. You find out your business partner has been cheating you for years. All of a sudden your world is turned upside-down. You're stunned, disbelieving, and finally heartbroken.

The image on the Three of Swords clearly describes this sudden pain. You literally feel as if someone has taken a sharp object and jabbed it through your heart. Even something as minor as a snippy remark can feel this way. Notice how this card contains just a heart and three swords. When your heart is breaking, you feel as if that is all you are—an open wound.

In readings, the Three of Swords often represents the nasty little curve balls that life can throw sometimes. Betrayal, abandonment, rejection, separation, a reversal of fortune. These hurts are painful because they hit you when you least expect them. If you have drawn this card, you may know what it refers to, but if not, the Three of Swords is a valuable warning. It is likely there is something amiss in your life that you are unaware of or unwilling to acknowledge. Curve balls hit us when we're looking the other way. Examine your situation carefully. Talk to the people in your life. Don't take anything for granted. Listen to your inner voice; it will help you locate the problem.

It is also possible that you are contemplating hurting someone else. With this card I think it is important to remember that each of us is capable of cruelty. We're all human, and we all make mistakes, sometimes serious ones. In the end, all we can do is trust in the goodness of life and try to live up to that ideal. When you slip, forgive yourself, and try to forgive others in turn, but, even better, head off trouble before it arrives.

Four of Swords

- REST
- CONTEMPLATION

- QUIET PREPARATION
  .

Actions

RESTING

taking a break
giving your body time to heal
avoiding overexertion
finding peace and quiet
relaxing body and soul
taking life easy

QUIETLY PREPARING

consolidating inner resources
making sure your base is secure
getting ready for the future
coming to terms with what is
tying up loose ends
stabilizing

CONTEMPLATING

gaining a better perspective
listening for your inner voice
taking time alone to think
standing back from the situation
examining your motivations
reviewing where you are

Opposing Cards: Some Possibilities

Magician—being active, focusing outward
Wheel of Fortune—rapid pace, lots of movement
Eight of Wands—making your move, rushing
Ten of Wands—overexerting, taking on too much
Two of Pentacles—having fun, balancing many activities

Reinforcing Cards: Some Possibilities

High Priestess—resting quietly, contemplating
Hermit—contemplating, being quiet
Hanged Man—rest, suspended activity
Four of Cups—contemplating, taking time alone
Six of Swords—rest, recovery
Seven of Pentacles—pausing to reflect, assess

Description

The Swords cards all stand for trials of some kind, but the Four suggests feelings of peace and stillness. Why is this card different? Because it represents the challenge to be quiet! Sometimes resting and doing nothing is the ultimate challenge. Activity can be a habit that is very difficult to break. There is always so much to do, and modern society beguiles us with its attractions and distractions. The result is that we forget to stop and be still.

In readings, the Four of Swords is often a sign that you need to slow down and get some rest. If you are recovering from an illness, allow yourself quiet time to heal. Even if you feel healthy, you are risking getting sick if you don't take a break.

The Four of Swords also represents taking time to think things over without hurry. It is important to step back and gain perspective. This is especially true when you are facing an ordeal or big event. You need quiet preparation time to gather your strength and center your energy. Picture an Olympic diver on the high board. She doesn't climb the ladder and then dash out. She stops, motionless as she readies herself for the burst of activity to come. This is the only way to bring the best to our endeavors.

Sometimes the Four of Swords implies that you are or could be shifting focus from the external to the internal. When we are silent, we can more easily go within. The knight in the picture appears to be praying or meditating deeply. Actually, he appears to be dead! For those who are addicted to activity, rest and quiet can seem like death, but that is certainly not the case. Stillness has its own rewards, but they must be recognized and sought.

Five of Swords

- SELF-INTEREST
- DISCORD

- OPEN DISHONOR

Actions

acting in your own SELF-INTEREST
  setting aside the concerns of others
  looking out for number one
  thinking of your own needs
  knowing you must concentrate on your-
    self
  encountering selfishness
  indulging in power plays
  gloating
  going for the win-lose result

experiencing DISCORD
  being in a hostile environment
  feeling people are set against each other
  choosing to battle
  having an "us-against-them" mentality
  recognizing ill will
  experiencing conflict

witnessing OPEN DISHONOR
  losing your moral compass
  letting ends justify means
  sacrificing integrity
  losing sight of what is right
  achieving a dubious victory
  knowing of criminal activity

Opposing Cards: Some Possibilities

Emperor—following the rules, obeying the law
Justice—having integrity, doing what is right
Temperance—working with others, harmony, cooperation
Six of Cups—innocent, well-intentioned, kind

Reinforcing Cards: Some Possibilities

Five of Wands—discord, people set against each other
Seven of Wands—"me-against-them" mentality, conflict
Seven of Swords—dishonor, separation from others

Description

The Five of Swords is about self-interest. Society tells us to think of others, yet we resist. How can we ignore our own concerns and still survive? This dilemma comes from our definition of self. If we view our self as our personality/body, our interests become those that relate to that self. Do I have enough to eat? Am I happy? Do I have all I want?

We may expand our concern to those we love, but, then, how can we stop there? We are connected to everyone in the long run. In truth, our self *is* the world. What we do to that world, we do to ourselves. This understanding is so basic, but so infuriatingly easy to forget day-to-day.

In readings, the Five of Swords can mean that you or someone else is forgetting this larger view of self. You are defining your interests too narrowly. If you try to get ahead in isolation, your actions will come back to haunt you, one way or the other.

Sometimes this card implies a *need* to put your own interests first. If you are being abused or taken advantage of, you must get free. If you are worn out by demands, take care of yourself. If it is your turn, step forward and claim your due. Just be aware that if you hurt others in the process, your victory will not feel complete.

The Five of Swords also represents hostility—from a cross word to warfare. When the cords that bind us are broken, we experience dis-cord. This card can signify dishonors that are fairly open. Cheats, lies, tricks, even crimes. You may be on the receiving end, or the perpetrator. Either way, hold to a larger view of who you are. Find the solution that is best for everyone . . . including yourself.

Six of Swords

- THE BLUES
- RECOVERY

- TRAVEL

Actions

feeling THE BLUES
  experiencing a low-level sadness
  just keeping your head above water
  working to get through the day
  feeling somewhat depressed
  avoiding the lows, but also the highs
  feeling listless
  functioning, but not much more

RECOVERING
  dealing with the effects of trauma
  getting over a tough time
  picking up the pieces
  starting to cope
  beginning to get your health back
  heading toward a more positive place
  feeling hope again

TRAVELING
  changing location
  moving from one place to another
  taking a trip
  experiencing a change of scene
  being uprooted
  going on a journey
  entering into a new frame of mind

Opposing Cards: Some Possibilities

Strength—having heart, unshakable resolve
Sun—vitality, enthusiasm
Four of Wands—excitement, celebration
Three of Cups—high spirits, exuberance
Two of Pentacles—fun

Reinforcing Cards: Some Possibilities

Ten of Wands—getting by, struggling along
Four of Cups—feeling listless, depressed, uncaring
Five of Cups—sadness
Eight of Cups—moving on, going on a trip
Four of Swords—rest, recovery
Nine of Swords—depression, sadness

Description

At one point in *The Pilgrim's Progress*, the hero Christian (who is also on a Fool's Journey) becomes mired in the Slough of Despond. He struggles for a time until drawn out by Help. Help tells him that "...many fears, and doubts, and discouraging apprehensions...settle in this place."[1]

The Slough of Despond is a good name for the Six of Swords. Sometimes this card represents a dull, listless state. Nothing is seriously wrong, but nothing is really right either. You're getting by, but not thriving. In the picture the figures in the boat seem sad and disengaged. Life is indeed uninteresting when we feel the blues.

In a more positive vein, the Six of Swords can indicate recovery. This is especially true when you have just experienced a tough time or psychological blow. During the crisis, you felt numb and disconnected; nothing mattered at all. Now you are beginning to heal and pick up the pieces of your life. The travelers in our boat are at least moving forward. They are headed toward a new place, even if they are not yet ready to eagerly embrace those shores.

In fact, the Six of Swords can indicate travel and moves of all kinds. This could mean an actual change of scene, relocation, or trip, but not necessarily. A journey can also take place on the inner planes as we move from one frame of mind to another.

Although the Six of Swords does not promise great joy, it also avoids the depths of despair. A slough is not a bottomless pit, but simply a hollow or depression. When you see this card, know that even though the situation is not ideal, you are moving toward a more positive place. Change is in the air, and new, more hopeful conditions lie ahead.

---

1. John Bunyan, *The Pilgrim's Progress.* Excerpt from the Norton Anthology of English Literature: vol.1, 3rd ed. (New York: W. W. Norton, 1974), p. 1780.

Seven of Swords

- RUNNING AWAY
- LONE-WOLF STYLE

- HIDDEN DISHONOR

Actions

RUNNING AWAY
    shirking responsibility
    sneaking off
    leaving
    avoiding obligations
    being afraid to face the music
    taking the easy way out
    hiding from the truth
    procrastinating

being a LONE WOLF
    feeling you don't need anyone else
    wanting independence
    deciding not to help
    keeping something to yourself
    preferring solitude
    staying aloof
    wanting to go it alone
    holding people at arm's length

choosing HIDDEN DISHONOR
    deceiving or being deceived
    covering your tracks
    maneuvering behind the scenes
    being two-faced
    seeing others take the rap
    controlling without appearing to
    avoiding a shameful secret
    lying or stealing

Opposing Cards: Some Possibilities

Hierophant—working within the group
Justice—accepting responsibility, being above board
Ten of Wands—meeting obligations, being responsible
Six of Cups—innocent, kind, open, noble

Reinforcing Cards: Some Possibilities

Hermit—being alone, staying away from others
Two of Swords—running from the truth
Five of Swords—dishonor, separation from others
Nine of Pentacles—relying on yourself, acting on your own

Description

The Seven of Swords is tied to the Five of Swords because both involve separation from others. On the Seven we see a man tiptoeing away from society (the colorful pavilions). He's taken some swords and seems rather pleased with his successful heist. He gives the impression of having secret, solitary plans.

This card sometimes represents the "lone-wolf" style—the desire to run lone and free. In films, the lone-wolf hero always acts totally on his own. He discovers, investigates and solves every problem using only his own wits and resources. He believes he's successful because he ignores the fumbling efforts of ordinary people.

In readings, the Seven of Swords can be a sign that you or someone else wants to be a lone wolf. You feel that you will be more effective and comfortable on your own. This approach is useful when you need to bypass an ineffectual group or assert your independence, but it can also be troubling. We can not be happy and productive for long without some commitment to others. If you feel inclined to act alone, make sure this isolation is really working for you.

Sometimes the Seven of Swords means that you are running from something—commitment, responsibility, hard work, love. You may be procrastinating, letting problems slip because you don't want to deal with them. Sometimes we just have to face what has to be faced. The Seven of Swords lets you know when you are making things worse for yourself and others by running away.

The Seven of Swords can also indicate a hidden dishonor—a choice you or another has made that does not do justice to the highest. We all make wrong choices that we want to hide. Some of these are minor, some serious. Your inner voice will tell you when this is happening. When you see the Seven of Swords, take a good look at what you're doing because hidden dishonors will eat away at your happiness and self-respect.

Eight of Swords

- RESTRICTION
- CONFUSION

- POWERLESSNESS

Actions

feeling RESTRICTED
    being fenced in by obstacles
    staying in a limited situation
    feeling trapped by circumstances
    experiencing few options
    being blind to freedom
    feeling persecuted

feeling CONFUSED
    being unsure which way to turn
    feeling at a loss
    lacking direction
    feeling overwhelmed
    floundering around
    needing guidance and clarity
    not understanding what is happening

feeling POWERLESS
    waiting for outside rescue
    doubting anything you do will help
    avoiding responsibility
    looking for a white knight
    feeling victimized
    accepting inaction

Opposing Cards: Some Possibilities

Magician—feeling powerful, knowing what's going on
Chariot—self-confidence, focus
Two of Wands—power, boldness
Four of Wands—freedom, lack of restriction
Three of Pentacles—competence, know-how, planning

Reinforcing Cards: Some Possibilities

Devil—confusion, restriction
Moon—confusion, lack of clarity
Ten of Swords—victim mentality, powerlessness

Description

The woman on the Eight of Swords is lost and alone. She can't see because she is blindfolded. She can't reach out because she is bound. She can't move freely because she is caught in a prison of swords. It seems she has wandered far from home—her place of security far away on the hill. How can she get back? She doesn't know which way to go. The Eight of Swords stands for those times when we feel lost, confused and powerless. Help and relief seem very far away.

Sometimes we feel restricted by circumstances. We wake up one day in an impossible situation. A dead end job. A troubled relationship. Mountains of debt. How did this happen? We have no idea. Even little problems can make us feel trapped. There just doesn't seem to be a way out. Other times life seems fine—on the surface. "I have everything I want. I should be happy, so what's the problem?" We just don't know. We're confused and unsure.

In readings, the Eight of Swords is often a sign that you are heading toward (or already in) a situation in which you will feel a lack of freedom and choice. Such situations are tricky because the more you get into them, the more restricted you feel. At each step, your options seem to narrow until you feel completely stuck.

When you see this card, remember that you do have choices, and you do have power. No matter how trapped you feel, you can find a way out if you believe it is possible. The young girl in the picture could free herself. She could wriggle free, tear off the blindfold, and kick down those swords. Solutions are not always easy, but they exist. Find your clarity of thought and purpose (the Swords ideal) and use them to take that first step toward home.

Nine of Swords

- WORRY
- GUILT

- ANGUISH

Actions

WORRYING
  doubting all will go well
  brooding
  making yourself sick over your troubles
  going over and over an issue
  feeling anxious and tense
  getting all worked up

feeling GUILTY
  regretting some offense
  refusing to forgive yourself
  wanting to turn back the clock
  focusing on your "sins"
  being hard on yourself
  denying that you did your best
  getting overwhelmed by remorse

suffering ANGUISH
  despairing
  feeling you've reached your limits
  having sleepless nights
  feeling depressed
  going through a dark night of the soul
  forgetting joy
  wanting to cry

Opposing Cards: Some Possibilities

Star—serenity, peace of mind
Judgement—lack of guilt, absolution
Three of Cups—being on top of the world, in the flow
Six of Cups—innocence
Ten of Cups—joy, peace, delight

Reinforcing Cards: Some Possibilities

Devil—despair, lack of joy
Ten of Wands—worrying
Three of Swords—anguish, heartbreak
Six of Swords—depression, sadness

Description

It makes sense that the figure on the Nine of Swords is in bed because it is during the night that our griefs and regrets come to mind most intensely. The quiet darkness strips away the distractions of the day, leaving us alone with our thoughts. Who has not lain awake at 4 A.M. filled with worries that refuse to go away? The Nine of Swords represents this unhappiness which can strike at any time.

Unlike the pain of the Three of Swords, which *seems* to come from without, the Nine of Swords represents the pain that we generate from within. What tortures we put ourselves through when our fears and doubts overwhelm us. Worry is probably the most common. Have I done enough? Will everything work out OK? What am I going to do? The thoughts go round and round—impossible to turn off.

Guilt is another source of pain. When we have done something that we feel is wrong or hurtful—or failed to do something we think we should have—the distress can be very real. It is worse when nothing we do relieves the bad feelings or makes them go away. Finally, there is just pure anguish. Sometimes the pain of life is so total that all we feel like doing is crying into our hands.

Needless to say, the Nine of Swords is not the most pleasant of cards, but it doesn't always indicate major distress. Often it is just a sign of some element of unhappiness or trouble—a vulnerable spot in your life. This card is often a warning from your Inner Guide that the path you are going down may be a difficult one. If you approach the Nine of Swords in this spirit—as a caution sign—you will be able to use it constructively. Examine your situation carefully to be sure you are making the best choices. Even a small change can make all the difference.

Ten of Swords

- BOTTOMING OUT
- VICTIM MENTALITY

- MARTYRDOM

Actions

BOTTOMING OUT
   having nowhere to go but up
   knowing it's darkest before the dawn
   being at the lowest point
   feeling things can't possibly get worse
   preparing for an upturn
   reaching the pits

feeling like a VICTIM
   bemoaning your fate
   feeling powerless
   seeing life as hostile
   suffering from an attack
   wondering "Why me?"
   feeling self-pity
   being on the receiving end

being a MARTYR
   putting your own interests last
   being self-deprecating
   feeling like a doormat
   taking a back seat
   letting others go first
   sacrificing

Opposing Cards: Some Possibilities

Chariot—self-assertion, power, victory
Two of Wands—power, self-confidence
Six of Wands—self-promotion, being on top of the world
Nine of Cups—satisfaction, happy with conditions

Reinforcing Cards: Some Possibilities

Hanged Man—sacrifice, martyrdom
Eight of Swords—victim mentality, powerlessness

Description

The Ten of Swords appears to be a card of terrible misfortune, but surprisingly, it often represents troubles that are more melodramatic than real. The man on this card has quite a few swords in his back. Wouldn't one be enough? Isn't ten a little excessive? Perhaps this gentleman's suffering—though sincere—is exaggerated as well.

One meaning of the Ten of Swords is hitting rock bottom. When one disaster follows another, we feel devastated at first, but eventually we throw our hands up and laugh. It's so bad, it's funny! In films, the hero says, "What else could possibly go wrong?" and we know that's a signal for the bucket of water to fall on his head. When you see the Ten of Swords, know that the last bucket has fallen, and you can expect a turn for the better.

This card can also show when you're in victim mentality. You're certain that the whole world is picking on you just to make your life difficult. I picture the man lifting his head and saying, "You think you've got it bad . . . a cut on the finger. I've got ten swords in my back . . . count 'em—ten! Then he drops his head back down with a sigh. When we're in victim mentality, we think everything is horrible, hopeless, and impossibly unfair.

Being a martyr is also a favorite Ten of Swords activity. In this case, the man would say with a weak wave of his hand, "No . . . you go on. Have fun. Don't think about me. I'll just stay here with these swords in my back . . . but I want you to enjoy yourself." Being a martyr in this sense is not the same as making a sacrifice for another with no strings attached. With the Ten of Swords, either is possible, but doing a good turn for someone else is more satisfying without the strings.

I don't mean to make light of misfortunes because, of course, there are many real tragedies in the world. Sometimes the Ten of Swords indicates a sad event, but you know when this is the case. There is not even a hint of laughter in your heart. Most of the time the Ten of Swords has a lighter side. It is as if your Inner Guide is gently kidding you about how you are handling your own personal tale of woe. When you see the Ten of Swords, check your attitude and know you've reached the point where things will definitely begin to look up.

Page of Swords

- USE YOUR MIND
- BE TRUTHFUL

- BE JUST
- HAVE FORTITUDE

Actions

USE YOUR MIND

    analyze the problem
    use logic and reason
    reexamine beliefs
    develop an idea or plan
    study or research the facts
    learn or teach
    think everything through

BE TRUTHFUL

    act honestly
    face the facts
    stop deceiving
    clear up any confusion
    expose what is hidden
    speak directly

BE JUST

    right a wrong
    act ethically
    treat others equally
    champion a cause
    try to be fair
    do what you know is right
    accept responsibility
    acknowledge the other point of view

HAVE FORTITUDE

    face problems squarely
    refuse to be discouraged
    meet setbacks with renewed energy
    keep a firm resolve
    move out of depression
    keep your chin up and head high
    keep trying

Court Card Pairs

The Page of Swords can form a pair with any other court card. Compare the ranks and suits of the two cards to see what such a pair might mean.

Description

The Page of Swords is a messenger bringing you challenges. He suggests that an opportunity for growth may come your way in the guise of a problem or dilemma. These challenges may not be your favorites. In fact, you probably will want to say "Thanks . . . but no thanks."

The Page of Swords asks you to embrace these difficult situations. Think of them as trials designed to test your mettle. If you accept and prevail, you will become stronger and more resilient. In meeting these challenges, you are encouraged to use the tools of the Swords suit—honesty, reason, integrity, and fortitude.

The Page of Swords can also stand for a child or young-at-heart adult whose interactions with you involve truthfulness, ethical behavior, discouragement, or matters of the mind. This relationship is likely to be troubled or difficult in keeping with the challenges of the Swords suit.

Sometimes the Page of Swords implies that your entire situation is one suffused with the spirit of learning, discovery, and mental activities of all kinds. At such times, use your mind and enjoy the delights of the intellect.

Knight of Swords

- DIRECT/BLUNT
- AUTHORITATIVE/OVERBEARING
- INCISIVE/CUTTING
- KNOWLEDGEABLE/OPINIONATED
- LOGICAL/UNFEELING

Actions

DIRECT/BLUNT

    is frank and outspoken/is tactless and rude

    gets straight to the point/may have a brusque manner

    does not mince words/does not spare the feelings of others

    lets others know where they stand/can't hold his or her tongue

    gives an honest answer/shows little discretion

AUTHORITATIVE/OVERBEARING

    speaks with assurance/tends to be domineering

    commands attention/forces a position on others

    acts with total certainty/expects immediate compliance

    gives orders naturally/does not welcome dissent

    has great influence/acts in a high-handed manner

INCISIVE/CUTTING

    has a keen, forceful intellect/is prone to biting sarcasm

    penetrates to the core/lacks sensitivity

    expresses ideas succinctly/can be critical

    is sharp and alert/has a barbed wit

    debates and argues well/derides stupidity

KNOWLEDGEABLE/OPINIONATED

    knows what he or she is talking about/believes he or she is always right

    can expound on any topic/lacks tolerance of other viewpoints

    is sought as an expert/must have the last word

    has well-reasoned positions/is arrogant

    is highly intelligent/can be dogmatic and close-minded

LOGICAL/UNFEELING

    reasons clearly/undervalues intuition

    analyzes information well/treats people like numbers

    concentrates on what is correct/doesn't temper justice with mercy

    can set aside emotional factors/is cut off from emotions

    makes sense out of confusion/is cold and aloof

Court Card Pairs

The Knight of Swords can form a pair with any other court card. Compare the ranks and suits of the two cards to see what such a pair might mean.

KNIGHT of SWORDS.

Description

On the positive side, the Knight of Swords is a master of logic and reason. He has a keen intellect that grasps the fine points of any subject. He speaks clearly, directly, and always with authority. His judgments are sure and free of emotion. Others rely on his lucid analyses of problems and solutions. On the negative side, this Knight is not a master of diplomacy. He can be downright tactless and rude. When he thinks you are wrong, you'll know it. He's convinced of his own superiority and has little tolerance for stupidity. He expects others to comply with his views. To him, feelings are irrelevant and illogical.

In readings, a Knight of Swords shows that his penetrating style is involved in the situation as an aspect of you, someone else, or the atmosphere in general. You need to ask yourself, "Is this Knight's energy helping or hurting?"

If his style is evident, then balance is needed. Are you always forcing your position on others? Do you get in trouble for saying what you think? Is your partner too cold and aloof? Do your colleagues tend to be critical rather than supportive? It may be time for a change.

If this Knight's energy is missing, a dose of clear-sightedness may be called for. Are you too emotional? Let your head rule your heart next time. Do you overvalue the opinions of others? Trust your own authority. Are you afraid to offend? Speak your mind. Let the Knight of Swords introduce you to his world of reason and self-assurance.

Queen of Swords

- HONEST
- ASTUTE
- FORTHRIGHT

- WITTY
- EXPERIENCED

Actions

HONEST

faces the truth, even if unpleasant
is up front with everyone
likes everything on the table
plays by the rules
avoids lies and deception

ASTUTE

sizes up a situation quickly
understands hidden motives and desires
is difficult to fool, trick, or con
figures out the unspoken rules and agendas
is quick on the uptake

FORTHRIGHT

is direct and open in all dealings
gets to the heart of the matter
acts without pretense or guile
is straightforward and no-nonsense
can be candid when necessary

WITTY

has a delightful sense of humor
diffuses awkward situations with a funny
    remark
never takes anything too seriously
laughs at everything, including him or herself

EXPERIENCED

has seen and done it all
has strength due to life's hard knocks
is free of self-righteous judgments
has realistic expectations

Court Card Pairs

The Queen of Swords can form a pair with any other court card. Compare the ranks and suits of the two cards to see what such a pair might mean.

Description

The personality of the Queen of Swords combines the positive air energy of the Swords suit with the inward focus of a Queen. You can always count on her to tell you exactly how it is. Above all else she admires honesty, and she lives by her commitment to being truthful. Lies, tricks, and games are of no interest to her, but she's not easy to fool. She is experienced in the ways of the world, good and bad. The Queen of Swords can size up a situation quickly. She understands human folly, but doesn't condemn it. She knows when cow manure is being thrown around and simply finds clever ways around it. She prefers being straightforward and direct. Her observations are candid, but never hurtful. In fact, this Queen has a delightful sense of humor. She likes a good laugh and always has a witty comeback ready-to-hand. She knows that life isn't meant to be taken too seriously. The Queen of Swords is refreshing in her candor and lack of pretense.

In readings, the Queen of Swords asks you to *think and feel* as she does. For example: Are you being completely honest? (Check this one first!) Do you see the humor in the situation? Are you getting right to the point? Have you figured out what's really going on? Are you letting yourself be fooled?

This Queen can also represent a man or woman in your life who is like her, or an atmosphere of honest, direct communication. In a reading, she tells you that her special energy has meaning for you at this time. Let yourself be inspired by this Queen in whatever form she appears in your life.

King of Swords

- INTELLECTUAL
- ANALYTICAL
- ARTICULATE

- JUST
- ETHICAL

Actions

INTELLECTUAL

    is comfortable in the world of the mind
    uses thought creatively
    grasps information quickly and completely
    inspires and challenges through ideas
    ably carries out research
    is knowledgeable

ANALYTICAL

    cuts through confusion and mental fog
    applies reason and logic
    is talented with games and other mental
       challenges
    easily breaks up complicated subjects
    is adept at argument and debate
    understands a problem quickly

ARTICULATE

    is adept at language and verbal skills
    communicates ideas successfully
    is a stimulating conversationalist
    often serves as a group spokesperson
    is a lucid writer and speaker

JUST

    renders honest, insightful judgments
    understands and honors all sides of an issue
    is concerned about truth and fairness
    views situations with a dispassionate eye
    is impartial and objective

ETHICAL

    is a moral/ethical leader
    encourages high standards
    works against corruption and dishonesty
    takes the high road in all dealings
    lives by his/her highest principles

Court Card Pairs

The King of Swords can form a pair with any other court card. Compare the ranks and suits of the two cards to see what such a pair might mean.

Description

The personality of the King of Swords is a combination of the positive air energy of the Swords suit and the active, outward focus of a King. He is a man of intellect who can absorb and work with information of all kinds. As a master of reason and logic, he analyzes any problem with ease. He can work out solutions quickly and explain them lucidly to others. In a chaotic situation, he cuts through the confusion and provides the clarity needed to move forward. Others seek him out to present their case as he speaks with eloquence and insight. He is always truthful and can be relied on to handle any situation fairly and honorably. When a judgment is called for, he can render an impartial but just decision. He is incorruptible and lives by the highest ethical standards. He encourages those around him to do the same, and they often live up to his expectations.

In readings, the King of Swords asks you to take the kinds of *actions* he might take. For example: telling the truth, thinking up a solution, communicating well, or judging fairly. This King can also represent a man or woman who is acting as he does, or an atmosphere of reason, honesty, and high standards. In a reading, he tells you that his special energy has meaning for you at this time. Let yourself be inspired by this King in whatever form he appears in your life.

Ace of Pentacles

- MATERIAL FORCE
- PROSPERITY

- PRACTICALITY
- TRUST

Actions

using MATERIAL FORCE
  focusing on concrete results
  having a real-world impact
  working with the physical
  achieving tangible results
  improving the body/health
  becoming involved with nature

PROSPERING
  having the means to reach a goal
  enjoying abundance
  drawing to you what you need
  flourishing
  seeing efforts rewarded
  increasing assets
  experiencing growth

being PRACTICAL
  using common sense
  getting down-to-earth
  taking advantage of what works
  being realistic
  grounding yourself in the real world
  accepting the tools at hand

proceeding with TRUST
  believing in the good faith of others
  feeling safe and protected
  knowing you have total security
  operating from a known position
  having a support system
  knowing the situation is stable
  consolidating a firm base

Ace-Ace Pairs

An Ace-Ace pair shows that a new spirit is entering your life. It draws on the energy of the Ace of Pentacles—prosperity, abundance, trust, security, groundedness—plus one of these:

Ace of Wands—creativity, excitement, adventure, courage, personal power
Ace of Cups—deep feelings, intimacy, attunement, compassion, love
Ace of Swords—intelligence, reason, justice, truth, clarity, perseverance

Description

The Ace of Pentacles is a symbol of possibility in the area of prosperity, abundance, trust, security, and groundedness. In readings, it shows that a seed of productivity has been planted in your life although you may not yet recognize it. When the seed sprouts, it could take almost any form. It might be a feeling of centeredness, desire for results, or need to focus on practical matters. On the outside, it could be an offer, gift, opportunity, encounter, or synchronistic event.

When you see this Ace, examine your life to see how its solid energy could work for you. Now is not the time for fantasy, drama, or daring. It is a time to be real and centered. Seek out comfortable, reliable experiences that make you feel secure. Build a foundation of trust in your life both within and without. Your common sense will tell you what to do. Focus on the natural world to help you stay grounded. Enjoy your body and the joys of material existence.

The Ace of Pentacles can be a sign that you will be able to make your dreams real. Your ideas are ready to be turned into something tangible. Figure out what will work and make it a reality. You can now attract all the wealth you need to get your projects going. Tap into the material force of the Ace of Pentacles, and all your enterprises will flourish.

Two of Pentacles

- JUGGLING
- FLEXIBILITY

- FUN

Actions

JUGGLING
   keeping everything in balance
   coping with demands
   getting people to work together
   making sure all areas are covered
   having a lot of irons in the fire
   moving forward smoothly
   emphasizing all aspects equally

being FLEXIBLE
   adapting quickly
   feeling free to try new approaches
   going with the flow
   refusing to let change throw you
   opening to developments
   seeing the possibilities
   handling challenges
   changing directions easily

having FUN
   doing something you enjoy
   getting a kick out of life
   taking time to play
   feeling in high spirits
   whistling while you work
   seeing the humor in the situation
   kicking back

Opposing Cards: Some Possibilities

Hierophant—following the program, being conventional
Five of Wands—being at cross-purposes, not working out
Four of Swords—rest, quiet, low activity
Six of Swords—the blues, feeling listless

Reinforcing Cards: Some Possibilities

Temperance—balance, finding the right mix
Four of Wands—fun, excitement, parties

Description

In the film *First Knight*, Lancelot takes on a challenge—to move down a line of swinging blades crossing in front of him at random intervals. He succeeds because he is alert, agile, and patient. He knows when to move and when to stay still. He glides through the dangers enjoying every moment of this deadly obstacle course. Lancelot has tapped the energy of the Two of Pentacles.

There is nothing quite like the feeling of being graceful and effective at the same time. On the Two of Pentacles we see a young man dancing as he juggles his worldly concerns. The infinity sign loops around the two pentacles to suggest that he could handle unlimited problems. In the background we see two ships riding the waves easily—cruising the ups and downs of life.

In readings, the Two of Pentacles lets you know that you can juggle all demands made upon you. In fact, you will relish the excitement of every hurdle. If you do not feel this level of confidence right now, this card asks you to believe in yourself. You have all you need to meet your every goal and more. Embrace the challenge.

The Two of Pentacles also reminds you to be flexible. Lancelot could not have navigated the swords walking in a straight line. He had to move freely and lightly in all directions as needed. You too must be supple if you want to prevail. Don't force your way through or you will be cut down. Now is not the time to be rigid. Know that sometimes a side step, or even a back step is the surest way forward.

The Two of Pentacles is also a symbol of fun, laughter, and good times. It is definitely a high-energy card. If you are feeling tired or depressed, this card may be a sign that greater vitality will be yours. If you are feeling revved already, the Two of Pentacles could be a warning against overstimulation. Be sure you get the rest you need so that you can enjoy the up energy of this card.

Three of Pentacles

- TEAMWORK
- PLANNING

- COMPETENCE

Actions

working as a TEAM
    coordinating with others
    finding all the needed elements
    functioning as a unit
    getting the job done together
    contributing to the group
    cooperating
    combining efforts

PLANNING
    organizing resources
    following a schedule
    operating in the know
    nailing down the details
    being an ant, not a grasshopper
    reviewing beforehand
    going over possible problems
    being prepared

being COMPETENT
    getting the job done
    carrying out an assignment well
    meeting your goals
    proving your ability
    achieving more than what's expected
    knowing what to do and how to do it
    being up to the job

Opposing Cards: Some Possibilities

Five of Wands—lack of teamwork, no cooperation
Seven of Wands—opposition, dissension
Eight of Swords—not feeling up to the job, lacking direction
Nine of Pentacles—doing it yourself, not focusing on teamwork

Reinforcing Cards: Some Possibilities

Hierophant—working in a team or group
Temperance—combining forces
Three of Wands—planning, preparing for the future
Three of Cups—working in a group

Description

In the TV show *Mission Impossible*, a crack team of specialists is always given a dangerous assignment. The team has to map out a strategy, co-ordinate resources, and draw on their skills and ingenuity to complete the mission. This is the Three of Pentacles in action: teamwork, planning, and competence.

The Three of Pentacles is one of the cards in the tarot that focuses on the group. (The Three of Cups and the Hierophant are the others.) As Pentacles are grounded and practical, this card represents a task-oriented team—people who are working cooperatively toward a common goal. There are few jobs that can be accomplished alone. We need the help of others to achieve our goals. Sometimes the Three of Pentacles is a sign that you will be more productive if you work with others. You don't have to do it all by yourself.

This card can also show a need for planning and preparation. Now is not the time to rush into something or begin a project with only a vague idea of what it's about. You need to think everything through, go over all the possibilities, and make sure you work out the details. Do your homework and your undertaking will flourish.

Another feature of the Three of Pentacles is competence—the ability to get the job done. How rare this is nowadays! This card tells you that you have the skills and knowledge you need. You can attract capable people and create a successful environment. Know that the situation is (or will be) in good hands, but be sure to concentrate on excellence in your work. Be proud of what you do and how you do it. Then you will accomplish your "impossible" mission.

Four of Pentacles

- POSSESSIVENESS
- CONTROL

- BLOCKED CHANGE

Actions

wanting to POSSESS
    keeping what you have
    getting your share
    acquiring material goods
    hanging on to someone
    being greedy
    penny-pinching
    declaring ownership
    saving

maintaining CONTROL
    wanting to be in charge
    denying weakness
    directing
    demanding compliance
    insisting on your own way
    imposing structure
    setting limits and rules
    creating order

BLOCKING CHANGE
    maintaining the status quo
    wanting everything to stay the same
    refusing to look at new approaches
    stagnating
    obstructing new developments
    holding on to the present
    resisting the flow

Opposing Cards: Some Possibilities

Fool—being spontaneous, impulsive
Empress—openhearted, lavish
Wheel of Fortune—movement, rapid changes
Hanged Man—letting go, not trying to control

Reinforcing Cards: Some Possibilities

Emperor—control, structure, order
Chariot—control
Two of Swords—stalemate, blockage
Ten of Pentacles—liking the status quo, conserving

Description

Spend time with a 2-year-old, and you will soon hear the sounds of the Four of Pentacles: "No!" and "Mine!" These are the cries of the ego, which is just developing in the young child. The ego tries to guarantee power by imposing its will. The desire for control is the hallmark of the Four of Pentacles.

Some control *is* valuable. In chaotic situations, a firm hand is needed to provide structure and organization. Too often, however, the urge for control gets out of hand, stifling creativity and individual expression. In readings, this card asks you to weigh carefully the level of control in your situation.

The Four of Pentacles can stand for issues of ownership. You may be involved in getting and keeping money or some other commodity. You may be having problems with possessiveness or jealousy. Use the energy of this card to preserve and defend, but not to lay claim. People need to be free to determine their own lives.

The Four of Pentacles also implies blocked change. It's as if the stubborn little man on the card is thwarting your every move. Opposition may come from those who want to maintain the status quo. It may also come from within yourself. Are you resisting change that is truly needed? We often cling to the familiar even when we know it's not for the best.

The lesson of the Four of Pentacles is that control is impossible. We stand in the world as in a great ocean. Who could manage or possess such power? The only way to keep from drowning is to ride the currents. The ocean will support us as long as we swim with the flow.

Five of Pentacles

- HARD TIMES
- ILL HEALTH

- REJECTION

Actions

experiencing HARD TIMES
    running into material troubles
    losing a job or income
    feeling insecure
    going through a period of hardship
    lacking what you need
    struggling to make ends meet

suffering ILL HEALTH
    feeling run down and tired
    refusing to take care of yourself
    neglecting your body and its needs
    feeling ragged around the edges
    seeking medical attention
    abusing your body

being REJECTED
    lacking support
    having the door slammed in your face
    taking an unpopular position
    being ostracized
    feeling excluded
    standing alone
    receiving disapproval

Opposing Cards: Some Possibilities

Strength—strength, stamina
Temperance—good health
Sun—vitality, strong constitution
Six of Wands—acclaim, recognition
Seven of Pentacles—material reward

Reinforcing Cards: Some Possibilities

Tower—hard times
Ten of Wands—struggling to make ends meet, hard times
Five of Cups—rejection, lack of support, loss of approval
Three of Swords—rejection, separation, lack of support

Description

The two figures on the Five of Pentacles are cold, hungry, tired, sick, and poor. They show us what it feels like to be without—to lack the basic ingredients of life. This is the specter that haunts so many in our world—a reality that is all too immediate. Those of us who are more fortunate may not have experienced this extreme, but we still recognize suffering. When we do not have what we want and need, it hurts.

In readings, the Five of Pentacles can represent several kinds of lack. First, there is poor health. It is hard to tackle life's challenges when we do not have our vitality and strength. This card can be a signal that you are neglecting the needs of your body. You are moving away from complete physical well-being, so you must take steps to discover and correct the problem.

This card can also be a sign of material and economic setbacks. There is no doubt that life is harder when we lack money or a decent job. When we are struggling to make ends meet, all other problems are magnified. Even if we are comfortable, we can still feel insecure, afraid that misfortune will take away all that we have worked for.

The Five of Pentacles can also represent rejection or lack of acceptance. We are social animals and feel pain when excluded from our group. We want to be included, not only for our emotional well-being, but also for mutual support. Being rejected can mean physical hardship as well.

The Five of Pentacles relates to material lack, but it also has a spiritual component. From the stained glass window, we can guess that these two figures are outside of a church. Comfort is so close at hand, but they fail to see it. The church symbolizes our spirits which are perfect and whole in every way. We are meant to enjoy abundance in all areas of life, but sometimes we forget that this is our birthright. Whenever you experience hardship, know that it is only temporary. Look for the spiritual center that will take you in and give you shelter.

Six of Pentacles

HAVING/NOT HAVING:
- RESOURCES

- KNOWLEDGE
- POWER

Actions

HAVING/NOT HAVING: RESOURCES
giving/receiving
taking care of/being taken care of
sponsoring/being sponsored
supporting/being supported
offering/receiving a gift or reward
acquiring/not acquiring what you need

HAVING/NOT HAVING: POWER
leading/following
dominating/submitting
acting with authority/deference
asserting/denying your wishes
coercing/being coerced
doing all the talking/listening

HAVING/NOT HAVING: KNOWLEDGE
teaching/learning
imparting/receiving information
becoming/finding a mentor
offering/taking advice
showing/being shown the ropes
knowing/not knowing a secret

Opposing Cards and Reinforcing Cards: Some Possibilities

Opposing and reinforcing cards do not work in the usual way with the Six of Pentacles because this card can mean either (or both) sides of the same issue—having or not having. The other cards in a reading can help you figure out which side applies in your case. The following cards also deal with this issue:

Empress—abundance, physical comfort
World—affluence, material fulfillment
Ten of Wands—struggling to make ends meet, hard times
Five of Pentacles—lack, not having
Seven of Pentacles—material reward, having
Ten of Pentacles—affluence, having

Description

The Six of Pentacles is a difficult card to describe because it falls in the shadowy area between the lack of the Five of Pentacles and the affluence of the Ten of Pentacles. These two cards represent the extremes of not having and having. The Six of Pentacles covers the huge middle ground where it is not exactly clear who has what.

On this card, a well-to-do gentleman is tossing a few coins to a beggar while another supplicant waits to the side. The giver holds the scales of justice as if claiming the right to decide who deserves blessings and who does not. In this picture we see both sides: what it means to give *and* to receive, to dominate *and* to submit, to be on top *and* to be on the bottom. It seems clear who has and who hasn't, but is it? Life is not that simple, and how quickly fortunes change.

In readings, the Six of Pentacles asks you to look very deeply into the whole issue of what *having* really means both materially (resources) and immaterially (knowledge, power, love). You may see yourself on one side or the other, but this card asks you to reconsider. Think of the successful businessman who suddenly declares bankruptcy. The tyrannical invalid who dominates through weakness. The teacher who learns from her students. The parent who controls by giving money.

The keywords for the Six of Pentacles include both the have and have not sides of each meaning. Sometimes this card is a clear sign one way or the other. You *will* get the gift, give advice or defer to another. In all cases, though, you should question the obvious and go deeper. Why are you in the situation you're in, and where is it leading? Who is really in charge? What's really going on?

Seven of Pentacles

- ASSESSMENT
- REWARD

- DIRECTION CHANGE

Actions

ASSESSING

    evaluating the status
    reflecting on progress to date
    reviewing what's been done
    pausing to check results
    making sure you're on course
    finding out where you stand
    taking stock

reaping a REWARD

    finally seeing some results
    enjoying the first fruits
    getting returns on investments
    receiving payoffs
    being able to let up a bit
    reaching a milestone

considering a DIRECTION CHANGE

    weighing a different approach
    pondering alternatives
    thinking about change
    opening to a new strategy
    questioning your choices
    standing at a crossroads

Opposing Cards: Some Possibilities

Wheel of Fortune—movement, action, direction change
Eight of Wands—rapid action
Five of Pentacles—lack of reward, hardship

Reinforcing Cards: Some Possibilities

Empress—material reward
Justice—assessing where you are, deciding a future course
Judgement—decision point
Four of Swords—rest, thinking things over

Description

On the Seven of Pentacles we see a man who has labored long and hard in his garden. The foliage is full, the blossoms are out—it seems that his work has paid off. Now he's taking a break to admire his handiwork. How satisfying it is to see such results! How rewarding is sweet success!

The Seven of Pentacles is a time-out card. It represents those moments after a rush of activity when we stop to catch our breath and look around. The man in the picture has paused to contemplate the fruits of his own labors, but he could also pick that fruit. In readings, the Seven of Pentacles can indicate a reward that will come your way, particularly as a result of your own efforts. Take it and enjoy.

This card is also a call for assessment. When we're busy, we don't take time to reflect on what we're doing and why. Are we still on course? Are we getting the results we want? Serious problems can develop if you don't take stock at key moments. This card asks you to take the time to be sure you're meeting your goals.

The Seven of Pentacles can also indicate a crossroads. In life, there's a tendency to continue with familiar routines. To go in a new direction isn't easy. The Seven of Pentacles may be telling you to figure out if you need a course correction, or even a complete about-face. You're not yet committed to a certain path, but you could be soon. Change is still possible.

The Seven of Pentacles is not a card of endings or final decisions. The game is not over, but only on hold for a moment. Once you've gotten your breath back and checked your strategy, be ready to jump back in and work even harder than before.

Eight of Pentacles

- DILIGENCE
- KNOWLEDGE

- DETAIL

Actions

showing DILIGENCE
    making an efort
    working hard
    applying yourself totally
    being absorbed in a project
    dedicating yourself to a task
    plugging away
    producing steady results

increasing KNOWLEDGE
    taking a course
    learning a new craft or skill
    receiving training
    pursuing greater understanding
    researching
    finding out the facts
    increasing expertise

paying attention to DETAIL
    being painstaking
    being extra careful
    approaching a task methodically
    getting down to the nitty-gritty
    handling all the loose ends
    checking and rechecking
    noticing the fine points

Opposing Cards: Some Possibilities

Four of Cups—lacking interest, not caring, apathetic
Seven of Cups—lazy, lacking drive

Reinforcing Cards: Some Possibilities

Magician—focus and concentration
Hierophant—learning, studying
Nine of Wands—keeping at it, persistence

Description

On the Eight of Pentacles we see a young man who is hammering away at a coin. He has finished six and has another coin to go. It is clear that he is in the middle of a project that absorbs all his attention. He's isolated himself from others (the town in the background) in order to concentrate. In this scene we see the essential elements of the Eight of Pentacles: hard work and attention to detail.

This card often implies a time of great diligence and focus. It advises you to *hammer away* at the business of the moment, whether a project, family difficulty, personal goal, or unpleasant duty. Sometimes blessings fall into our laps to be enjoyed. Other times we must put out great effort to obtain them. The Eight of Pentacles represents moments when you must give 110 percent. Just buckle down and do it. Fortunately, this kind of work is invigorating and leads to superb results. The labor of the Eight of Pentacles is deeply satisfying and productive.

The Eight of Pentacles can also symbolize the impulse to learn—to broaden horizons (to use an old-fashioned term). Sometimes we need to develop new skills. We do research, dig out facts, or search for greater expertise. The Hermit is looking for inner knowledge. The man on the Eight of Pentacles seeks external knowledge—the how and why of the material world.

This card can also show the need for meticulous attention. People who are painstaking are often dismissed as nitpickers, but their extra effort ensures everything is as it should be. It's a matter of caring—taking the time to check the little details. Now is not the time to be slipshod or casual. Look for errors, and tie up loose ends. The key to success is an extraordinary effort. Whatever your task, the Eight of Pentacles tells you to give it your all in every way.

Nine of Pentacles

- DISCIPLINE
- SELF-RELIANCE

- REFINEMENT

Actions

being DISCIPLINED
    exercising self-control
    showing restraint
    reining in impulses
    sacrificing to reach a goal
    sticking to a program
    taking a step-by-step approach

RELYING ON YOURSELF
    handling the situation alone
    acting on your own
    falling back on your own resources
    doing it all by yourself
    wanting to be alone
    feeling sure your way is best

pursuing REFINEMENT
    achieving a comfortable lifestyle
    avoiding the coarse and unsavory
    being tactful and diplomatic
    seeking high-minded activities
    enjoying the finer things of life
    remembering to be gracious
    enjoying leisure

Opposing Cards: Some Possibilities

Empress—earthy sensuality
Seven of Cups—being undisciplined, self-indulgent
Three of Pentacles—working in a team, doing with others

Reinforcing Cards: Some Possibilities

Chariot—self-control, discipline
Seven of Swords—relying on yourself, acting on your own

Description

The woman on the Nine of Pentacles is taking a leisurely stroll through the gardens of her estate. She is clearly a lady of refinement and grace, so it is incongruous to see on her left hand a bird trained to hunt and kill on command. Falconry is an unusual hobby for a gentlewoman, but it is the key to the special nature of this card.

On one hand, the Nine of Pentacles represents all that is gracious, high-minded, and civilized. Art, music, and other forms of beauty are very much part of our physical world (Pentacles). Coins are present in this scene, but they are toward the ground. The business of life is important, but we don't have to focus on practical matters all the time. We can enjoy the finer things of life. In readings, the Nine of Pentacles can imply an interest in these areas. It is also a sign that you may need to reject the coarse or offensive and seek the highest.

The Nine of Pentacles can also be a sign of discipline and self-control. This woman enjoys her cultured life because she has mastered her baser instincts. Her impulses work for her because they do not rule her. The falcon symbolizes all that is dark and unruly in human nature. Our shadow side can serve us well, but only when it is directed. Sometimes the Nine of Pentacles suggests that you must show restraint and self-control if you are to achieve your best efforts. You may have to "sacrifice" for the moment, but the results will be worth it.

This card is also a sign of self-reliance. Sometimes you must trust your own ability to handle a situation. Resist the temptation to let others do for you. You need to take matters into your own hands. Our elegant lady has done just that. She trusted in her own grit and determination, and now she enjoys all the best life has to offer.

Ten of Pentacles

- AFFLUENCE
- PERMANENCE

- CONVENTION

Actions

enjoying AFFLUENCE
    having material abundance
    being free from money problems
    enjoying business success
    feeling financially secure
    seeing your ventures flourish
    having a run of good fortune

seeking PERMANENCE
    looking for a solution that will last
    creating a lasting foundation
    feeling secure as things are
    being concerned with the long term
    having an orderly family life
    moving beyond makeshift arrangements
    nailing down the plan

following CONVENTION
    staying within established guidelines
    proceeding according to the rules
    taking part in traditions
    becoming part of the Establishment
    being conservative
    trusting in the tried-and-true
    continuing in known patterns

Opposing Cards: Some Possibilities

Two of Wands—being original, avoiding convention
Three of Wands—exploring, going into untested areas
Five of Pentacles—hard times, material lack

Reinforcing Cards: Some Possibilities

Empress—affluence, luxury, physical comfort
Hierophant—conforming, following rules, conservative
Lovers—permanent unions, family ties
World—affluence, material fulfillment
Four of Pentacles—enjoying the status quo, conserving

Description

On many cards, we see a cluster of buildings off in the distance. In the Ten of Pentacles, we finally arrive in that village—in the middle of the marketplace. The family we see is carrying on the affairs of everyday life. A patriarch, dressed in a luxurious robe, pats his hounds as he watches over the younger generations. A man and woman converse in passing as their child plays at their feet. Coins (money) are in the air.

The Ten of Pentacles stands for the ultimate in worldly and material success. Sometimes I jokingly call it the "fat cat" card because it reminds me of the aura of prosperity that surrounds wealthy men and women of business. This is the card you want to see if you are wondering how your latest enterprise will turn out. Wealth and affluence are yours.

When we achieve material success, we naturally want it to last. This is the conservative, Establishment side of the Ten of Pentacles. Why rock the boat when life is fine just the way it is? In readings, this card often stands for convention—following established guidelines and maintaining the status quo. Fat cats are rarely radicals; they love tradition and the tried-and-true. Sometimes it is important to trust the known ways, but only when change is inadvisable.

The Ten of Pentacles is also concerned with permanence. Change is an unavoidable part of life, but constant change is uncomfortable. We need stability and the chance to work for a secure foundation in life. In readings, this card may be telling you to concentrate on the long term. Work toward a lasting solution. Now may be the time to settle down and make the arrangements that will work for you far into the future.

Page of Pentacles

- HAVE AN EFFECT
- BE PRACTICAL
- BE PROSPEROUS
- BE TRUSTING/TRUSTWORTHY

Actions

HAVE AN EFFECT

make your plans real
mold the physical world
use your body
experience nature
achieve tangible results
act on your dreams
set events in motion

BE PRACTICAL

take a realistic approach
apply the tools at hand
find a solution that works
use common sense
stop daydreaming
work with what you have
concentrate on what's effective

BE PROSPEROUS

draw to you what you need
increase your means
grow and expand
enrich yourself
go out to meet success
seek abundance
become secure

BE TRUSTING/TRUSTWORTHY

accept that the solution is well in hand
have faith in others
accommodate uncertainty
accept others at their word
keep your word
prove yourself dependable
stick by your commitments
establish credibility

Cour Card Pairs

The Page of Pentacles can form a pair with any other court card. Compare the ranks and suits of the two cards to see what such a pair might mean.

Description

The Page of Pentacles is a messenger bringing you opportunities for prosperity. He delivers real chances to experience wealth, abundance, security, and solid achievement—the wonders of the Pentacles suit. In your readings, this Page suggests that an opening may appear that promises enrichment, comfort, trust, or the chance to make your dreams real. When you see such a chance, act on it!

The Page of Pentacles can also stand for a child or young-at-heart adult whose interactions with you involve stability, trust, commitment, safety, and material needs. Sometimes the Page of Pentacles implies that your entire situation is suffused with the spirit of physical enjoyment. At such times, feel free to have fun with your body, skills, and possessions in a lighthearted way. Revel in the delights of being alive on the Earth at this time.

Knight of Pentacles

- UNWAVERING/STUBBORN
- CAUTIOUS/UNADVENTUROUS
- THOROUGH/OBSESSIVE
- REALISTIC/PESSIMISTIC
- HARDWORKING/GRINDING

Actions

UNWAVERING/STUBBORN

is dogged in pursuit of a goal/is hardheaded and obstinate
will not quit/digs into a position
stands firm against opposition/must have his or her own way
stays fixed to a chosen course/refuses to listen to reason
keeps true to personal convictions/resists compromise

CAUTIOUS/UNADVENTUROUS

checks and double-checks/is too conservative
examines all angles beforehand/misses chances by waiting
proceeds slowly and carefully/is reluctant to try something new
prefers the safe, known path/settles for safe, small gains
is prudent and careful/is afraid of risking

THOROUGH/OBSESSIVE

takes care of every detail/does not know when to quit
is meticulous/is too picky
wraps up all loose ends/must have everything just so
never leaves a job half done/is inflexible and compulsive
is painstaking/insists on perfection
completes anything started/can't leave well enough alone

REALISTIC/PESSIMISTIC

is willing to look at the facts/concentrates on what's wrong
faces the truth/thinks others are dreamers
is not lured by false hopes/sees a glass as half empty, not half full
assesses circumstances candidly/takes the gloomy view
predicts problems in advance/dooms a project from the start

HARDWORKING/GRINDING

becomes dedicated to a task/focuses too narrowly on work
is diligent and industrious/can be humorless and grim
produces as much as two people/sees playtime as wasteful
tackles any chore vigorously/drives everyone too hard
is tireless and unflagging/forgets life should be fun

Court Card Pairs

The Knight of Pentacles can form a pair with any other court card. Compare the ranks and suits of the two cards to see what such a pair might mean.

Description

On the positive side, the Knight of Pentacles is like a bulldog. Once he bites down, you can be sure he won't let go. He's dogged in pursuit of his goals. A hard worker, he has tremendous stamina and dedication. Every job is always completed down to the last detail. He's careful and prudent, never wasteful. He knows the facts and is immune to false promises. On the negative side, this Knight is a bit stodgy and dull. He's not known for his playful sense of humor. Work always comes first. He tends to be inflexible and obsessive about little details. Stubborn to a fault, he refuses to give in even when wrong, something he'll never admit. He doesn't like change or risk and will always take the gloomiest view.

In readings, a Knight of Pentacles shows that his cautious style is involved in the situation as an aspect of you, someone else, or the atmosphere in general. You need to ask yourself, "Is this Knight's energy helping or hurting?"

If his style is evident, then balance is needed. Are you working too hard? Do you refuse to listen to reason? Do you have a perfectionist in your life? Is the atmosphere around you one of gloom and doom? It may be time for a change.

If this Knight's energy is missing, a dose of prudence may be called for. Are you spending too much? Maybe it's time to slow down. Do you give up too soon? Dig in and refuse to quit. Is your work often careless, late, or incomplete? Next time resolve to work up a sweat and get the job done. Let the Knight of Pentacles introduce you to his world of care and persistence.

Queen of Pentacles

- NURTURING
- BIGHEARTED
- DOWN-TO-EARTH

- RESOURCEFUL
- TRUSTWORTHY

Actions

NURTURING

gives love and support
creates a warm, secure environment
makes people feel better
responds to the natural world
has a green thumb
has a way with children and animals

BIGHEARTED

will do any service for others
is a soft touch
always has an open door and welcoming
    smile
gives freely and abundantly
is warm, generous, and unselfish

DOWN-TO-EARTH

handles problems matter-of-factly
allows others to be themselves
has no pretensions or affectations
takes a simple, sensible approach
appreciates all the senses

RESOURCEFUL

finds a use for whatever's at hand
is handy and versatile
makes a little go a long way
gets around every obstacle
comes up with what's needed

TRUSTWORTHY

keeps confidences and secrets
is loyal and steadfast
comes through in a pinch
keeps faith with others
is true to his/her word

Court Card Pairs

The Queen of Pentacles can form a pair with any other court card. Compare the ranks and suits of the two cards to see what such a pair might mean.

Description

The personality of the Queen of Pentacles combines the positive earth energy of the Pentacles suit with the inward focus of a Queen. If you were to visit the Queen of Pentacles, the first thing she would say is, "Come in, come in. It's great to see you. Have a bowl of soup!" No one is more welcoming and nurturing than she. Her greatest pleasure is to care for others—making sure they are happy and secure. Her home is always overflowing with children, pets, plants, and footloose friends. She is warm and generous to all. In day-to-day matters, she is sensible and practical. She doesn't have a lot of time for elaborate plans and other craziness. If something needs doing, she just takes care of it without a lot

of fuss and bother. There is a down-to-earth, matter-of-factness about her. She is always loyal and steadfast. Because she is trusting by nature, others trust her completely. When you are hurting or in need, the Queen of Pentacles will calm your fears and share your troubles.

In readings, the Queen of Pentacles asks you to *think and feel* as she does. For example: Are you feeling warm and caring toward others? Are you being sensible? Have you been true to your word? Do you feel generous? Can you be counted on when times are tough?

This Queen can also represent a man or woman who is like her, or an atmosphere of warmth, trust, and security. In a reading, she tells you that her special energy has meaning for you at this time. Let yourself be inspired by this Queen in whatever form she appears in your life.

King of Pentacles

- ENTERPRISING
- ADEPT
- RELIABLE

- SUPPORTING
- STEADY

Actions

ENTERPRISING

   makes any venture successful
   finds opportunity everywhere
   attracts wealth
   takes an idea and makes it work
   is a natural manager and business person
   has the Midas touch

ADEPT

   is informed about practical matters
   has a wide range of natural abilities
   has quick reflexes
   is skillful with his/her hands
   handles any situation competently

RELIABLE

   meets all commitments and promises
   assumes responsibility
   is dependable and unfailing
   can be counted on in a crisis
   serves as a rock for others to lean on

SUPPORTING

   encourages the accomplishments of others
   readily jumps in to help
   is a philanthropist
   gives generously of time and attention
   sponsors worthwhile projects

STEADY

   works toward a goal with firm resolve
   avoids mood and behavior swings
   has regular habits and activities
   maintains a calm, even approach
   is a stabilizing influence

Court Card Pairs

The King of Pentacles can form a pair with any other court card. Compare the ranks and suits of the two cards to see what such a pair might mean.

Description

The personality of the King of Pentacles is a combination of the positive earth energy of the Pentacles suit and the active, outward focus of a King. He might as well be called King Midas as he turns everything he touches to gold (riches of all kinds). He finds opportunity everywhere and succeeds at whatever he sets his mind to. He is enterprising and adept. Whatever the task, he handles it competently, drawing on his wide range of skills and practical knowledge. He's a jack-of-all-trades—and master of all as well. He is always dependable and responsible. Others rely on him completely because he never fails them. He gives generously of his time and resources because he knows that by giving more, you receive more.

He encourages others in their accomplishments and lends his support whenever it is needed. He has a steady and even temperament that adds an element of stability to any situation. When he has set a goal for himself, he pursues it with firm resolve until he's successful.

In readings, the King of Pentacles asks you to take the kinds of *actions* he might take. For example: keeping a commitment, fixing something that's broken, making money, or sponsoring a new enterprise. This King can also represent a man or woman who is acting as he does, or an atmosphere of steady, reliable competence. In a reading, he tells you that his special energy has meaning for you at this time. Let yourself be inspired by this King in whatever form he appears in your life.

V

THE CELTIC CROSS SPREAD

The Celtic Cross

Introduction

The Celtic Cross is probably the oldest and most popular pattern for reading the tarot. It has survived so long because the layout of the cards is simple, but powerful. A strong energy has built up around this spread due to its use by so many people over the years.

Celtic Cross Spread

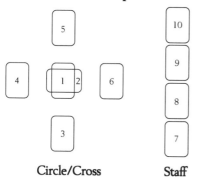

Circle/Cross   Staff

You can think of the Celtic Cross as divided into two sections: the Circle/Cross (six cards) on the left, and the Staff (four cards) on the right.

The Circle/Cross simulates the Celtic cross found throughout Ireland. This cross has a circle linking the four perpendicular spokes. The circle and cross symbolize the joining of spirit and matter and the unity of all events in time. (See the example cross on page 276.)

The feminine energy of the circular section works in unison with the masculine energy of the Staff section. These two parts of the Celtic Cross mirror the dual nature of manifested reality—the polarities that abound in the human psyche.

The Circle/Cross section is made up of two crosses—a central one (two cards) nested within a larger cross (six cards). The smaller cross represents the heart of the matter—what is most central to you at the time of the reading. It is the hub around which the wheel of your life is turning.

The larger cross consists of two lines that overlay the minicross. The horizontal line shows time moving from your past on the left into your future on the right. The vertical line is your awareness moving from your unconscious on the bottom to your conscious mind on the top. Together these six cards give you a snapshot of your inner and outer environment at the time of a reading.

The cards of the Staff section comment on your life and lie outside of the immediate situation. Here, your Inner Guide helps you understand what is shown in the Circle/Cross section. You receive guidance about yourself and others, your life lessons, and your future direction.

There are a number of versions of the Celtic Cross. The differences are usually in Positions 3-4-5-6. I use a circular placement to emphasize how the unconscious and the past (Cards 3 and 4) lead

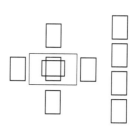

Smaller Cross

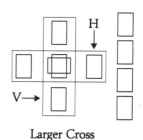

Larger Cross

This is the High Cross of Muredach. (From Derek Bryce, *Symbolism of the Celtic Cross*, York Beach, ME: Samuel Weiser, 1995, p. 113.)

to the conscious and future (Cards 5 and 6). I have also added some meanings to Card 9. This position traditionally means "hopes and fears," but I also use it as a lesson or guidance card. It is always possible to adapt a spread to your own needs as long as you decide on any changes before you do a reading.

Interpretation of the Celtic Cross

Here is one approach to interpreting the Celtic Cross.

1. Look at the six cards of the Circle/Cross section. They show what is going on in your life at the moment of the reading.
2. Examine the cards in pairs, perhaps in the following order:
   a. Look at Cards 1 and 2 to find out the central dynamic.
   b. Look at Cards 3 and 5 to find out what is going on within you at different levels.
   c. Look at Cards 4 and 6 to see how people and events are flowing through your life. From these six cards, create a description of your immediate situation.
3. Consider the Staff section of the spread, perhaps in this order:
   a. Look at Cards 7 and 8 to find out more about the relationship between you and your environment.

b. Look at Card 10—the projected outcome. How do you feel about it? What does it say to you?

4. Review the cards to discover the factors leading to the outcome. See if one card stands out as key. Also:

a. Compare the projected outcome (Card 10) to a possible alternative outcome (Card 5).

b. Consider how the near future (Card 6) contributes to the projected outcome (Card 10).

c. See if Card 9 tells you something you need to know. Do you have a hope or fear that is relevant?

Tarot Keywords Celtic Cross Spread

POSITION 1	POSITION 2	POSITION 3
Heart of the Matter Present Environment (Outer) Present Environment (Inner) Primary Factor	Opposing Factor Factor for Change Secondary Factor Reinforcing Factor	Root Cause Unconscious Influence Deeper Meaning Unknown Factor
POSITION 4	**POSITION 5**	**POSITION 6**
Past Receding Influence Resolved Factor Quality to Let Go	Attitudes and Beliefs Conscious Influence Goal or Purpose Alternate Future	Future Approaching Influence Unresolved Factor Quality to Embrace
POSITION 7	**POSITION 8**	**POSITION 9**
You as You Are You as You Could Be You as You Present Yourself You as You See Yourself	Outside Environment Another's Point of View Another's Expectations You as Others See You	Guidance Key Factor Hopes and Fears Overlooked Factor
	POSITION 10	
	Outcome (Overall) Outcome (Inner State) Outcome (Actions) Outcome (Effects)	

Celtic Cross Position 1

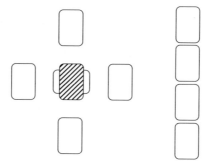

• HEART OF THE MATTER
• PRESENT ENVIRONMENT
  (OUTER)

  HEART OF THE MATTER
      central issue
      major concern
      basic worry or upset
      primary focus
      focal point
      fundamental problem

  PRESENT ENVIRONMENT (OUTER)
      "that which covers you"
          —traditional
      surrounding circumstances
      immediate problem at hand
      what's going on around you
      what you're dealing with
      external factors

• PRESENT ENVIRONMENT
  (INNER)
• PRIMARY FACTOR

  PRESENT ENVIRONMENT (INNER)
      internal factors
      how you feel about the situation
      key personal quality
      basic state of mind
      emotional state
      what's going on inside of you

  PRIMARY FACTOR
      major influence
      dominant characteristic
      outstanding feature
      most important element
      most striking quality

Celtic Cross Position 2

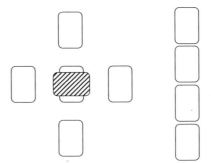

• OPPOSING FACTOR
• FACTOR FOR CHANGE

OPPOSING FACTOR
    "that which is crossing you"
      —traditional
    contrary element
    source of resistance
    balancing tendency
    moderating influence
    rival or subversive agent

FACTOR FOR CHANGE
    something out of left field
    unpredictable element
    new consideration
    unbalancing force
    surprise
    what's rocking the boat

• SECONDARY FACTOR
• REINFORCING FACTOR

SECONDARY FACTOR
    tangential concern
    another source of information
    side issue
    subordinate problem
    minor factor

REINFORCING FACTOR
    supporting feature
    additional emphasis
    cooperating person
    extra attraction
    magnifying force
    related issue

Placement:
To place card 2 correctly, rotate the card 90° clockwise and lay it on top of card 1. Card 2 is reversed if the top of the card's image is on the left after placement.

Celtic Cross Position 3

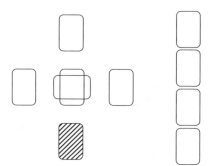

• ROOT CAUSE
• UNCONSCIOUS INFLUENCE

ROOT CAUSE

   source of the problem
   basis of the situation
   why things are as they are
   childhood or past life (karmic)
      influence
   reason behind events
   starting point

UNCONSCIOUS INFLUENCE

   "that which is beneath you"
      —traditional
   unrecognized motivations
   unacknowledged goals
   most basic impulses
   driving needs or desires
   denied or rejected aspects of self

• DEEPER MEANING
• UNKNOWN FACTOR

DEEPER MEANING

   larger picture
   fundamental pattern
   all-embracing point of view
   soul purpose
   underlying context
   what's really going on

UNKNOWN FACTOR

   hidden influence
   unrecognized contribution
   undiscovered participant
   concealed agenda
   behind-the-scenes machinations

Celtic Cross Position 4

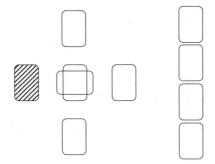

- PAST
- RECEDING INFLUENCE

SOMETHING RELATED TO THE PAST
quality
person
belief
event
opportunity
orientation
concern
hope
fear

RECEDING INFLUENCE
feature that is losing importance
fading concern
former focus
someone/something going away
falling star

- RESOLVED FACTOR
- QUALITY TO LET GO

RESOLVED FACTOR
fully realized quality
completed task
what's been wrapped up
what can be set aside
what's been taken care of

QUALITY TO LET GO
outmoded approach
what's no longer useful
unnecessary baggage
someone/something no longer
    needed
factor to be discarded

Celtic Cross Position 5

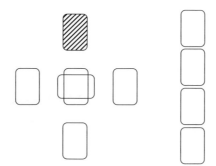

• ATTITUDES AND BELIEFS
• CONSCIOUS INFLUENCE

ATTITUDES AND BELIEFS
  what you accept as true
  assumptions
  convictions
  how you view what is happening
  delusions or illusions
  where you are placing your trust

CONSCIOUS INFLUENCE
  what's on your mind
  what you're focusing on
  what you're worried about
  what you're obsessed about
  what you acknowledge
  what is known

• GOAL OR PURPOSE
• ALTERNATE FUTURE

GOAL OR PURPOSE
  aspirations
  what you intend to achieve
  expectations for the future
  what you've set your heart on
  preferences
  desired result

ALTERNATE FUTURE
  "what could come into being"
      —traditional
  potential development
  different possibility
  another option
  what you *think* will happen
  future you are consciously projecting

Celtic Cross Position 6

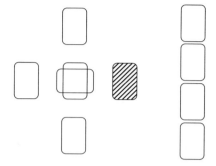

- FUTURE
- APPROACHING INFLUENCE

SOMETHING RELATED TO THE FUTURE
  quality
  person
  belief
  event
  opportunity
  orientation
  concern
  hope
  fear

APPROACHING INFLUENCE
  feature that is gaining importance
  developing concern
  coming focus
  someone/something coming nearer
  rising star

- UNRESOLVED FACTOR
- QUALITY TO EMBRACE

UNRESOLVED FACTOR
  unrealized quality
  incomplete task
  what is still pending
  what must be considered
  what needs to be taken care of

QUALITY TO EMBRACE
  valid approach
  what will be useful
  desirable attribute
  someone/something that is needed
  factor to be welcomed

Celtic Cross Position 7

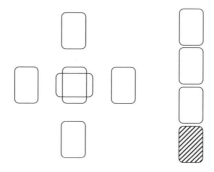

- YOU AS YOU ARE
- YOU AS YOU COULD BE

- YOU AS YOU PRESENT YOURSELF
- YOU AS YOU SEE YOURSELF

YOU AS YOU ARE

 personal style
 your temperament or disposition
 your approach to the problem
 your unique orientation
 your point of view
 your way of being
 your position or stance

YOU AS YOU COULD BE

 inner resource to tap
 talent or ability you can use
 what you are capable of
 an ideal to live up to
 a possible approach
 what you want to be
 your goal for yourself

YOU AS YOU PRESENT YOURSELF

 your public face
 how you think you should be
 mask you show the world
 what you do for appearance' sake
 role you accept
 self-imposed duty
 your false self

YOU AS YOU SEE YOURSELF (TRADITIONAL)

 your self-image
 your beliefs about yourself
 your sense of where you are
 your fears about yourself
 your assumptions about yourself
 how you limit yourself
 how you magnify yourself

Celtic Cross Position 8

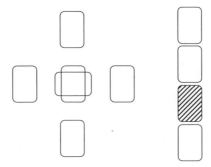

- OUTSIDE ENVIRONMENT
- ANOTHER'S POINT OF VIEW

OUTSIDE ENVIRONMENT
> "that which surrounds you"
>> —traditional
> atmosphere
> emotional climate
> physical and social milieu
> setting for the situation
> playing field
> context in which you must operate

ANOTHER'S POINT OF VIEW
> how another sees the situation
> the other person's side
> another slant on the problem
> different outlook
> an objective opinion

- ANOTHER'S EXPECTATIONS
- YOU AS OTHERS SEE YOU

ANOTHER'S EXPECTATIONS
> what others want from you
> demands placed on you
> what another thinks you should be
>> or do
> claims of others on you
> outside restrictions imposed on you
> your assigned role

YOU AS OTHERS SEE YOU
> "how others see you"—traditional
> how you are coming across
> how you're being assessed
> public opinion about you
> impression you create
> effect you have on others

Celtic Cross Position 9

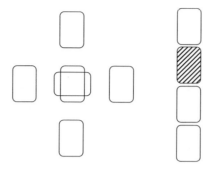

• GUIDANCE
• KEY FACTOR

• HOPES AND FEARS
• OVERLOOKED FACTOR

GUIDANCE

what you might do
how best to proceed
how you can make a change
word of warning
truth of the matter
different approach
helpful suggestion
honest assessment

KEY FACTOR

fundamental aspect
lesson to be learned
what explains everything
clue to what is happening
what you need to know
connecting link

HOPES AND FEARS (TRADITIONAL)

what you're afraid of
what you suspect is true
what you're avoiding
personal demon
what you long for
your dream
your ideal
your secret desire

OVERLOOKED FACTOR

something you haven't considered
missing piece of the puzzle
someone else who has a role to play
something else to consider
element of surprise
underestimated influence

Celtic Cross Position 10

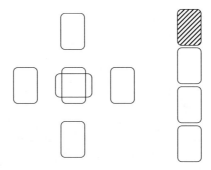

- OUTCOME (OVERALL)
- OUTCOME (INNER STATE)

- OUTCOME (ACTIONS)
- OUTCOME (EFFECTS)

OUTCOME (OVERALL)
  the most likely result
  what may come to pass
  how the situation may be resolved
  where everything is leading
  probable resolution

OUTCOME (INNER STATE)
  how you will end up feeling
  what your mood will be
  understanding you will gain
  lesson you will absorb
  attitude you will assume
  quality or ability you will realize

OUTCOME (ACTIONS)
  what you may have to do
  how you may succeed or fail
  conduct you will have to adopt
  required behavior
  what you may accomplish
  approach you may have to take

OUTCOME (EFFECTS)
  how someone else will be affected
  how the environment will change
  what others will do
  possible countermeasure or backlash
  possible benefit or reward
  improvement that will occur
  change in status

Jill's Readings

Introduction

Jill's tale is a series of three readings I did for a friend over the course of a year. These readings illustrate how the tarot can reflect developments over time. Every reading is a snapshot of a given moment. As events unfold, the snapshots change, but there is a common thread that connects them. In this series about one woman's experience, you can see how new elements interact with those that endure. (Reversed cards were not used.)

In the interpretations, phrases in SMALL CAPITALS are meanings taken from card information pages. *Italic* phrases are taken from position pages. I recommend laying out the cards selected so you can experience these readings too.

Jill's First Reading

This first reading took place in January 1990 as an Open Reading for Jill (not her real name). Jill had been adopted at eleven months. She wanted to learn all she could about her first year. For several months, she had been trying to gain information about her birth mother and, to a lesser extent, her birth father.

Jill tried to go through the agency that handled her adoption, but found that most of the information was closed to her. At the time of the reading, she had decided to pursue legal options to gain access. These are the cards she drew:

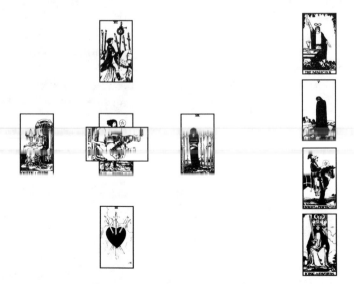

Celtic Cross with cards from Jill's first reading.

When these cards were laid down, both of us were immediately drawn to the Three of Swords—the *root cause* of the situation. This card perfectly symbolizes the HEARTBREAK and LONELINESS Jill must have felt as a baby being abruptly separated from her birth parents and foster family. Note the three swords—Jill and her two parents—piercing their communal heart.

The BETRAYAL meaning is also important. At some level, Jill feels betrayed by many people: her adoptive parents who deny her search, the agency who thwarts it, and her birth parents whom Jill may *unconsciously* resent for leaving her.

The many court cards suggest a need for balance. First, there is the central Cups/Pentacles pair (Cards 1 and 2). They symbolize the conflict between Jill's wish to fantasize about the future (Cups) and her need to be realistic (Pentacles). This theme will turn out to be a *primary focus* for Jill in the months to come.

The Page of Pentacles shows Jill's need to focus on PRACTICAL matters in order to win her legal case and learn about her origins. The Knight of Cups shows her countertendency to dream UNREALISTICALLY about what finding her birth mother will be like. He suggests that Jill lacks moderation in her emotions. As a Knight, he shows that her hopes are OVERLY ROMANTIC.

This idea is reinforced by the Queen of Cups as Card 4. The word "mother" popped into my mind in relation to this card. It occurred to me that the Queen of Cups had a special meaning in this case. She is the dream mother Jill hopes to find; one who is completely LOVING and TENDERHEARTED. This desire from the *past* is propelling Jill into her current situation.

Another important pair is the King of Swords as Card 7 and the Knight of Pentacles as Card 8. The King of Swords suggests that Jill *sees herself* as the agent of HONESTY and JUSTICE in this situation. She feels it is her right to learn the truth about her first year of life. Also, in the week before the reading, Jill had prepared a position paper for the court. She used the talents of the King of Swords—his keen ANALYTICAL ABILITY, INTELLECT, and WRITING SKILLS.

The Knight of Pentacles suggests that *other people may be seeing* Jill as TOO SERIOUS and DRIVEN. Since they do not appreciate her intensity, they *judge* her as TOO OBSESSED to compromise. Whether or not this view is justified, it is valuable information. If Jill alienates the agency and the legal system, she reduces her chances for success. The Knight of Pentacles hints that Jill should temper any appearance of INFLEXIBILITY with a moderated, reasonable approach.

The Five of Cups as Card 9 is the *key to the whole situation*. It represents LOSS, beginning with the original loss of her birth parents. Now, Jill must be willing to let go of her dream mother so a true relationship can form with her actual birth mother, whoever she may be. Jill is also *afraid* she may LOSE her court case.

The Eight of Swords suggests that some confusing moments *lie ahead*. There will be times when Jill feels POWERLESS as she tries to balance her conflicting feelings. Also, outside forces may temporarily RESTRICT her search.

On the other hand, the Six of Wands as Card 5 and the Magician as Card 10 could not be more positive. The Six of Wands shows the strength of Jill's *conscious belief* in her ability to overcome her legal obstacles and emerge TRIUMPHANT. She knows she can achieve the victory predicted by the Magician. As the only major arcana card in the reading, the Magician shows the extra dimension of POWER waiting for Jill when she realizes her goal. If she can consolidate her inner strengths and accept her losses consciously, she will meet with great success.

Jill's Second Reading

In June 1990, I did an Other Reading about Jill and her situation. The events which had transpired were so dramatic that I felt drawn to see what the tarot would say about them.

In March, Jill met with a judge who was so convinced by the validity of her search that she ruled the adoption files should be opened. Through hard work, Jill located her birth parents within three weeks. Her father was reluctant to speak with her at first, but her mother welcomed her warmly after a surprise meeting in a distant city.

I truly felt Jill had realized the positive outcome projected for her in the first reading. She trusted her abilities and accomplished all her goals in a very short time; however, this drama was about to take an unexpected turn.

Jill and her birth mother quickly formed a close relationship. While Jill was staying with her mother, her birth father reestablished contact. Her parents spoke to each other for the first time in over thirty years, and soon they renewed their original romantic relationship! It was at this time that I decided to do a reading. I wanted to understand the highly charged energy that surrounded this situation. The question I wrote was, "What is the nature and cause of the intertwining life dramas of Jill, her birth mother, and her birth father?" Here are the cards I chose:

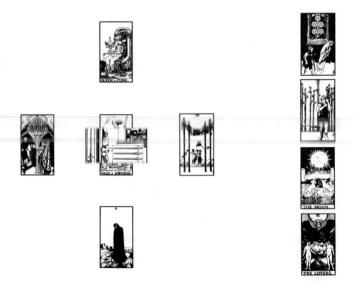

Celtic Cross with cards from Jill's second reading.

We again see a Page as Card 1. Jill's *situation* is still an *opportunity to act*, but this time she is facing a CHALLENGE. Jill must be TRUTHFUL with herself and approach this situation with FORTITUDE and CLARITY OF THOUGHT (Swords).

The Four of Swords as Card 2 tells her how to *support* herself through this period. She must EXAMINE HER ACTIONS AND MOTIVATIONS scrupulously. She must also NURTURE A STILL, QUIET CENTER in herself so that she can ride this emotional roller coaster.

In Cards 3 and 5 we see the links between this reading and the first. In Card 5, we again see the "dream mother"—the Queen of Cups. It seems that Jill has not let this ideal go, but has instead placed it firmly in *her conscious mind*. She is *thinking and feeling about* her birth mother most of the time.

In January, the Five of Cups showed that transmuting emotional loss is a *key lesson* for Jill in this drama. Now, this card has moved to Card 3. The regret Jill feels about her birth has become lodged firmly in her *unconscious*. At a *deep level*, she is mourning the loss of her loved ones and the dream of what might have been. This reenactment of her birth triangle is also triggering a fear that she will LOSE her parents again.

The Three of Pentacles as Card 4 suggests that the TEAMWORK Jill has enjoyed with her birth parents may become *a thing of the past*. The position of the figures on this card is revealing. Two are together while the other stands alone. The solitary figure is half turned away as if she can't decide if she is part of the twosome or not. In studying this card, I noticed for the first time the tipped cup in the right hand of the lone figure. How clearly it echoes the overturned cups in the Five of Cups and the losses they represent!

The Four of Wands as Card 6 is cause for CELEBRATION. Whatever else Jill's situation may bring, it seems that the *near future* will be EXCITING.

Cards 7 and 8 carry extra weight because they are major arcana cards. They spell out an important conflict between Jill and her environment. *Jill's point of view* is the Lovers. She wants to forge the bonds of LOVE and RELATIONSHIP that were denied her originally. She is also coming to terms with the fact that her parents are becoming lovers *literally*.

Unfortunately, *Jill's environment* is one of FEAR and ILLUSION. The Moon symbolizes the UNCERTAINTIES that arise when events are not what they seem and people do not mean what they say. In this case, there is no willful deceit, just lack of clarity. No one means any harm, but everyone is unsure of their real needs.

It appears that Jill is heading toward some REJECTION as pictured in the Five of Pentacles (Card 10). The lack of unity showing up throughout this reading suggests that Jill could *find herself* LEFT OUT IN THE COLD, SHUNNED as the odd person out.

Jill's strength lies with the TRUTH. The Page of Swords (Card 1) reminds her of the central need for CLARITY and HONESTY. In the meantime, Jill should prepare for the worst. The Nine of Wands as Card 9 *tells her* she must be DEFENSIVE and prepare to draw on her hidden reserves. There may be CELEBRATION in the *near future*, but there will also be hard times as Jill seeks to find her way with truth in her new relationships.

Jill's Third Reading

The third reading for Jill was held in her presence in November 1990. In July, Jill's birth father visited her mother, and the budding romance between the two blossomed. In August,

Jill and her mother traveled to the distant state where her father lived. There were positive aspects to the trip, but the visit took a troubling turn toward the end. Jill experienced the rejection anticipated in the second reading when her father's door was literally slammed in her face one night. She was turned out onto the street when the tensions between them reached a climax.

Jill's mother never returned from that trip. She left her husband and all her belongings to move in with Jill's father. From that point on, Jill's interaction with the two was often tense. There were several dramatic, even frightening, occurrences that were very upsetting to Jill. At the time of the reading, she wanted very much to find out where this situation was heading. The question she wrote was: "How will my relationship with my birth mother and birth father develop in the future?"

Here are the cards she drew:

Celtic Cross with cards from Jill's third reading.

We can see that the energies of Jill's situation are still in evidence. There are four repeat cards. The Eight of Swords has moved from Card 6 (reading 1) to Card 5. The RESTRICTION that was in *the future* is now *the basis of the situation*. The emotional events of the past year have been so turbulent that Jill feels POWERLESS at a *fundamental level.*

The Nine of Wands has moved from Card 9 (reading 2) to Card 5. This card was a warning to Jill to take care of herself and PREPARE FOR THE WORST. Well, she has certainly started to *think along those lines!* Having been burned, she knows she has to be strong and DEFENSIVE emotionally.

The Four of Wands has moved from Card 6 (reading 2) to Card 4. The CELEBRATION over the reunion *is fading*. The excitement of the good times has *moved through* Jill's life and is now *way behind her*.

Cards 7 and 8 show that *Jill's expectations* still do not match *her parents'*. Jill longs for a SECURE, ORDERLY family life (Ten of Pentacles). She wants a solution that will ENDURE—nothing more than the chance to experience the ORDINARY ROUTINES of a normal family.

Her parents, however, are locked into an OBSESSIVE RELATIONSHIP symbolized by the Devil. What Jill viewed as the Lovers in reading 2 is really the BONDAGE of two souls who do not have enough self-understanding to create a love that includes their daughter.

Jill needs a resolution, and there are two cards that suggest it is coming. First is the Eight of Wands as Card 1. This card shows that a CONCLUSION is likely. Jill will be able to COMPLETE UNFINISHED BUSINESS if she takes QUICK, DECISIVE ACTION.

Death shows that a major ENDING is approaching in the *near future*. Perhaps the three will suffer a PARTING OF THE WAYS. Maybe Jill will make a TRANSITION into a new kind of relationship with her parents.

The Empress as the *outcome* or *resolution* is a positive sign because it shows that the ideal of the Mother is the understanding awaiting Jill in this situation. The Empress is the archetype of MOTHERING—the ability to love, cherish, and nurture despite all temptations away from that response. Jill felt this card also meant a refocusing on her own role as a mother.

How is Jill to proceed if she wants to bring about this positive resolution? The key lies in the two Pentacles court cards. The Page as Card 9 is the fourth repeat card; it appeared first as Card 1 (reading 1). It reinforces the idea that *Jill's lesson* is about TRUST and the ABILITY TO ACT ON YOUR DREAMS.

Jill found her birth parents despite many formidable obstacles, but she discovered that the reality was not the same as her fantasy. She learned to trust herself and not rely on the support of others to see her through. The King of Pentacles as Card 2 tells Jill not to seek salvation through other people. She must develop within herself the mature (kingly) Pentacles qualities of STEADINESS AND DEPENDABILITY.

The Page is *encouraging her* to claim her power and FIND A SOLUTION THAT WORKS. She must release her dream of an ideal family once and for all so she can relate to her actual parents with all their faults and limitations.

Although this reading is about love and the ties that bind people from birth, there is not a single Cups card. These cards of love and emotion are totally absent. The lessons of love are not always easy. For Jill, they have taken the form of challenges that have drawn out her inner reserves and made her a stronger and wiser person.

APPENDICES

The Fool's Journey

The Fool's Journey is a metaphor for the journey through life. Each major arcana card stands for a stage on that journey—an experience that a person must incorporate to realize his wholeness. These 22 descriptions are based on the keywords for each major arcana card. The keywords appear as SMALL CAPITALS in the text. A card's number is in parentheses.

The Fool

We begin with the Fool (0), a card of BEGINNINGS. The Fool stands for each of us as we begin our journey of life. He is a fool because only a simple soul has the innocent FAITH to undertake such a journey with all its hazards and pain.

At the start of his trip, the Fool is newborn—fresh, open, and SPONTANEOUS. The figure on Card 0 has his arms flung wide, and his head held high. He is ready to embrace whatever comes his way, but he is also oblivious to the cliff edge he is about to cross. The Fool is unaware of the hardships he will face as he ventures out to learn the lessons of the world.

The Fool stands somewhat outside the rest of the major arcana. Zero is an unusual number. It rests in the exact middle of the number system—poised between the positive and negative. At birth, the Fool is set in the middle of his own individual universe. He is strangely empty (as is zero), but imbued with a desire to go forth and learn. This undertaking would seem to be FOLLY, but is it?

Magician and the High Priestess

On setting out, the Fool immediately encounters the Magician (1) and the High Priestess (2)—the great balancing forces that make up the perceived world. It is a feature of the material universe that as soon as we name some aspect of experience, we automatically evoke its opposite.

The Magician is the positive side. He represents the ACTIVE, masculine power of creative impulse. He is also CONSCIOUS AWARENESS. The Magician is the force that allows us to impact the world through a CONCENTRATION of individual will and POWER. The High Priestess is the negative side. She is the MYSTERIOUS UNCONSCIOUS. She provides the fertile ground in which creative events occur. The High Priestess is our unrealized POTENTIAL waiting for an active principle to bring it to expression.

The words *positive* and *negative* do not imply "good" and "bad." These are human distinctions that do not apply in the tarot. The Magician and the High Priestess are absolutely equal in value and importance. Each is necessary for balance. We may view the negative as our Shadow, but without shadows, we cannot see the light, and without a ground of potential, we cannot create.

The Empress

As he grows, the Fool becomes more and more aware of his surroundings. As with most babies, he first recognizes his MOTHER—the warm, loving woman who nourished and cared for him. He also comes to know Mother Earth, who nurtures him in a larger sense.

The Empress (3) represents the world of NATURE and SENSATION. A baby delights in exploring everything he touches, tastes, and smells. He cannot get enough of the sights and sounds that enchant his senses. It is natural to delight in the ABUNDANT goodness of Mother Earth who surrounds us with her support.

The Emperor

The next person the Fool encounters is the FATHER in the figure of the Emperor (4). He is the representative of STRUCTURE and AUTHORITY. When a baby leaves his mother's arms, he learns that there are patterns to his world. Objects respond in predictable ways that can be explored. The child experiences a new kind of pleasure that comes from discovering order.

The Fool also encounters RULES. He learns his will is not always paramount, and there are certain behaviors necessary for his well-being. There are people in authority who will enforce such guidelines. These restrictions can be frustrating, but through the patient direction of the Father, the Fool begins to understand their purpose.

The Hierophant

Eventually, the Fool ventures out of his home into the wider world. He is exposed to the beliefs and traditions of his culture and begins his formal EDUCATION. The Hierophant (5) represents the organized BELIEF SYSTEMS that begin to surround and inform the growing child.

A Hierophant is someone who interprets arcane knowledge and mysteries. On Card 5 we see a religious figure blessing two acolytes. Perhaps he is inducting them into church membership. Although this image is religious, it is really a symbol for initiations of all kinds.

The child is trained in the practices of his society and becomes part of a particular culture and worldview. He learns to identify with a GROUP and discovers a sense of belonging. He enjoys learning the customs of his society and showing how well he can CONFORM to them.

The Lovers

Eventually, the Fool faces two new challenges. He experiences the powerful urge for SEXUAL union with another person. Before, he was mainly self-centered. Now he feels the balancing tendency, pictured in the Lovers (6), to reach out and become half of a loving partnership. He yearns for relationship.

The Fool also needs to decide upon his OWN BELIEFS. It is well enough to conform while he learns and grows, but at some point, he must determine his own VALUES if he is to be true to himself. He must start to question received opinion.

The Chariot

By the time the Fool becomes an adult, he has a strong identity and a certain mastery over himself. Through discipline and WILLPOWER, he has developed an inner control which allows him to triumph over his environment.

The Chariot (7) represents the vigorous ego that is the Fool's crowning achievement so far.

On Card 7, we see a proud, commanding figure riding VICTORIOUSLY through his world. He is in VISIBLE CONTROL of himself and all he surveys. For the moment, the Fool's ASSERTIVE success is all he might wish, and he feels a certain self-satisfaction. His is the assured confidence of youth.

Strength

Over time, life presents the Fool with new challenges, some that cause suffering and disillusionment. He has many occasions to draw on the quality of STRENGTH (8). He is pressed to develop his courage and resolve and find the heart to keep going despite setbacks.

The Fool also discovers the quiet attributes of PATIENCE and TOLERANCE. He realizes the willful command of the Chariot must be tempered by kindliness and the SOFTER POWER of a loving approach. At times, intense passions surface, just when the the Fool thought he had everything, including himself, under control.

Hermit

Sooner or later, the Fool is led to ask himself the age-old question "Why?" He becomes absorbed with the SEARCH for answers, not from an idle curiosity, but out of a deeply felt need to find out why people live, if only to suffer and die. The Hermit (9) represents the need to find deeper truth.

The Fool begins to LOOK INWARD, trying to understand his feelings and motivations. The sensual world holds less attraction for him, and he seeks moments of SOLITUDE away from the frantic activity of society. In time he may seek a teacher or GUIDE who can give him advice and direction.

Wheel of Fortune

After much soul-searching, the Fool begins to see how everything connects. He has a VISION of the world's wondrous design; its intricate patterns and cycles. The Wheel of Fortune (10) is a symbol of the mysterious universe whose parts work together in harmony. When the Fool glimpses the beauty and order of the world, if only briefly, he finds some of the answers he is seeking.

Sometimes his experiences seem to be the work of fate. A chance encounter or miraculous occurrence begins the process of change. The Fool may recognize his DESTINY in the sequence of events that led him to this TURNING POINT. Having been solitary, he feels ready for MOVEMENT and action again. His perspective is wider, and he sees himself within the grander scheme of a universal plan. His sense of purpose is restored.

Justice

The Fool must now decide what this vision means to him personally. He looks back over his life to trace the CAUSE AND EFFECT relationships that brought him to this point. He takes RESPONSIBILITY for his past actions so he can make amends and ensure a more honest course for the future. The demands of JUSTICE (11) must be served so he can wipe the slate clean.

This is a time of DECISION for the Fool. He is making important choices. Will he remain true to his insights, or slip back into an easier, more unaware existence that closes off further growth?

Hanged Man

Undaunted, the Fool pushes on. He is determined to realize his vision, but he finds life is not so easily tamed. Sooner or later, he encounters his personal cross—an experience that seems too difficult to endure. This overwhelming challenge humbles him until he has no choice but to give up and LET GO.

At first, the Fool feels defeated and lost. He believes he has SACRIFICED everything, but from the depths he learns an amazing truth. He finds that when he relinquishes his struggle for control, everything begins to work as it should. By becoming open and vulnerable, the Fool discovers the miraculous support of his Inner Self. He learns to surrender to his experiences, rather than fighting them. He feels a surprising joy and begins to flow with life.

The Fool feels SUSPENDED in a timeless moment, free of urgency and pressure. In truth, his world has been TURNED UPSIDE-DOWN. The Fool is the Hanged Man (12), apparently martyred, but actually serene and at peace.

Death

The Fool now begins to ELIMINATE old habits and tired approaches. He cuts out nonessentials because he appreciates the basics of life. He goes through ENDINGS as he puts the outgrown aspects of his life behind him. This process may seem like dying because it is the death of his familiar self to allow for the growth of a new one. At times this INEXORABLE CHANGE seems to be crushing the Fool, but eventually he rises up to discover that Death (13) is not a permanent state. It is simply a TRANSITION to a new, more fulfilling way of life.

Temperance

Since embracing the Hermit, the Fool has swung wildly back and forth on an emotional pendulum. Now, he realizes the BALANCING stability of TEMPERANCE (14). He discovers true poise and equilibrium. By experiencing the extremes, he has come to appreciate moderation. The Fool has COMBINED all aspects of himself into a centered whole that glows with HEALTH and well-being. How graceful and soft is the angel on Card 14 compared to the powerful but rigid ruler on the Chariot (Card 7)?[1] The Fool has come a long way in realizing the harmonious life.

Devil

The Fool has his health, peace of mind, and a graceful composure. What more could he need? On everyday terms, not much, but the Fool is courageous and continues to pursue the deepest levels of his being. He soon comes face to face with the Devil (15).

The Devil is not an evil, sinister figure residing outside of us. He is the knot of IGNORANCE and HOPELESSNESS lodged within each of us at some level. The seductive attractions of the MATERIAL world bind us so compellingly that we often do not even realize our slavery to them.

We live in a limited range of experience, unaware of the glorious world that is our true heritage. The couple on Card 15 are chained, but acquiescent. They could so easily free themselves, but they do not even apprehend their BONDAGE.[2] They look like the Lovers, but are

---

1. Rachel Pollack, *Seventy-Eight Degrees of Wisdom*, Part 1 (London: Aquarian Press, 1980), p. 65.
2. Rachel Pollack, *Seventy-Eight Degrees of Wisdom*, Part 1 (London: Aquarian Press, 1980), p. 102.

unaware that their love is circumscribed within a narrow range. The price of this ignorance is an inner core of despair.

Tower

How can the Fool free himself from the Devil? Can he ever root out his influence? The Fool may only find RELEASE through the SUDDEN CHANGE represented by the Tower (16). The Tower is the ego fortress each of us has built around his beautiful inner core. Gray, cold, and rock-hard, this fortress seems to protect but is really a prison.

Sometimes only a monumental crisis can generate enough power to smash the walls of the Tower. On Card 16 we see an enlightening bolt striking this building. It has ejected the occupants who seem to be TUMBLING to their deaths. The crown indicates they were once proud rulers; now they are humbled by a force stronger than they.

The Fool may need such a severe shakeup if he is to free himself, but the resulting REVELATION makes the painful experience worthwhile. The dark despair is blasted away in an instant, and the light of truth is free to shine down.

Star

The Fool is suffused with a SERENE calm. The beautiful images on the Star (17) attest to this tranquility. The woman pictured on Card 17 is naked, her soul no longer hidden behind any disguise. Radiant stars shine in a cloudless sky serving as a beacon of HOPE and INSPIRATION.

The Fool is blessed with a trust that completely replaces the negative energies of the Devil. His faith in himself and the future is restored. He is filled with joy and his one wish is to share it GENEROUSLY with the rest of the world. His heart is open and his love pours out freely. This peace after the storm is a magical moment for the Fool.

Moon

What effect could spoil this perfect calm? Is there another challenge for the Fool? In fact, it is his bliss that makes him vulnerable to the ILLUSIONS of the Moon (18). The Fool's joy is a feeling state. His positive emotions are not subject to mental clarity. In his dreamy condition, the Fool is susceptible to fantasy, distortion, and a false picture of the truth.

The Moon stimulates the creative IMAGINATION. It opens the way for bizarre and beautiful thoughts to bubble up from the unconscious, but deep-seated FEARS and anxieties also arise. These experiences may cause the Fool to feel lost and BEWILDERED.

Sun

It is the lucid clarity of the Sun (19) that directs the Fool's imagination. The Sun's illumination shines in all the hidden places. It dispels the clouds of confusion and fear. It ENLIGHTENS, so the Fool both feels *and* understands the goodness of the world.

Now, he enjoys a vibrant energy and enthusiasm. The Star's openness has solidified into an expansive ASSURANCE. The Fool is the naked babe pictured on Card 19, riding out joyously to face a new day. No challenge is too daunting. The Fool feels a radiant VITALITY. He becomes involved in grand undertakings as he draws to himself everything he needs. He is able to realize his GREATNESS.

Judgement

The Fool has been REBORN. His false ego-self has been shed, allowing his radiant, true self to manifest. He has discovered that joy, not fear, is at life's center.

The Fool feels ABSOLVED. He forgives himself and others, knowing that his real self is pure and good. He may regret past mistakes, but he knows they were due to his ignorance of his nature. He feels cleansed and refreshed, ready to start anew.

It is time for the Fool to make a deeper JUDGMENT (20) about his life. His own personal day of reckoning has arrived. Since he now sees himself truly, he can make the necessary decisions about the future. He can choose wisely which values to cherish, and which to discard.

The angel on Card 20 is the Fool's Higher Self CALLING him to rise up and fulfill his promise. He discovers his true vocation—his reason for entering this life. Doubts and hesitations vanish, and he is ready to follow his dream.

World

The Fool reenters the World (21), but this time with a more complete understanding. He has INTEGRATED all the disparate parts of himself and achieved wholeness. He has reached a new level of happiness and FULFILLMENT.

The Fool experiences life as full and meaningful. The future is filled with infinite promise. In line with his personal calling, he becomes actively INVOLVED in the world. He renders service by sharing his unique gifts and talents and finds that he prospers at whatever he attempts. Because he acts from inner certainty, the whole world conspires to see that his efforts are rewarded. His ACCOMPLISHMENTS are many.

• • •

So the Fool's Journey was not so foolish after all. Through perseverance and honesty, he reestablished the spontaneous courage that first impelled him on his search for Self, but now he is fully aware of his place in the world. This cycle is over, but the Fool will never stop growing. Soon he will be ready to begin a new journey that will lead him to ever greater levels of understanding.

Tarot Suit Qualities

Each of the four suits in the tarot has its own special quality or energy. You can get a feel for these energies by looking over the word lists in this appendix. Each list has words that show the different facets of a suit's character. These words are just my suggestions. If your intuition guides you differently, trust your own impressions first.

There is a positive and negative list for each suit. This split is not ideal because it implies good and bad. In the tarot, qualities are neither good nor bad, they just are. We humans judge qualities based on their impact on us. Our language reflects these judgments, so we have positive and negative expressions for every quality. We also view traits differently depending on our circumstances. Is being *aggressive* positive or negative? It all depends.

Wands–Positive

adventurous
aggressive
ardent
attractive
audacious
avid
bold
brave
buoyant
charismatic
charming
cheerful
confident
courageous
creative
daring
eager
ebullient
energetic
enthusiastic
exuberant
extroverted
fiery
forceful
heroic
inspiring
intrepid
inventive
magnetic
optimistic
original
outgoing
passionate
risk-taking
self-assured
self-confident
undaunted
valiant
wholehearted

Wands–Negative

aggressive
brash
cocky
dare-devilish
devil-may-care
foolhardy
hasty
headstrong
heedless
hot-headed
hot-tempered
impatient
impetuous
impulsive
imprudent
incautious
irresponsible
nervy
overconfident
overzealous
precipitous
presumptuous
rash
reckless
restless
rootless
self-absorbed
superficial
thoughtless
unprepared

Cups—Positive

aesthetic
affectionate
agreeable
amiable
benevolent
calm
caring
compassionate
concerned
considerate
diplomatic
dreamy
emotional
empathetic
forbearing
gentle
good-hearted
gracious
healing
humane
imaginative
inner
intimate
introspective
intuitive
joyful
kind
loving
mellow
merciful

mild
nice
pacific
patient
peaceful
perceptive
psychic
quiet
refined
responsive
romantic
sensitive
soft
spiritual
subjective
sweet
sympathetic
telepathic
tender
tenderhearted
tolerant
understanding
wise

Cups–Negative

broody
delicate
doleful
escapist
fanciful
fragile
frail
gushy
huffy
hypersensitive
hysterical
impressionable
indolent
introverted
lazy
maudlin
melancholic

mopish
moody
morose
narcissistic
overemotional
overrefined
petulant
passive
sulky
sullen
temperamental
thin-skinned
touchy
vapory
waspish
wishy-washy

Swords–Positive

analytical
articulate
astute
authoritative
clearheaded
clever
dignified
direct
discerning
dispassionate
equitable
ethical
evenhanded
forthright
frank
honest
honorable
impartial
incisive
intellectual
just
keen-minded
knowledgeable
learned

literate
logical
lucid
magisterial
mental
moral
objective
observant
outspoken
penetrating
perspicacious
quick-witted
rational
reasonable
smart
trenchant
truthful
unbiased
unprejudiced
well-informed
witty

Swords–Negative

abstruse
aloof
arrogant
autocratic
biting
blunt
cold
condescending
controlling
cool
critical
cutting
detached
distant
dogmatic
domineering
high-handed
imperious
insensitive

intolerant
judgmental
opinionated
overbearing
overintellectualizing
patronizing
remote
standoffish
thoughtless
unaffectionate
unfeeling
unresponsive
unsparing

Pentacles–Positive

able
adept
adroit
assiduous
bighearted
capable
careful
cautious
competent
concrete
conscientious
constant
dogged
efficient
enterprising
dependable
determined
down to earth
factual
firm
generous
handy
hardworking
industrious
loyal
magnanimous

meticulous
nurturing
orderly
organized
painstaking
persevering
practical
productive
proficient
prudent
realistic
reliable
resolute
resourceful
responsible
sensible
skillful
solid
stable

stalwart
staunch
steadfast
steady
sturdy
supporting
tenacious
thorough
trusting
trustworthy
unwavering

Pentacles–Negative
bullheaded
colorless
compulsive
conventional
drab
gloomy

grim
grinding
hardheaded
humorless
inflexible
intractable
intransigent
materialistic
mulish
obdurate
obsessive
obstinate
ordinary
overcautious
overorganized
pedestrian
perfectionistic
pertinacious
pessimistic

pigheaded
prim
prosaic
rigid
staid
stiff
stiff-necked
stodgy
stubborn
timid
unadventurous
unbending
uncompromising
unexciting
unimaginative
unquestioning
unromantic
unspontaneous
unyielding

Suit Pair Meanings

Wands/Cups

Fire/Water
Outer/Inner
Aggressive/Passive
Extrovert/Introvert
Passionate/Tender
Eros/Agape
Intense/Mild
Energetic/Restful
Militant/Peace-Loving
Individual/Group
Competitive/Cooperative
Actions/Feelings
Overt/Covert
Direct/Indirect

Wands/Swords

Fire/Air
Hot/Cool
Passionate/Reserved
Engaged/Detached
Charisma/Authority
Partisan/Unbiased
Inspiration/Analysis
Artist/Critic

Wands/Pentacles

Fire/Earth
Showy/Sedate
New/Old
Risk/Security
Impetuous/Deliberate
Inspiration/Perspiration
Adventurous/Cautious

Liberal/Conservative
Original/Traditional
Big Picture/Detail
Cursory/Thorough
Fast/Slow
Optimistic/Pessimistic

Cups/Swords

Water/Air
Feelings/Thoughts
Right Brain/Left Brain
Love/Truth
Emotion/Logic
Intuition/Reason
Heart/Head
Connection/Separation
Mercy/Justice
Subjective/Objective
Intimacy/Distance
McCoy/Spock

Cups/Pentacles

Water/Earth
Spirit/Matter
Religion/Science
Dreamy/Down-to-Earth
Fantasy/Reality
Delicate/Tough
Flexible/Firm
Soft/Hard
Romantic/Practical
Sentimental/Matter-of-Fact
Play/Work

Swords/Pentacles

Air/Earth
Theory/Practice
Abstract/Concrete
Mental/Physical
Book Learning/Common Sense

Thinking/Doing
Ideas/Implementation
Perfection/Compromise
What is Right/What Works
Ideals/Realities

Court Card Rank Pair Meanings

King/King

Adult/Adult
Two equals
Two mature, well-developed, but
  different aspects of self
Masculine/Masculine
Focus of a King is doubled
Concern with external events
Interaction in real world

Queen/Queen

Adult/Adult
Equal partners
Two mature, well-developed, but differ-
  ent aspects of self
Feminine/Feminine
Focus of a Queen is doubled
Concern with inner states

King/Queen

Man/Woman
Masculine/Feminine
Outer/Inner
Aggressive/Passive
Extrovert/Introvert
Direct/Indirect
Intense/Mild
Individual/Relationship
Actions/Feelings
Doing/Being
Logical/Intuitive
Competitive/Cooperative
Strong/Gentle
Offense/Defense

King-Queen/Knight

Adult/Teen–Young Adult
Moderate/Immoderate
Conservative/Liberal
Old/Young
Traditional/New
Establishment/Challenger
Slow/Fast
Cautious/Adventurous
Security/Risk
Stable/Unstable

King-Queen/Page

Adult/Child
Serious/Lighthearted
Responsible/Carefree
Restrained/Unrestrained
Dignified/Uninhibited
Grown-up/Childish
Planned/Spontaneous
Jaded/Innocent
Sedate/Showy
Ant/Grasshopper

Knight/Knight

Adult/Adult
Teen/Teen
Two extreme, opposing sides of self
Two people/groups fixed in different
  positions with little common ground
Focus of a Knight is doubled

Knight/Page

Adult/Teen/Older Child—Younger Child
Drastic/Mild
Obsessive/Easygoing
Grim/Merry
Pessimistic/Optimistic
Complicated/Simple
Questioning/Accepting

Page/Page

Child/Child
Two childlike people
Focus of a Page is doubled
Powerful opportunity with two different
  aspects

Shuffling Methods

Card Player's Method

The Card Player's Method is commonly used to shuffle everyday playing cards. Hold about half the cards face down in each hand and intermingle them as they drop to the surface of the table. This technique mixes the cards thoroughly, but it can be awkward because most tarot cards are bigger than normal. This method is also hard on your cards. They tend to form a bend in the middle. The Card Player's Method is effective, but somewhat mechanical in spirit.

Insertion Method

Hold about half the deck in each hand, and insert one half in a scattered fashion down through the other half. You can hold the cards on their long or short side. This method is fast, efficient, and composed with a lot of hand-to-card contact. Be careful with the edges as they can fray over time.

Cowie Push/Put Method

I discovered this style in a book by Norma Cowie.[1] Her technique thoroughly mixes the cards with maximum hand contact and little or no damage. Hold the deck face down in your dominant hand. Push some cards from the top with your thumb into your other hand. Then, push again, but this time to the bottom of the new pile. Continue alternating a push to the top, then one to the bottom until all the cards have been transferred. At this point, put the entire deck back into your dominant hand and start over. This method can be difficult at first. You may push too many at a time or drop some, but your technique will improve with practice.

Scrambling Method

The Scrambling Method is about as basic as you can get. Spread all the cards face down on the floor or table, and start scrambling. This technique creates a good mix with few ill effects on the cards. The main drawback is that you need room. This shuffle also has a rather uncomposed feel which some find objectionable.

To Avoid Reversed Cards

Start with your cards all facing the same direction. Every time you divide the deck before shuffling, make sure the two piles stay facing the same way.

To Get Reversed Cards

Every time you divide the deck before shuffling, rotate one of the piles 180 degrees.

---

1. Norma Cowie, *Tarot for Successful Living* (White Rock, British Columbia: NC Publishing, 1979), pp. 23–25. Used by kind permission.

The Question Reading:
A Step-by-Step Procedure

Here are the steps for a tarot reading you do for yourself based on a written question (see lesson 8).

To begin, have ready:

> your written question
> your tarot cards
> the layout for the spread you have chosen
> the card and spread information pages, if desired

1. Setting the mood
    Prepare the environment according to personal preference.
    Sit down with some empty space in front of you.
    Relax and still your mind. Breathe deeply several times.

2. Asking your question
    Remove cards from container.
    Hold cards cupped in one hand. Place other hand on top.
    Close your eyes.
    Say an opening statement out loud, if you wish.
    Read your question out loud, or say it from memory exactly as written.

3. Shuffling the cards
    Shuffle the cards until you feel ready to stop.
    Concentrate on your question while shuffling, but without strain.

4. Cutting the cards
    Place cards face down in front of you with short edge toward you.
    Cut the deck in one unplanned action as follows:
      Grab some number of cards from the complete pile.
      Drop this smaller pile to the left.
      Grab part of the second pile. Drop this new pile to the left.
      Regroup cards into one pile in any fashion.

5. Laying out the cards
    Hold cards in your hand with short edge toward you.
    Turn over the top card as you would turn the page of a book.
    Lay out cards according to the spread you have chosen.
    Turn reversed cards around if you are not using them.

6. Responding to the cards
   Note your responses to individual cards.
   Note your response to the whole pattern of cards.

7. Analyzing the cards
   Analyze individual cards:
      Find the information page for the card.
      Read over keywords and actions.
      Look for actions that hit home.
      Write down thoughts and feelings, if you wish.
      Consider card orientation—upright or reversed?
   Analyze card relationships.
   Use principles of interpretation.
   Note additional insights.

8. Creating the story
   Tell your story spontaneously out loud.
   Tape your story, if you wish.

9. Writing the summary statement
   Think about the theme or message in your reading.
   Answer question in a written summary statement (1–2 sentences).

10. Finishing up
    Write down cards and their positions.
    Clear the deck.
    Gather cards together.
    Hold cards cupped in one hand. Place other hand on top.
    Close your eyes.
    Say out loud what you have learned from the reading.
    Express gratitude to your Inner Guide.
    Put cards back into container.
    Restore environment, if necessary.

11. Using what you have learned
    Decide on one or two actions to take based on the reading.
    Write down intended actions.
    Later, relate developments in situation to the reading.

The Other Reading: A Step-by-Step Procedure

Here are the steps for a tarot reading you do for yourself based on a written question about another subject (see lesson 9).

Choose the subject of your reading—person, couple, group, place, news event, and so on.
Check your involvement.

Switch to a Question Reading if you answer yes to any of these:

Do I feel *strong emotions* when I think about this subject in this situation?

Do I have a vested interest in this situation?

Do I desire a particular outcome in this situation?

Write a question focusing on what interests you about your subject.

To begin, have ready:

your written question

your tarot cards

the layout for the spread you have chosen

the card and spread information pages, if desired

1. Setting the mood

   Prepare the environment according to personal preference.

   Place a picture or object of the subject nearby, if you wish.

   Sit down with some empty space in front of you.

   Relax and still your mind. Breathe deeply several times.

2. Asking your question

   Remove cards from container.

   Hold cards cupped in one hand. Place other hand on top.

   Close your eyes.

   Say an opening statement out loud, if you wish.

   Read your question out loud, or say it from memory exactly as written.

   Say why you are doing an Other Reading about this subject.

   Request guidance in the best interest of all concerned.

   Mention your good intentions toward the subject.

3. Shuffling the cards

   Shuffle the cards until you feel ready to stop.

   Concentrate on your question while you shuffle, but without strain.

4. Cutting the cards

   Place cards face down in front of you with short edge toward you.

   Cut the deck in one unplanned action as follows:

   Grab some number of cards from the complete pile.

Drop this smaller pile to the left.

Grab part of the second pile. Drop this new pile to the left.

Regroup the cards into one pile in any fashion.

5. Laying out the cards

Hold cards in your hand with the short edge toward you.

Turn over the top card as you would turn the page of a book.

Lay out cards according to the spread you have chosen.

Turn reversed cards around if you are not using them.

6. Responding to the cards

Note your responses to individual cards as they relate to the subject (and you).

Note your response to the whole pattern of cards.

7. Analyzing the cards

Analyze individual cards:

Find the information page for the card.

Read over keywords and actions.

Look for actions that hit home about the subject's situation.

Write down thoughts and feelings, if you wish.

Consider card orientation—upright or reversed?

Analyze card relationships.

Use principles of interpretation.

Note additional insights.

8. Creating the story

Tell the story spontaneously out loud as it relates to the subject.

Tape the story, if you wish.

9. Writing the summary statement

Think about the theme or message in the reading.

Answer question in a written summary statement (1—2 sentences).

10. Finishing up

Write down cards and their positions.

Clear the deck.

Gather cards together.

Hold cards cupped in one hand. Place other hand on top.

Close your eyes.

Say out loud what you have learned from the reading.

Express gratitude to your Inner Guide.

Put cards back into container.

Restore environment, if necessary.

11. Using what you have learned

Think how the lesson of this reading applies to your life.

Follow subject's situation to see how it relates to reading.

The Open Reading: A Step-by-Step Procedure

Here are the steps for a tarot reading you do for yourself that is not based on a question (see lesson 10).

To begin, have ready:

> your tarot cards
> the layout for the spread you have chosen
> the card and spread information pages, if desired

1. Setting the mood
   Prepare the environment according to personal preference.
   Sit down with some empty space in front of you.
   Relax and still your mind. Breathe deeply several times.

2. Making your statement
   Remove cards from container.
   Hold cards cupped in one hand. Place other hand on top. Close your eyes.
   Say an opening statement out loud, if you wish.
   Say a general message of intent.

3. Shuffling the cards
   Shuffle the cards until you feel ready to stop.
   Keep your mind free and open while you shuffle.

4. Cutting the cards
   Place cards face down in front of you with short edge toward you.
   Cut the deck in one unplanned action as follows:
   Grab some number of cards from the complete pile.
   Drop this smaller pile to the left.
   Grab part of this second pile. Drop this new pile to the left.
   Regroup cards into one pile in any fashion.

5. Laying out the cards
   Hold cards in your hand with the short edge toward you.
   Turn over the top card as you would turn the page of a book.
   Lay out the cards according to the spread you have chosen.
   Turn reversed cards around if you are not using them.

6. Responding to the cards
   Note your responses to individual cards.
   Note your response to the whole pattern of cards.

7. Analyzing the cards
   Analyze individual cards:
      Find the information page for the card.
      Read over keywords and actions.
      Look for actions that hit home.
      Write down thoughts and feelings, if you wish.
      Consider card orientation—upright or reversed?
   Analyze card relationships.
   Use principles of interpretation.
   Note additional insights.

8. Creating the story
   Tell your story spontaneously out loud.
   Tape your story, if you wish.

9. Writing the summary statement
   Think about the theme or message in your reading.
   Write a summary statement of 1–2 sentences.

10. Finishing up
    Write down cards and their positions.
    Clear the deck.
    Gather cards together.
    Hold cards cupped in one hand. Place other hand on top.
    Close your eyes.
    Say out loud what you have learned from the reading.
    Express gratitude to your Inner Guide.
    Put cards back into container.
    Restore environment if necessary.

11. Using what you have learned
    Let the message of the reading guide you in a general way.
    Later, relate developments to what you learned in the reading.

Bibliography

Alighieri, Dante. *The Purgatorio*. John Ciardi, trans. New York: New American Library, 1957.

Almond, Jocelyn, and Keith Seddon. *Understanding Tarot*. St. Paul, MN: Llewellyn, 1991.

Bunyan, John. *The Pilgrim's Progress*. Excerpt from *The Norton Anthology of English Literature*: vol. 1, 3rd ed. New York: Norton, 1974.

Calvino, Italo. *The Castle of Crossed Destinies*. New York: Harcourt Brace Jovanovich, 1969.

Connolly, Eileen. *Tarot: The Handbook for the Journeyman*. North Hollywood, CA: Newcastle, 1987.

———. *Tarot: A New Handbook for the Apprentice*. North Hollywood, CA: Newcastle, 1979.

Cortellesi, Linda. *The User-Friendly Tarot Guidebook*. Worthington, OH: Chalice Moon Publications, 1996.

Cowie, Norma. *Tarot for Successful Living*. White Rock, British Columbia: NC Publishing, 1979.

D'Agostino, Joseph D. *Tarot: The Path to Wisdom*. York Beach, ME: Samuel Weiser, 1994.

Denning, Melita, and Osborne Phillips. *The Magick of the Tarot*. St. Paul, MN: Llewellyn, 1983.

Dummett, Michael. *The Visconti-Sforza Tarot Cards*. New York: George Braziller, 1986.

Fairfield, Gail. *Choice-Centered Tarot*. North Hollywood, CA: Newcastle, 1985.

Garen, Nancy. *Tarot Made Easy*. New York: Simon & Schuster, 1989.

Gerulskis-Estes, Susan. *The Book of Tarot*. Dobbs Ferry, NY: Morgan & Morgan, 1981.

Giles, Cynthia. *The Tarot: History, Mystery & Lore*. New York: Simon & Schuster, 1992.

Gray, Eden. *A Complete Guide to the Tarot*. New York: New American Library, 1970.

———. *Mastering the Tarot*. New York: New American Library, 1971.

———. *The Tarot Revealed*. New York: New American Library, 1960.

Greer, Mary K. *Tarot For Yourself: A Workbook for Personal Transformation*. North Hollywood, CA: Newcastle, 1984.

Greer, Mary K., and Rachel Pollack. *New Thoughts on Tarot*. North Hollywood, CA: Newcastle, 1989.

Haga, Enoch. *Tarosolution: A Complete Guide to Interpreting the Tarot*. Livermore, CA: Enoch Haga, 1994.

Kaplan, Stuart R. *The Encyclopedia of Tarot: Volumes 1–3*. Stamford, CT: U.S. Games Systems, Inc., 1978, 1986, 1990.

Kaser, R. T. *Tarot in Ten Minutes*. New York: Avon, 1992.

Konraad, Sandor. *Classic Tarot Spreads*. Atglen, PA: Whitford, 1985.

Louis, Anthony. *Tarot Plain and Simple*. St. Paul, MN: Llewellyn, 1996.

Masino, Marcia. *Easy Tarot Guide*. San Diego: ACS Publications, 1987.

Myers, I. B. *The Myers-Briggs Type Indicator*. Palo Alto, CA: Consulting Psychologists Press, 1962.

Nichols, Sallie. *Jung and Tarot: An Archetypal Journey*. York Beach, ME: Samuel Weiser, 1980.

Pollack, Rachel. *Seventy-Eight Degrees of Wisdom: A Book of Tarot. Part 1: The Major Arcana*. London: Aquarian, 1980.

———. *Seventy-Eight Degrees of Wisdom: A Book of Tarot. Part 2: The Minor Arcana and Readings*. London: Aquarian, 1980.

Reps, Paul. *Zen Flesh, Zen Bones*. Tokyo: Tuttle, 1957.

Rorschach, Hermann. *The Rorschach (R) Test*. Switzerland: Hans Huber, 1927.

Sharman-Burke, Juliet, and Liz Greene. *The Mythic Tarot: A New Approach to the Tarot Cards.* New York: Simon & Schuster, 1986.

Simon, Sylvie. *The Tarot: Art, Mysticism, Divination.* Rochester, VT: Inner Traditions, 1986.

Waite, Arthur Edward. *Pictorial Key to the Tarot.* York Beach, ME: Samuel Weiser, 1993.

Wang, Robert. *Qabalistic Tarot: A Textbook of Mystical Philosophy.* York Beach, ME: Samuel Weiser, 1983.

Woudhuysen, Jan. *Tarot Therapy: A New Approach to Self Exploration.* Los Angeles: Jeremy P. Tarcher, 1979.

Index

Joan Bunning grew up in Washington, DC during the 1950s. She received her B.A. in Social Psychology from Cornell University and has worked as a writer, computer programmer, and website developer. In September 1995, Bunning launched the "Learning the Tarot" website at www.learntarot.com. Her on-line course, which includes sample readings and other tarot-related material, has helped thousands of people worldwide discover the personal value of the tarot. She lives in Virginia with her husband, two sons, and two dogs.